MW00634715

DIRTY POOLE

DIRTY POOLE

a sensual memoir

Wakefield Poole

MAPLE SHADE, NEW JERSEY

Dirty Poole

First edition published by Alyson Books, 2000.
This edition published in 2011 by Lethe Press, Inc.
118 Heritage Avenue • Maple Shade, NJ 08052-3018
www.lethepressbooks.com • lethepress@aol.com
ISBN: 1-59021-229-0
ISBN-13: 978-1-59021-229-5

Set in Hoefler Text, Broadway, and Edwardian Script.
Interior design: Alex Jeffers.
Cover design: C.J. Reinhart.
Cover photos: Peter Fisk.

LIBRARY OF CONGRESS CATALOGING-IN-PUBLICATION DATA
available on request

To

Marvin Shulman,

for everything,

and

my nephew, Bill,

who once said, "I don't envy your life,
Uncle Wake, only the people you've met."

Contents

Chapter One

Rolling out the Red Carpet

New York City, 1971

I spent one of those nights you spend waiting for the alarm to go off, half worrying about not sleeping, half wanting the night to end. The wait was finally over. Peter removed his arm from under my head, touched the alarm button, and gently slipped out of bed. We'd been lovers since the summer of '69 and were comfortable with each other. We'd also been through a lot to get that way, and although we didn't know it, the fun was just beginning, especially since my first movie was opening in New York City that day.

I had publicly come out of the closet the week before. It started with a *Variety* review of my movie *Boys in the Sand* on December 22, 1971—the publication's first-ever review of a hardcore all-male film—and was topped off in a Sunday edition of *The New York Times* with a sixth of a page advertisement for the film's opening, the first gay display ad ever accepted by the *Times*. To this day, I don't know how we got such good placement. The ad looked classy, so maybe they just didn't read the copy. Or perhaps someone had let it slip by. I'd like to think some gay man in the advertising department had pulled some strings. If that is what happened, I'm forever grateful.

The provocative and stylish ad, a drawing by Ed Parente, depicted an attractive, mustached man in a Speedo, from his thighs up. His nipples were prominent, and a lightning bolt ran across his crotch at an angle to the top of his bathing suit. He wore a banner of shells over one shoulder, leather thongs tied around his wrists, and held a beach ball against his right hip. An art deco border framed the ad, making it eye-catching.

The ad appeared on the first page of the movie ads between, and of equal size to, *X, Y and Zee*, starring Elizabeth Taylor, and the John Cassavetes film *Minnie and Moskowitz*. *Nicholas and Alexandra* took up the top half of the page. My name appeared above the title, out there for all to see. I was proud of the film and never considered not putting my name on it. People who knew me would be intrigued and, I'd hoped, curious to see what I'd done. What good is a movie if no one sees it?

I hadn't really been in the closet or pretended to be anything or anyone other than who I was. I didn't label myself. The majority of my sexual experiences had been homosexual, and even though it was my preference, I didn't limit myself to men sexually or emotionally. My sexuality probably added mystery to my persona and in turn attracted both men and women who might not have otherwise had any interest. But this was after Stonewall, when gay pride was just taking hold. We were feeling good about ourselves, and most of all we felt hope. Without hope, there would have been no gay movement. It was time to make a declaration. So many people were demanding their freedom. And it was time.

The phone rang and jolted me from sleep. It was Marvin. He wanted to make sure Peter and I were up and about. Really, he just wanted to talk. "I'm going to run out to Lamston's and to the florist," he said. "I just wanted to check in before I left the office to see if you needed anything."

I told him we were on schedule and that everything was fine. "Don't worry, I've got the print sitting by the front door, and I won't be late. But what if nobody comes?" I said, laughing.

"Good-bye, girl," he said as he hung up the phone. Obviously, he didn't want to deal with that possibility. Marvin Shulman, one of the funniest and most interesting people I'd ever met, had been a friend as well as my business manager for more than ten years. His generosity allowed me to live and maintain a comfortable lifestyle, even when it appeared I'd never work again.

Marvin became my partner in the movie and also came out publicly in the credits. He even listed his own name as the producer of *Boys in the Sand*. Although we didn't realize it then, this day would forever change our lives. Marvin had quite a talent for choosing clients, mostly from his friends, who he thought not only had talent but also potential for making money. He had many clients and did taxes for hundreds of singers, dancers, and actors. Some of us were friends as well.

Tom Porter (a production stage manager), Paul Jasmin (an artist and photographer), and Michael Bennett, Larry Fuller, and I (choreographers and directors) all supported each other as colleagues, professionally, and through Marvin, as our manager, financially. We would remain like this for many years.

I got out of bed and went downstairs to put on some coffee. It was a nice clear day outside, cold but not windy. The weather certainly would have no effect on the box office, an excuse we couldn't use if no one showed up. We'd already had so many screenings that most of our friends had already seen the movie. I hoped this wouldn't affect ticket sales for the premiere.

Jack Deveau, a longtime friend of Marvin's, had hosted a screening in his penthouse and invited about twenty of his friends. Cal Culver, A.K.A. Casey Donovan, the star of the movie, was invited as guest of honor. It was a big success, and I heard later that in Jack's bedroom Cal entertained each and all who were interested. All were interested! We should have known from that screening what a gem we had in Casey. Everyone wanted to fuck him. Cal called me the next morning to say he'd had one of the best times of his life.

Robert L. Green, a fashion editor and friend of Marvin's, took great care in whom he invited to his own screening. It was shown during a brunch, and I'm sure it was the first porno-chic party ever thrown. The guest list included people in the fashion industry: models, photographers, stylists, makeup artists, and magazine editors, people who talk about everything that's happening. It was a very "in" group, and the reaction was unanimous: They loved it. Most of the guests at Robert's screening already knew Cal. He was also a model who appeared regularly in ads for Bloomingdale's, so there was a lot of discussion as to whether making this movie would damage his modeling career. As it turned out, it did. But eventually Cal became an underground superstar and launched a career in pornographic films, both straight and gay.

We had a small screening at Marvin's apartment for some of his straight clients and friends. This took a lot of courage on Marvin's part. Still, the positive reaction was the same. But we still didn't know how well the film would go over publicly. Then we held a press screening at the Rizzoli screening room. Our press agent, Robert Ganshaw, saw to it that all the critics were made aware of our efforts and urged them to attend the screening. Most of them came. Most also chose not to review or even write about it. The gay press, however, gave us more coverage than we could have asked for.

We wanted an audience of first timers—those who had never been inside a porno theater. Most of the gay theaters at the time were depressing and dirty and located in out-of-the way places. People went to cruise and meet others, not to see movies, and the atmosphere was almost always sleazy. Marvin and I wanted something else; we didn't want to feel like second-class citizens. So we rented the 55th Street Playhouse across the street from Marvin's apartment. Andy Warhol sometimes exhibited his films there, but lately the theater had been showing Chinese movies. We made a deal with Frank Lee, who held the lease, and our work began. We did a lot of cleaning, fixing, and even a little painting. Peter brought some posters from Triton Gallery to brighten up the lobby walls. The location was perfect, and now the theater's atmosphere was at least pleasant, if not plush. Marvin and I wanted everything to be first class—or at least to appear so. We had to make a little magic. So we left nothing to chance.

On the day of the premiere, I was reading the morning paper when Peter came downstairs, ready for work. He was part owner of Triton Gallery, a theater and movie poster shop. He planned to go to work that day as usual, even though he was one of the film's stars. He took the name Peter Fisk for the film, not so much because he was ashamed but because he thought Peter Schneckenburger was a bit much. We all agreed.

Peter helped me bring all the elements of the movie together. The old cliché "I couldn't have done it without him" certainly held true in this case. Peter poured himself a glass of juice and sat next to me. He asked what Marvin had wanted, and I said he was just nervous, like me. I poured him a cup of coffee.

"I'll try to get up there before the first show starts," he said. We finished our coffee in silence. I have no idea if he had any second thoughts about being in the movie. If he did, he didn't share them with me. He kissed me good-bye and left.

At noon my first movie was premiering. It was X-rated, but it was a movie, made exactly the same way all movies are made. Unlike live theater, it was finished, no changes. All I could do now was show up and observe. I had the cab let me off in front of the Wellington Hotel on Seventh Avenue. When I walked around the corner to 55th Street, I saw the marquee:

WORLD PREMIERE
WAKEFIELD POOLE'S
BOYS IN THE SAND
ALL-MALE IN COLOR

I was frightened, proud, excited, anxious—so many things at once. Most of all, I felt a great sense of accomplishment. Frank Capra once said that just finishing a film, any film, is a minor miracle. When I walked into the theater, I found Marvin on his knees, arranging flowers in a large vase. He was making his magic and had worked wonders on the lobby.

"Marvin, I never know when I'm going to find you on your knees!" I announced as I handed the print of the film to the projectionist. We'd been warned not to let the print out of our hands overnight because someone could duplicate it without our knowledge. Pirate prints could suddenly be playing in every gay theater in the country.

At that time there were maybe ten gay theaters across the nation, in the major cities, so if we wanted to make any money at all, we had to be careful. Everyone should be suspect. The ticket taker, the projectionist, the manager, even the owners were not to be trusted. This would be our first of many cases of "porno paranoia."

In the early '70s, pornography was still taboo, and across the country raids occurred frequently, so we had some fear. Even though it never influenced the content or how we promoted the movie, the danger of being busted was always present.

"The lobby looks terrific, Marvin," I said. "What a difference."

"Go up and look at the bathrooms if you want to see a *big* difference. You could eat off that floor...and you probably will."

I wanted to speak to the projectionist anyway, so I headed upstairs to check out the john. It was not only clean but also had been lightly sprayed with deodorant and was stocked with soap and towels. We'd decided to start the program with a ten-minute film called *Andy*, which I'd made as a birthday present for Andy Warhol, a documentary of his retrospective at the Whitney Museum. I wanted the audience to think they were going to see a solo jerk-off short featuring a young stud named Andy. Instead they got a short subject that could be shown at Cinema One. It set a different mood and made the audience really look at what they were seeing. I asked the projectionist to splice it onto the front of the print, then went downstairs.

Peter had arrived and planned to sit with me. With all the editing and screenings, we must have seen the film fifty times, but we wanted to sit through the premiere together.

At 11:45 it was time to open the doors. There was no line outside, but the minute the doors opened, people started to filter in. Most had their $5 in hand so that they could rush in unnoticed from passersby. No one lingered at the box office. Even customers were caught up in the paranoia of the times. In minutes the theater was half filled, and they were still coming. We knew for sure now that we'd have a decent crowd for the opening.

Marvin decided to hang around the lobby while Peter and I took our seats. By the time the feature started, the house was packed. Usually when people go to porno movies they sit alone, but today it was so crowded that people were forced to sit next to each other.

The audience's reaction was overwhelming. They even laughed at the right places, which was good, since we had included a lot of humor: calendar pages burning in the sand to denote the passage of time, Casey throwing a pill that turned into an Italian stud in a swimming pool, and our recognizing our insecurities in the way we cruise. But I didn't want to include anything degrading about the sex or the situations in which the actors were involved. It all worked marvelously.

For the most part, the audience stayed in their seats and watched the movie without getting up to cruise or check out the john. It was so crowded that people couldn't change seats as they usually did; they had to stay put and watch the movie.

When the film ended the audience burst into applause, which I hadn't expected. Peter and I walked into the lobby but couldn't find

Marvin anywhere. Mr. Louie, the theater manager, told us Marvin had gone to his office to arrange for a security guard. We were taking in so much money that the theater didn't want to be responsible in case of a robbery. The tickets for the second show were selling steadily too, so it seemed our movie might have legs. But how long would this success last?

I said good-bye to Peter, and he went back to Triton. I wanted him to stay and enjoy our success, but he wasn't yet ready to be recognized. He was now a porno star, and it would take him time to become comfortable with it. He knew his life would never be the same again, but he didn't realize it would be so instantaneous. As he left the theater I saw two guys recognize him and follow him down the street.

Marvin came back a little later with a smile on his face I'd never seen. "I can't believe this. Can you? They think we'll bring in at least $5,000 today. The security guard is on his way, and everything's taken care of. All we have to do is collect the money and enjoy it."

Cal came in looking like a million dollars, greeting me with a big kiss. He wasn't alone. "Wakefield, this is Jerry Douglas. He directed me in *Circle in the Water*. We're going to make a film together."

"Welcome," I said, offering my hand. "The second show is about to start, so you'd better find a seat. It's pretty full in there." I gave Cal a hug and whispered "Thank you" in his ear.

Cal had made a movie titled *Casey*, so he decided to take the name of the character he played as his porno name. Voilà! Casey Donovan was born.

The second show had started, and people were still coming in. We had done it. Even the feeling in the theater was different. There was no depressing sense of gloom or guilt in the air. People were actually smiling at each other.

Marvin approached me and said Michael Bennett wanted us to come to his place to celebrate with a glass of champagne. Michael lived directly across the hall from Marvin, and his terrace overlooked 55th Street. A few minutes later, on that cold December day, Michael, Marvin, and I were toasting our good fortune on his terrace, looking down at people getting out of cabs and entering the theater. Michael had set up a small table, complete with linen cloth, champagne flutes, and a crystal cigarette cup filled with joints. It was perfect.

Michael had begun his meteoric rise to fame with four shows running on Broadway: *Promises, Promises*; *Company*; *Follies*; and *Twigs*. After our toast he put his arms around me and said, "Welcome to the mushroom." I never quite understood the meaning of that remark, but its effect was pleasant. We laughed and enjoyed the moment.

Who'd have thought everything I had done up to this point would result in my making a hit porno movie? I certainly had no idea—not even a year before—that my life would bring me here.

The Poole family with dog Midgie in 1942. Clockwise from top left: Hazel,Walter, Wakefield, Pat, and Marilyn.

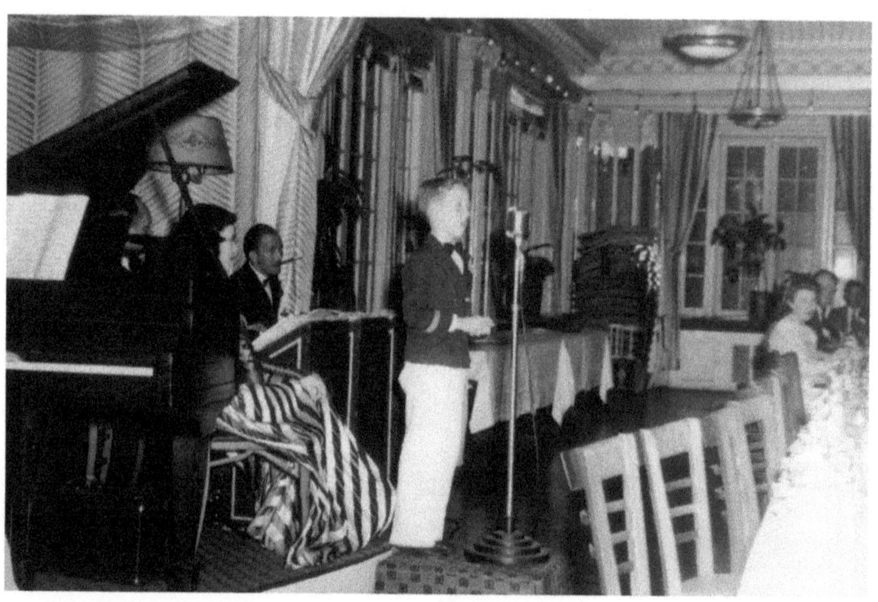

Young crooner Wakefield Poole entertains the audience at the Mayflower Hotel, Jacksonville, Florida, 1947.

Chapter Two

A Normal Start

Salisbury, N.C., 1944

Jack Brady was my first boyfriend. We were both eight years old, and I can't remember a time when we weren't friends. We did everything together. Jack's house stood directly behind ours, separated by a large field that our families used for a victory garden.

My father was a policeman, and I remember him as he directed traffic in the middle of Main Street. He was tall and thin and cut quite a figure in his uniform. Horns would honk, hands would wave, and every once in a while "Hey, Slick, how ya doin'?" could be heard over the traffic. My mother called him Walter, but to everyone else he was Slick or Bub. I went to a lot of movies since he got me in for free. He'd place me in a seat, tell the usher to watch me, then pick me up later.

The State Theater was my favorite because it had a stage act, a glorified burlesque show featuring animal tricks, magicians, and a big finale. I saw Sally Rand do her famous fan dance there. It was the most beautiful thing I had ever seen. A few days later at a baseball game, there she was. Sally Rand, in broad daylight, fully clothed, throwing out the first ball. I even got her to sign an autograph on a telegram form. I kept it for years, and meeting her still remains a vivid memory.

My mother, Hazel, had beautiful black hair and an olive complexion, which in the summer turned a golden brown. I always regretted that I didn't inherit her genes; I was a miniature of my dad: fair skin and light-brown hair. My sisters, Marilyn and Pat, were a mixture of both.

Altogether, we made an attractive family. All my memories of this time are static, fragmented without linear sense. Good times! Swimming in the quarry lake at the farm, playing cowboys and Indians, listening to music on the Victrola, and, most of all, eating. Bad times! Getting punished for breaking into the hen house to steal eggs for mud pies and being spanked with a hickory switch for some minor offense. One day, though, stands out clearly in my mind.

One afternoon in the early spring of my eighth year, a series of events occurred that would change my life forever. I was going to sing at Catabah College's *Spring Follies* that night. For some reason I had been invited to participate, probably because of my expert rendition of "God Bless America," which I had sung in church a few months before. I was a bass baritone, while the other boys were still singing soprano. That night, I would stand on a real stage for the first time and sing "Long Ago and Far Away." Until then, playtime with Jack.

Jack's driveway was our favorite place to play. We'd gotten all our cars and trucks out of the box and were digging under a root to make an underpass for our highway when we noticed Monroe Kress come out of his house next door. Monroe had four brothers and two sisters. He was fourteen, the youngest and the best looking. He went into the family's dog shed and began to sweep. Mr. Kress loved to hunt and kept his three dogs in a playhouse he had built for his daughters years before. The playhouse was elegant, with a front door, windows, and even a porch. Southerners treat their dogs well!

After a lot of sweeping and cleaning, things grew quiet in the doghouse, just quiet enough to get my interest. I didn't know what it was at the time, but I could feel a sexual energy and was drawn to it. Jack and I went over to the fence.

"Whatcha doin'?" I called out.

"Just resting," Monroe said.

"Can we come inside?" Jack nudged.

We kept on until he finally gave us permission to enter the gate, crawl through the dog run, and enter the shed. When we got inside it was pretty dark, and it took us a second to get used to the light.

"Sit down right there and be quiet," Monroe commanded. "You wanna see what I'm doing, so watch!"

We sat. Then, as my eyes adjusted to the light, I began to make out his figure. Monroe was sitting on the floor in the corner. His legs were spread apart as far as the walls would let them, and in his hands was the biggest dick I'd ever seen. Apart from Jack and a few cousins, I hadn't seen many. His was certainly the oldest I'd seen, and if that's what "growing up" meant, I couldn't wait.

Jack and I both sat in the semidarkness with our mouths open, barely breathing, as he slowly moved his hand up and down. First one hand, then the other. Sometimes even both. I was truly awed. It wasn't until his stroke grew faster that I noticed a swelling of my own. It was the first time I had gotten an erection without doing anything. I didn't understand what was causing it, but I liked it a lot. Suddenly Monroe began to mutter things I couldn't understand. Once, I thought I heard him swear. I know I heard him say "God" and "Ah, Jesus" a couple of times.

Outside, the sky was growing dark, and we heard rain hit the doghouse roof. Thunder cracked, and rain began to pound harder over our heads, which seemed to urge Monroe on even more. His strokes grew faster, and suddenly his body stiffened. He let out a sound from deep down, and out shot an eruption, a stream of white fluid. It flew all over the place, like fireworks. I almost fainted. It was truly miraculous. I sat there with my little boner, knowing I had seen something quite special.

Monroe pulled a rag from his pocket and began to clean himself. "Someday soon you'll be able to do that. Both of you," he said as he put himself back in his pants.

I didn't want it to end. Couldn't he do it again? I could only think, *When will we be able to join in this miraculous event?* Later I would think of a million questions I should have asked. I also knew he had shared a personal moment with us and it wasn't likely to happen again. I was sorry about that.

Jack and I made our way out through the run. Monroe went into the house as we stood in the drizzling rain watching him disappear through the screen door. Too overwhelmed to talk about what had occurred, I said good-bye and ran up the path toward home. "See you later," Jack cried out as the rain fell down even harder.

It was still raining as Mom and I ran out to the taxi. Daddy was suppose to pick us up in the patrol car and take us to the college for the *Follies* but couldn't get away. We rode in silence, listening to the wipers beat out an irregular rhythm against the strains of "Bésame Mucho" coming from the radio. I couldn't stop thinking about the adventure in the doghouse. I wanted to talk to Jack. Had he seen anything like it before? Did he feel the same excitement I did? Would ours get that big? I had so many questions.

When we arrived backstage at the auditorium, it was total chaos. Lights were switching on and off. People were running around shouting orders, carrying things, and some were half dressed. Some were rehearsing while others talked in groups. Backstage! It was a sight I would see many times, but this first time was frightening. How would this show ever get on? Someone took us in hand, led us to a room, and started to put makeup on my face. When she was done I looked in the mirror. No freckles. Hey, I liked this more and more every minute. The pace of all this activity grew and grew until everything stopped abruptly and then grew quiet. All that crazy energy had transformed into palpable excitement. The show had started.

In no time I was in the spotlight and the band was playing my intro. I was on stage alone and couldn't see a thing. I could only feel a hot white light around me. Then an amazing thing happened. It was over! The audience was clapping and whistling, and I didn't even remember singing. It was over. As I came offstage everyone touched me and told me how great it was. What a fuss! My mom just stooped down, took me in her arms, and held me close for a few seconds. Then she stood up and led me to the dressing room. If this was show business, I liked it a lot.

When we got home the rain was still coming down hard. I got into the house and was immediately told to get out of my wet clothes and into a hot tub. Then my mother told me I could go to Jack's to spend the night. What a surprise! I wasn't about to ask why, but I knew something was going on. I was getting out of the tub when I heard my dad and Uncle Ray arguing. They must have arrived while the bath was running. I heard a lot of cursing and yelling followed by a lot of shushing and commotion. Things would calm down, but before long the volume would rise to an understandable level again, "...woman in the police car?" Uncle Ray's voice cut through again. Then more commotion. I kept hearing one word I didn't know, *fuck*.

After I was dressed I was given an umbrella, led to the back door, and told, "Everything's going to be all right. Just go right in. They're waiting for you."

I never heard anything more about that night, except later someone said that Uncle Ray chased Daddy with a butcher's knife. Someone also told me my dad wasn't a policeman anymore.

I spent the weekend at Jack's. We had a chance to talk and experiment with the new activity we had learned from watching Monroe, but we were really disappointed when all our efforts produced nothing but skin burns and sore arms. Monroe had said, "Someday you'll be able..." If only we had asked when, we could have saved ourselves a lot of pain.

I told Jack about what happened at my house and what I'd heard that night, but we couldn't make any sense of it. He did tell me *fuck* was what a man and a woman did together to make babies. Wow! This became major fuel for my fantasies.

To this day, what really happened that night has remained a family secret. Not one of my relatives will admit that they know exactly what occurred. My Uncle Clayton even recalls something about there being twin girls involved, so the stories grow. My mother's relatives are all gone now, and the secret remains a secret. One thing that's not secret is that my dad was quite a ladies' man. As a child, I was following his lead.

I had two female friends at the time: Nancy Brown from church and Liddy from my second-grade class. She lived across the street, so she would be the one I would ask to have my baby. The following week in class I took a piece of paper, wrote "Wanna fuck?" and passed it down the row to Liddy. It had almost gotten there when the teacher caught sight of it and snatched it. I froze as she unfolded the note. I'll never forget how the color of her face changed as she read it. I thought it would end with her head exploding.

Instead, she walked over, took me by the arm, and led me to the principal's office. I didn't think I had done "something bad" as she had told the principal. Besides, Liddy hadn't even seen the note. My mom had to come pick me up.

Many years later, watching the *Today* show, I'd learn that Liddy, my Liddy, had become the U.S. Secretary of Transportation and president of the American Red Cross. Liddy Hanford had become Elizabeth Hanford Dole, senator's wife, servant of the people, a staunch Republican, and a presidential candidate.

One day after the letter incident, I was taken to stay at my grandparents' farm while the rest of my family visited relatives in Florida. If this was their way of punishing me, it was far too severe for the crime. My family had gone to Florida to investigate the possibility of our relocating there. When they returned they informed me that the decision had been unanimous and that we would move there. I didn't get to vote. I wasn't too happy about leaving Jack, but a deal was struck that he could visit whenever his parents allowed.

We finished out the school year before leaving Salisbury.

It was a perfect early summer's day when we arrived in Jacksonville. As we drove down Riverside Avenue, I was speechless. The street was lined with enormous oak trees; their limbs, laden with Spanish moss, hung over the street, making a sort of tunnel. Hibiscus, of various shades of pink and red, flanked both sides of the street. These ranged in size from small shrubs to bushes of eight or nine feet tall, all covered in blossoms.

Rays of sun found their way through the moss to play over the flowers like tiny spotlights. A blooming dogwood tree appeared now and then. I will never forget this first impression of our new home. It was so different from the red hills of North Carolina.

As promised, in late June, Jack arrived by bus. My God, he was a handsome boy. He was supposed to stay just a week, but more than a month passed before his mom called to say she missed him and that he would have to come home. It was great having him there and even better sleeping with him every night. Before he left for North Carolina, though, we both experienced our first orgasms. I was first.

"What was it like?" whispered Jack.

"It happened so fast, I'm not sure," I answered. "It hurt! Yeah, it hurt. But felt good too. Real good."

A few nights later Jack would have his. I was relieved because he was beginning to worry. Ten years old, and we had already begun to fret about orgasms. We had matured sexually at an early age, and since that day in the doghouse, there had never been a more determined pair. It had been a good summer, but eventually Jack and I would grow apart. Distance made things too hard. Friends have to be together or things change, despite what they want.

I would see Jack just once more, when we were both twenty years old and I was living in New York. My Grandmother Melton died, so I met my family in Salisbury for the funeral. I called Jack, and we agreed to meet after dinner that night.

At the appointed time I was waiting in the Empire Hotel lobby. I thought about my great-uncle George, my dad's uncle who lived in this hotel. He was quite a character and was always immaculately dressed but usually in bright colors: yellow slacks, bluejacket, white shirt, an outrageous tie, a vest, and shoes with spats. At the end of his watch fob hung a miniature chamber pot with a $100 bill stuffed inside. He was striking, to say the least. Everyone called him Lord Salisbury, and when there was a parade in town, he would always be the last one marching, throwing brand-new pennies into the crowds. The kids loved him. I regret that I was so young when I knew him because I'm sure he had some good stories to tell. He was the black sheep of the family, and I was next in line for his title.

A car pulled up in front of the hotel, and Jack stepped out. He had grown even more handsome over the years. He looked like Paul Newman. I had developed a habit of comparing people to movie stars, but this likeness was uncanny.

"Wakie?" he asked, holding out his hand.

"Jack." I clasped his hand in mine.

There was a moment's pause, then I pulled him into a bear hug. My mind jumped back to the old days as I felt his body next to mine. He had brought some buddies with him and said we should all go have a few beers and then see what we could do about getting laid. After drinks at a local juke joint, we drove several miles out of town. I didn't know what was going on, so I stayed real cool.

Jack pulled off the highway and turned off his headlights as he continued down a dirt road. He slowed, pulled to a stop under a big tree, then flashed his lights. In a minute or two I heard footsteps coming up the road toward the car.

"Who's there?" came a woman's voice out of the dark.

"Jack!" he answered. "Come on over here."

"I can't do nothing tonight, Jack. I got the rag on."

Dropping by like this was evidently a common occurrence since there were no amenities or small talk. Jack turned on his parking lights and into the glow appeared an average-looking girl in her teens. She had on a faded cotton housedress, which was tight fitting but had a stretched-out look to it. Jack slid out of the seat and stood by the open door facing into the car.

"Well, I guess you'll have to use your mouth," he said devilishly as he unzipped his fly. "I'm horny as hell, and I'm not alone." He reached into his pants, and I held my breath. Then I saw his dick in his hand. It wasn't totally erect yet, so it just hung off the front of his hand. The girl worked her way inside the open door, sat on the running board, and took him into her mouth. I have no idea what the guys in the backseat were doing, since my mind was trying to deal with the moment at hand. My own dick was rock-hard. I could only see the back of her head move. I raised my eyes up to see Jack looking straight at me. He motioned with his head for me to join him.

I got out of the car, walked around the back to the driver's side, and stood next to him. With absolutely no shame, he reached down and unzipped my fly. He took out my dick and, holding it in his hand, offered it to her. "Try some Yankee dick, honey," Jack said.

She took me into her mouth. There I was on a dirt road with Jack, one of his arms around me, the other playing with his dick, and a teenage girl giving me a blow job. It didn't take me long to get off. When I did, she took me down her throat and kept me there until I began to go limp. She immediately moved onto Jack and brought him off just as quickly.

"Like ol' times, huh, Wakie?" he whispered under his breath as he put his dick back into his pants and zipped up. Jack was straight, but he sure was hot.

When I hear people talk about sexual orientation and gays recruiting straights, I think of Jack. The things we did together as kids didn't affect him the same way they affected me, but we both remembered. Queers are born, not made.

Some years later I asked around about Jack. I was told that he was married, had two daughters, and was living in Winston-Salem, N.C.

It had been an eventful year. We moved to Florida, President Roosevelt died, the war ended, and I had my first orgasm. Jacksonville was a military town, with three major naval bases within a forty-square-mile-area: the reason most fathers kept a tight rein on their daughters.

At that time young girls did not venture out alone, period. But as a nine-year-old boy, I was allowed to go almost anywhere. It didn't make sense to me, but I was glad to be a boy. I rarely stayed home, as I was always out searching for a new adventure.

Saturday mornings were another matter entirely. I never missed my favorite radio shows, *Let's Pretend*, *First Nighter*, and *Grand Central Station*. But by afternoon I would be on my way downtown. I could take care of myself. My many afternoons spent alone at the movies in Salisbury had provided good training. I had no fear of getting lost, no fear of people, no real fear at all. The few fears I had were of unreal things, stories my sisters told me, monsters from movies, and the like. I looked forward to my Saturdays since they were mine.

One Saturday I turned on the radio a little early. Right before *Let's Pretend*, I heard the end of a local program called *Crusader Kids*, a talent contest with the theme song "School Days." I decided to check it out the following week—another new adventure.

The next week I walked to the station. Behind double glass doors, etched with the letters WJAX, was a wide staircase and, at the top, two more glass doors. When I entered I saw a woman talking on the phone. Her hair was gray; she wore a soft, filmy dress; and from the way she sat, very straight, I could tell she wore a corset. She smiled at me as she hung up.

"I'd like to sing on the radio," I blurted. She looked around. I think she was surprised I had come alone.

"I'm Irene Lake. What's your name?"

"Wakefield Poole, ma'am." I offered my hand.

I liked her immediately, and I could tell she liked me too. She told me she was the pianist for the show. I said I didn't have any music. All I had with me was nerve, and that could leave me at any minute.

"What would you like to sing?" She took a dainty handkerchief out of her sleeve and lightly dusted the keys of the biggest piano I'd ever seen.

"Do you know 'Ah! Sweet Mystery of Life'?" I asked.

"Now let's see...what key?" Mrs. Lake muttered as she played a few cords, then nodded for me to begin.

"A little lower, please. Much lower," I said.

Mrs. Lake modulated to an even lower key, and this time I didn't wait for a nod. I opened up and began to sing. She broke into a broad smile but continued to play, urging me on to the end. She took out the little handkerchief, wiped her forehead and hands, then returned it to her sleeve. "Very nice, Wakefield," she said. "I think we can use you on the program."

"Today?" I answered. "I'd love to."

Mrs. Lake let me use the phone to call my mom. At first my mother didn't believe me. Then, when she finally did, she had to get off the phone to call everyone to listen.

We went into another studio where there were about twenty people. Some children, a few parents, and even a little girl in a hillbilly costume. Mrs. Lake sat me next to her at the piano. I was on last, and when it was time for me to sing, she showed me where to stand. It went even better than the rehearsal.

After the commercial the announcer gave the results of the judges. Third place went to a little girl who did a recitation. Second place went to a teenager who sang "La Vie En Rose."

"And first place," the announcer said, "goes to our young bass baritone, Wakefield Poole."

The audience broke into applause, then Mrs. Lake played the intro to "School Days." As we started to sing, the announcer made his closing remarks, and then it was over.

A man handed me an envelope containing fifteen dollars in savings stamps, the first prize, and the first "money" I had ever earned. It had been so easy. I thanked Mrs. Lake.

"You're more than welcome," she said. "Your mother should be proud of you. You're quite talented and such a sweet boy."

Over the next few years I would appear regularly on *Crusader Kids*. Each series ran twelve weeks. Depending on how you placed, you could win anywhere between $50 and $100. It was fun—and profitable. I liked singing, I liked winning, and I liked the money.

Suddenly, my mom got phone calls asking me to sing at this meeting and that function, until I was making quite a bit of money with little effort. She wanted me to have a fairly normal childhood, so these offers were carefully screened and I was allowed to sing only once a week. This left me plenty of time to go to school, make friends, be a son to my parents, and a brother to my sisters.

I made friends with Sandra Hicklin, who lived up the street. She was in my class and was a lot like me. She was inquisitive, fun, spoiled, and an only child used to having her way. I had two sisters, but I was used to getting my way too. This made for a volatile relationship. After a few years of playing the romance of kids, we became the best of friends. We still went to school dances and did things together, but we both knew that romance, for us, would be found elsewhere. It was a friendship we each found both pleasant and useful.

One Saturday afternoon after the radio show, I went to the Arcade Theater to see *Frankenstein*. Most kids went to Saturday-morning matinees in their neighborhoods, but I liked to go to the regular movies downtown. I enjoyed being with adults.

I walked out of the bright sun, through the black-velvet drapes, and into the dark theater. Waiting a second for my eyes to adjust, I caught a slight chill from the change of temperature and decided to go to the bathroom before the show.

When I walked into the men's room, I saw two sailors inside. One stood at the sink combing his hair, and the other was at one of the urinals. I stepped up next to him, unzipped, and started to take a leak. The sailor at the sink turned off the water and left. The bathroom suddenly grew quiet, and all I could hear was the sound of my urine hitting the bowl. I realized that there was no sound coming from the sailor next to me. I glanced over. Out of the corner of my eye, I saw him trying to hide a slight erection with his hand and not doing a good job of it. Without thinking, I turned my head slightly toward him to get a better look.

He noticed that I was looking, then took a small step back. Then he changed hands to allow me an unobstructed view. The flap of his sailor pants was totally unbuttoned, revealing snow-white boxer shorts out of which hung an incredibly beautiful dick. Why I found it beautiful, I didn't know, but my mind flashed back to that day in the doghouse with Monroe. I was so excited that I reached out and took it in my hand. He was surprised at my action. He wasn't smiling, but when he turned to face me, a strange feeling of warmth overwhelmed me.

Suddenly there was a sound at the door. He turned quickly to face the urinal just as the door opened. A man entered and went straight for the toilet, dropped his pants, and sat down. I noticed there was a hole in the wall of the booth about the size of a billiard ball, and then I saw the man's eye look through the hole at us.

During this the sailor had buttoned his pants and walked over to the sink. When I turned to look at him, he nodded for me to follow, then opened the door and left. I walked out and found the sailor waiting at the top of the aisle inside the theater. When I reached him, he put his arm on my shoulder and led me to a seat. After a while he leaned over and spoke for the first time.

"How much time do you have?"

"I have to be home by dark," I answered without hesitation. "Do you have some place we can go?"

"I have a room at the Roosevelt Hotel. Wanna go up?"

"Yeah." I had never been so excited in my life.

We sat for a minute or two before getting up. Then, together, we left the theater. Crossing Adams Street, he told me to be natural and act like he was my big brother when we entered the hotel. Things went well, and without any problems, we arrived at his room.

Once inside, he removed his uniform. I undressed as well. I could hardly take my eyes off him. There he was, a naked man, standing before me. He took me in his arms, kissed me, then led me to the bed. I had never kissed a grown man like this before, but I liked it very much.

We kept it up for more than an hour, taking turns doing things to each other. He would do something, then I would eagerly follow his lead. I learned more about sex in one afternoon than I had ever imagined. I know now I should have been frightened, but I wasn't. I wasn't forced to do anything. I was the aggressor. Nothing we did seemed ugly, and nothing hurt me. He was kind and gentle, and it was totally enjoyable.

When we were finished I asked him all sorts of questions. I told him this was the first time I'd been with an adult but that I'd thought about it. He seemed amused when I told him about the doghouse episode and Jack. Then I asked him about the man in the men's room looking through the hole. He explained that it was a glory hole and that guys used it to have oral sex. He also said I should be careful if I decided to use one. He knew this wasn't a one-time thing for me. He was very nice and talked to me in a way I had never been talked to before—like a grown-up.

It was getting late, and I realized I had to get home. I didn't want to, but I rolled off the bed and put on my clothes anyway. When we kissed good-bye I couldn't resist touching him once more. He laughed, opened the door, and I left him there in his snow-white shorts with a semi-hard-on.

I got home just before dark, and my mother was just before getting angry. When she asked where I had been, I lied to her for the first time.

"The movie was so good, I stayed to see it twice," I answered innocently. "I'm sorry I worried you. Next time I'll call." And I would.

This experience changed the way I felt about myself sexually. Sex was no longer something I did with my friends but something adults did as well and did better. I began to see sexual situations where I had never imagined them.

Almost every men's room in the city had glory holes. I had never paid any attention to them before, but now I saw them everywhere—in theaters, in city parks, at bus stations, even the public library. From this time on, most of my adventures would end up with me in one of these places. The sex was usually impersonal, with no direct communication.

I started to look for signs: uniforms, shoes, wedding rings, anything to give them some identity. So many married men cruised these places that I thought it was commonplace, something all men did. For the longest time I even feared I might run into my dad in one of these places. I wouldn't know for a few years that there were straights and queers and that I definitely belonged to the latter. At this time, though, I felt no fear, guilt, or shame about my actions. I assumed that under the right circumstances all men liked sex with other men. I had sex regularly with a man who was married, had six children, and even owned a second house to entertain his male friends. This may sound strange to many, but in all my sexual dealings with adults, I was always the aggressor. I was never a victim of child molestation. Just the opposite—I was relentless in my pursuit of adult companionship.

It was during a fourth-grade class play that things began to change for me. Actually, it was my voice that changed. It was part of growing up, and I was all for that.

Katherine Bagaley of the Bagaley Juvenile Theater offered me a scholarship to her school. The school taught tap, ballet, acrobatics, and dramatics, and within a month I began my first dance class. Again, something so simple, but my life would never be the same. I knew I was a dancer. Even when my voice settled and I started to sing again, I was still a dancer. Dancing made me feel like nothing else could. It was even better than sex. Well, maybe not better but different and just as good.

From that moment on, dancing and sex would occupy most of my time. After I started to take dancing classes, people began to call me a sissy. I had been called names before, but this time the taunting had a hateful, superior edge to it. I found some humor in it, though. I'd been having sex secretly with men and boys for years, and no one knew. But they were calling me a sissy for being a dancer. Right name. Wrong game.

After two months at the school, I moved to the advanced class. By my third year I was teaching the class.

When I was fifteen, Miss Bagaley took me to New York to study dancing. The trip was unbelievable. I started to get stronger and stronger and more sure every day that this was what I was meant to do.

At this point in my life, dancing became my primary motivation. School became a place just to make friends and have fun. After school I reserved my time for dancing.

My teenage years were not filled with torment and emotional crisis. I had close friends, others who had goals and serious ambitions like me. Ann Koscielny and Helio DeSoto were both studying to become concert pianists. Sandra Hicklin and Beverly Jones were both sensitive and eager to get everything out of life. And we were all a little boy crazy. Sisi, Helio's sister, became a welcome tagalong. The six of us made up our gang. It would change sometimes to include a new boyfriend here or there, but even today we remain the best of friends.

My spare time was limited, but I joined the chorus at school, coached the majorettes, and worked with the drama club. I also saved a little time to go to the park or the bus station to pursue my sexual activities, which were becoming more frequent as I grew older.

Despite increased name-calling, I performed in many school plays. I was always happy with my performances, even though I had to dodge pennies thrown by hecklers and endure loud hoots and laughter. When I was in my junior year, I exacted my revenge. I was asked to be the master of ceremonies for the junior-senior prom floor show. At the end of the show I walked onstage in my white dinner jacket to wrap up the proceedings.

"I want to take this opportunity to thank you all for your appreciation of my performances throughout our years together," I proclaimed. "I've received so much from you over the years that I want to give you something in return."

With this remark, I put my hands in my jacket pockets, and with one grand gesture, I showered the audience with brand-new pennies. If it worked for Uncle George in Salisbury, it should work for me here. Two black sheep using pennies to gain acceptance. There was a dreadful moment of silence. Then, after the shock, the entire audience laughed, applauded, and stood up—the only standing ovation I ever received at school. It was worth waiting for.

Simple fact: I was the best ballroom dancer in school. For that reason, I was quite popular. I liked girls a lot and never had any trouble having a good time. I was at the age when kissing and petting was part of the dating process. It was pleasant but totally different from the kisses I received from my male partners. With men, it was an interlude before or during sex. With girls, it held the promise of things to come.

My sexual activities were still mostly limited to men's rooms and parks and were for the most part impersonal. It's hard to get personal through a glory hole. But it made everything easy. No commitment, no identity, nothing but sex. It was exciting to have sex with people and then not recognize them if you should pass them on the street. Judgments and personal tastes didn't confuse the game. There were no "I like blonds" or "I like redheads." There was only a dick and a hole in the wall. The rest was up to you.

Many times I would agree to meet someone face-to-face. When

we met, the men were always surprised by how young I was. I knew nothing about laws concerning sex with minors, so I didn't understand when immediately some would say they had to go back to work, or make some other excuse. I assumed they didn't find me attractive or didn't like my hair or something. Others weren't bothered by my age.

Early on I learned to deal with rejection. In 1951, when I was fifteen, I began to notice a growing trend in all the men's rooms I had cruised for the past five years. It started the same way at all of them. More and more, a nasty janitor would storm into the room, banging the door as he announced, "All right, you fairies. Outta here! We're closing up for cleaning."

Toilets would flush, and the place would clear out in seconds, which always amazed me. Rushing out would mean you were responding to him and that you were what he said you were. But I never rushed out in these instances and, defiantly, even took time to comb my hair. After a short walk I could always go right back, but it would be the same routine every few hours.

Then one day the glory hole would be boarded over, even if the stalls had steel walls. They riveted some; they welded others. This was definitely a sign that things were changing, that the good times were coming to an end. Nasty notes began to appear on the walls: FAGS, GET OUT! or KILL QUEERS. One by one, the bathrooms became almost dangerous, and with these changes came the fear that you could be arrested at any moment. Suddenly these places became instruments of entrapment and harassment. Police hid in mop closets, peeped through tiny holes in partitions, and observed through transoms. Sexual activity in these places all but stopped.

I was shocked. I not only lost my major source for sex but also discovered that all men didn't do the things I loved doing. What I loved doing, they said, was nasty, degenerate, and a crime against nature. I knew I was different, but anything that felt so good couldn't be that bad.

After putting a lot of thought into what might have brought about these drastic changes, I formed a theory. The first time I had sex through a glory hole was in 1946. The war had ended, but there were still thousands of servicemen coming through Jacksonville on their way home from overseas. We still had the same military bases, only now we had more transients. But when the bases scaled down and the numbers were smaller and more permanent, the purge began.

By 1952 the only place left untouched was the men's room at the naval air station bus depot. All sailors coming into town on leave, going to the beaches, or returning to their bases after a hard night of drinking, had to pass through the bus station. Except for occasional harassment from porters, things there were the same as they had always been. This gave me the idea that the government knew about the sexual activity in these places and found it to their advantage to look the other way. It would also explain how some of these holes got there in the first place.

Most of the bus depot toilet stalls were made of steel or marble but there, almost always, bigger than life, would be a hole. How could anyone unconnected with the building drill through steel or chip through marble undetected? I've known some determined queens, but none who would take the time to chip through marble! As long as the servicemen were getting blown in some bathroom, they wouldn't be out getting the young girls of the city in trouble.

In 1952 I met Beverly. The first time I saw her, she was standing by the piano in chorus class. She had books in her arms and a way of holding them that directed all the boys' eyes right to her breasts. The bell hadn't rung yet for class to begin, so several guys were talking and laughing around her. Our eyes met for a moment; she smiled and continued talking. It was a scene right out of one of those B teenager movies.

She looked just like Susan Hayward, wearing a tight-fitting gray skirt that flared out at the knees, a pink angora sweater, and a scarf around her neck. Her hair was shoulder-length but swept to one side.

I had never seen anyone so sexy except in the movies. But she was trouble. She was a senior, and I was a sophomore. After we went steady for a year, she broke my heart and married an older man. This was the first time someone had broken my heart, and I knew it wouldn't be the last.

During my senior year, I received an offer to do winter stock at the Palm Beach Playhouse. The season was filled with big stars and great plays: *Born Yesterday*, with Charlton Heston, Jan Sterling, and Paul Douglas; *Mr. Roberts*, also with Heston; *The Man*, starring John

Barrymore Jr. and Sylvia Sydney; and, my favorite, *Life With Father*, featuring Billie Burke. We were to do two musicals, *Annie Get Your Gun* and *Carousel*.

Billie, who had played Glinda, the Good Witch of the North, in *The Wizard of Oz*, immediately took a liking to me. She must have been in her late seventies, and she walked, though not too well, with a cane. She was a hypochondriac and draped her dressing room with white muslin. I was one of the few people allowed in, and I felt honored.

Her transformation for the role was miraculous. She wrapped her legs from thigh to ankle with elastic bandages, applied her makeup, and put on a wig, and when she walked onstage she was thirty again. To this day, I have never seen magic quite like that. Witnessing her in action was worth the price I would later have to pay.

When I returned home ten weeks later, even though I had completed all my work and was in the top third of my class, school administrators informed me that I had not been in attendance a sufficient number of days and, therefore, would not be allowed to graduate. But I wasn't about to wait another year to go to New York. I would continue to teach dancing, save my money, and leave for the city when I had enough.

I was getting out socially since the bathroom scene was gone. I soon discovered there were other people like me and that they had their own little society. Some had lovers, some just had roommates, and some were still living at home like me.

One night I had dinner at the home of Bob Smith and Gene Braddock, two gay lovers I had met. They had been together several years and were the first gay couple I recall knowing. They were wonderful together, and I was envious, especially since I had a crush on Bob. When it came time to leave, Bob Hughes, another friend, asked for a ride home and suggested that we stop at the Standor Bar for a nightcap. We weren't there more than five minutes when a friend of his invited us to a party.

There were about thirty guys at the party, all crammed into a two-bedroom bungalow, and I recognized some of their faces from the bus station. It had been a long day, and nothing was really happening at the party. We were just about to leave when we heard a loud knock at the door. The host opened the door to reveal two policemen. "OK, boys," said one of the cops pushing his way into the living room. "The party's over! Get out your IDs and file out."

"Come on, Bob," I said as I pulled out my driver's license. "Let's get out of here."

One of the cops took down my name, and as I passed through the door, flashbulbs went off, I felt a hand grab my arm, and before I knew what was happening, I was loaded into a paddywagon. We were being arrested.

As soon as the wagon was packed with very worried-looking guys, we were driven to the county jail and booked on a crimes against nature charge. I had enough money on me to arrange for my own bail, so I didn't have to spend the night there.

I discovered that one of the guests at the party had brought a marine with him. When someone made a pass at him, he ran from the house, immediately called the police, and told them a bunch of fairies had tried to molest him. The charge was absurd, so I wasn't worried—that is, until I arrived home at seven in the morning.

My mom and dad were sitting at the table having coffee as I walked in the door.

"Well, Bub," my dad said calmly, "Where the hell have you been all night? Your mom has been worried sick."

"In jail," I answered straight out.

"On what charge?"

"Crimes against nature," I responded, not really sure what that meant. I hadn't done anything wrong, so I felt no need to lie to them. "Nothing was going on," I explained. "At least I didn't see anything. Bob and I realized that it wasn't our kind of party. We were bored and on our way out when the police came. They arrested thirty of us, and we have to be in court Monday morning at ten o'clock. That's all there is to it, I swear!"

"I believe you, son," he said as he went to the phone to call Eliot Norton, his lawyer.

Sometime later, when we arrived in court, we discovered the other guys had all hired one lawyer to represent them. Only one other person, Richard Cawley, had his own lawyer. We took a seat and waited for the trial to proceed. They called the case, and the judge asked that the group of us come to the front. All thirty of us stood and filed up to stand in front of the judge. My father and Norton walked up with me, joining the others.

Sgt. Bacon, the arresting officer, was asked to verify the charges. When he finished, the judge asked him to be more specific about what he had observed upon entering the house.

"There were two guys dancing with each other, and several had no clothes on."

"Who, Sgt. Bacon?" the judge interrupted. "Point them out, and tell me what they were doing."

There was a moment's hesitation before the officer responded. Then he pointed and said, "That older guy there was dancing nude on top of the dining room table." He was pointing to my father.

When my dad realized the officer meant him, he lunged forward. Fortunately, Norton prevented him from reaching the officer. We had another stroke of luck. My dad had sold the judge his Chrysler at the car lot where he worked.

"Sgt. Bacon," the judge reprimanded, "I know this man. He's the father of one of the accused and wasn't even at the party. There's no crime against nature here, and I'm releasing all these young men. I'll see you later in my chambers." Then he turned to face us. "I know there are some queers among you and that some of you are just nice young boys caught in a bad situation. I can only say that you should be more careful." I felt like he was looking directly at me. "I don't want to see any of you again."

We were all relieved. In that day gay rights victories were unheard of. There were no rights for gays, but still we were all elated over this first taste of justice.

Then later that afternoon the *Jacksonville Journal* hit the newsstands. ALL-MALE PARTY RAIDED read the headline of the front-page story. All the charges were printed, followed by the names, addresses, ages, and even phone numbers of all who were there. Not one word was mentioned about the case being thrown out of court.

Norton threatened a lawsuit, so a retraction was printed on the back page the following Friday. It was about the size of a want ad.

The damage was done. Several people left town and moved away for good. My phone rang constantly with prank calls, and Miss Bagaley refused to speak to me. I was told she took down all the pictures of me that were hanging in the reception room of her school. I never saw her again. But my mom and dad were supportive as always. It would have been so easy for me to leave for New York a little earlier than planned, but I wasn't ready. I stayed and took all my licks.

The funniest part of the whole episode was that two of my good friends from school, Helio DeSoto and Harry Goodwin, were forbidden by their parents to associate with me any longer. Harry had been at the party too but jumped out the window and got away. His parents didn't know about his being there, so Harry couldn't put up any resistance. Ironically, a few months later they both were arrested during a raid at Lukeys, a lesbian bar on Phillips Highway. I was sitting and watching in a car across the road as police carried them off to jail. Another few minutes and I would have been right there with them.

I bailed them out of jail and took them home so that they could tell their parents. Maybe the time was right to take off for the big city. I started to think seriously about it. It was October, and it took me until January to get ready.

Edith Schiller-Fehl

Edith Schiller-Fehl

Wakefield Poole head shot and promotional photo for his appearance on the Virginia Atter TV show, Jacksonville, Florida, 1952.

Edith Schiller-Fehl

Wakefield Poole and Anne Phillips in a promotional photo for the Ballet Guild of Jacksonville, circa 1954.

Chapter Three

Running Wild

Jacksonville, Fla., 1955

It was sprinkling as we drove to the airport. It seems that every time something major happens in my life, it's accompanied by rain. It was also January, and there was a chill in the air. My mom was unusually quiet; her "baby" was leaving. I realized my departure would be hard on her, but I was more excited than ever, even though I tried not to show it. After repeating "I'm going to live in New York" over and over in my mind, I realized my longtime dream was becoming a reality. Even though I knew I would miss my family, I felt no sadness about leaving home. It was still dark when we arrived at the airport. We said our good-byes, and I boarded the plane bound for the city that would make all my dreams come true.

After the flight I found my luggage and took my seat on the bus that would take me to Manhattan. Dawn was just breaking. When I first caught sight of the skyline, it was flooded with sunlight against a dark western sky, and most of the lights in the city were still burning. What a picture!

The Sloane House YMCA lobby was filled with people buzzing about. I paid for a week in advance and received the key to my room. Room? It was about the size of a closet, with a single bed, a small chest, and a cupboard to hold about three hangers of clothes. I unpacked my bags and went down the hall to take a shower.

The bathroom was huge and had at least a dozen washbasins in a row.

On each side of the sinks were the showers. The shower room itself was twice as big as my room. Six showerheads were mounted on the wall, and two of them were in use. I removed my towel and stepped under the warm and relaxing spray. I noticed the two men in the shower with me were soaping themselves vigorously and had raging hard-ons. I was shocked. After all, this was the YMCA. I had always thought of it as a religious institution and had never heard stories of sexual escapades in the Y. This should have been my first clue as to how naïve I was. I realized I had interrupted something when I came in, so I quickly finished my shower and left them to their pleasure.

On my way back to my room, I noticed that some of the room doors were open. Inside, most of the occupants were lying on their beds, naked, with just a towel across their laps. I hurried back to my room, as my towel was starting to stand away from my body. It was the first time in my life that I remember being truly embarrassed.

My God, I thought, *it's only one o'clock in the afternoon.* Did this go on all the time? It did. The YMCA was a huge building with many floors. Was this happening all over? It was. The idea was staggering. You could find sex any time of the day or night. I needed this?

One afternoon I called Tom Ayers, an actor I had worked with in Palm Beach. Tom was the perfect juvenile lead type: short, cute, kind, and full of personality. He invited me to his apartment on the Upper East Side. By the time I arrived it was mid afternoon. Tom was ironing his shirts, getting ready to go out of town on another job. While we were talking the phone rang.

"Hello," Tom answered. There was a pause. "I'm here getting ready to go to Pittsburgh and talking to Wakefield Poole." Another pause. "No, he's right here. I swear! I'll let you talk to him." He handed me the phone.

"Hello," I said, not knowing who was on the other end.

"Hi, I'm Bob Stone, a friend of Tom's. Are you really Wakefield Poole?"

"Yes, I am."

"Well, one night your name came up in conversation. It's got to be one of the greatest names I've ever heard. I was calling to ask Tom to go to a movie. Since he's busy, why don't you join me? There's a double bill I want to catch: *Stalag 17* and *Member of the Wedding*."

I made plans to meet Tom's friend, then hung up the phone. Tom explained that one night while talking about unusual names, he had offered mine to some friends, and Bob said he just had to meet me.

Tom wrote down the address, told me Bob was an actor, and said he'd be back in a month.

I made my way downtown to Bob's apartment. I rang the bell, and the door opened to reveal a tall and not terribly attractive older man. But the moment he spoke, his looks became unimportant. He had the most beautiful speaking voice, deep and rich, covering you all over. I liked him immediately.

Bob and I had some tea and talked comfortably. As the time passed I found myself more and more attracted to him. At one point he reached out and touched my arm. His hands were massive, but his touch was gentle. He was not at all as he appeared. I was truly amazed by this man, and by the time we left for the movie theater, I wanted him badly.

We took our seats during the opening credits of *Stalag 17*. A few minutes into the film, I recognized Bob on the screen. He was the actor playing the mute. He was terrific, but it was ironic that with that incredible voice he didn't get to speak at all. Then *Member of the Wedding*, the second film, began. At one point during the movie, I was noticeably moved. Bob reached over and took hold of my hand, which he continued to do until the end of the picture.

Walking back to his apartment, he said he was upset they had cut the scene in the movie in which Ethel Waters sings "Song of the Sparrow." Once inside, he made us a drink and, excusing himself, went to the telephone. He dialed, and after a few seconds I heard him speak. He was speaking to Ethel Waters! She hadn't seen the re-release of the film but had heard what they had done and was resigned that nothing could be done about it. When they were finished talking, Bob asked if she would say hello to someone, then handed me the phone.

Was this a New York thing? Twice in one day I was talking on the phone with someone I'd never met. I don't remember what I said to her or what she responded, but at the end I do remember she said, "Well, sugar, you have a nice evening, and tell Bob next time not to wait so long to call, you hear?"

I hung up the phone and sat next to Bob on the sofa. In less than a minute his arm was around my shoulder, and in less than that we were undressing, a fitting end to a wonderful afternoon. I would see him many times, and each time would be as interesting and wonderful as the time before.

I decided I had better get on with my life. But I didn't know how to find out about auditions or any of the things that were necessary. The only thing I knew was where to take classes, so I enrolled at the International School of Dance at Carnegie Hall with just enough money to last six or eight weeks. I could only afford to take one class a day, so I mixed it up. Three days a week I took ballet and two days I took what was then called modern jazz. The jazz class, taught by Frank Wagner, was held late in the afternoon and was filled with working dancers and actors. There was no music, but usually the class was accompanied by one or more drummers.

On numerous occasions Marlon Brando would sit in with his bongo drums. He was dating Viola Essen, who owned the studio, so he was around a lot. A staircase at one end of the studio led up to a private sitting room where Viola would rest and entertain guests between classes. Often, about twenty minutes into the class, the door to the sitting room would open and Brando would descend, drums in hand. He'd move quietly into the corner with the other drummers and play until the class was finished. After a few private words with the drummers, he'd disappear up the stairs. The class was always fun, but when he joined in, the excitement level would always rise.

The second week at the Sloane House, I met Tony Bianchino. He had been there six months and showed me where to eat and do my laundry and pointed out the local pawnshop. One night he took me to my first gay bar in the city, the Terrace on West 45th Street. The minute I walked in the door, my eyes fell on the bartender, who was about thirty years old, tall, blond, attractive, and who wore the tightest pants I'd ever seen. Nothing was left to the imagination. I introduced myself, and he told me his name was Mike Bayens. Right away I knew I would be waiting until four o'clock for him to get off work. After breakfast at Toffenetti's we went up to Mike's apartment on West 75th Street.

We were barely in the door before we were in each other arms. All night we had been like racers at the starting line waiting for the gun to go off. In no time at all we were standing naked before each other, our clothes at our feet. We didn't even turn on the lights.

Three days later I moved in with him, and within a month I had taken a waiter job at the Terrace.

For the first time, I became a night person and liked it. We worked through the night, fucked until dawn, and slept most of the day. Mike became my mentor, exposing me to new things from Mahler to Mabel Mercer. We were never apart. We had such a good life that I put my aspirations on the back burner, and now I was taking just two classes a week. There wasn't enough time for everything.

We were together less than a year when I told Mike I had to get back to serious study. I couldn't do it—working nights and wanting to be with him the rest of the time. I said I couldn't live with him anymore and told him I'd start looking for a new place to live.

A few days later Tom Mathews, a friend of ours, was coming over to go with Mike and me to an afternoon movie. At the last minute Mike excused himself from joining us. He told me he'd found a new place to live and that by the time I got back from the movie, he'd be gone. He said he'd leave his new address on the table and would let me know when he got his phone. Then the downstairs buzzer went off. It was Tom. I hugged Mike and left the apartment.

Tom and I walked through the park to the East Side. He was raving about a new Maria Callas recording he had heard the night before, and, voila, there it was, in the window of a little record shop. We changed our plans on the spot. I bought the record, and we decided to go back to the apartment. Chinese food and Callas. What could be better?

We had been gone only an hour. As I opened the door the smell of gas overwhelmed me. My eyes began to water, and I felt a stinging sensation in my throat. Tom was coughing and saying "Oh, my God!" over and over. I ran to the window and opened it wide. The kitchen door had been jammed closed and pieces of towel were sticking out from the crack under the door.

"Call an ambulance!" I yelled as I tried to break down the door. Shocked, Tom stood motionless, so I turned around and smacked him. He finally moved to the phone. The door had been nailed from the inside, so I had to kick it in. I found Mike slumped forward in a kitchen chair, his head lying on the open oven door.

I broke the kitchen window and dragged Mike into the living room. He was over six feet tall, so it wasn't easy. His color was ashen, he was foaming at the mouth, and he didn't appear to be breathing. I turned him over and started to give him artificial respiration.

In no time the apartment was filled with policemen and emergency workers. Pure chaos. After much activity they told me Mike was coming around, then put him on a gurney and took him out. Tom went with Mike, and as quickly as they had come, everyone left. There I was, completely alone, not even knowing where they had taken him.

Suddenly, reality caught up with me, and I began to shake and sob. I really lost it. How could I have not seen this coming? *Poor Mike,* I thought. *What have I done?*

I had no one to talk to in New York except Sonny DeSoto, a friend who played piano for ballet classes. I picked up the phone and dialed his number. I must have sounded distraught, because after our talk he called my parents in Florida and told them what had happened.

It was several hours before Tom called to say that Mike would live and that he was in the psychiatric ward at Bellevue Hospital. I never saw Mike or Tom again.

Eighteen hours later, my father rang the downstairs buzzer. He packed my bags, and in less than an hour Sonny, my father, and I were driving home to Florida. I don't remember much about this except they said that I had an emotional breakdown. Now, a little more than a year after I had left home, I was returning to Florida, having accomplished nothing.

More than thirty years later I was having dinner with my friend, Ron Parisi, when the phone rang. It was Mike. He asked if I remembered him. I assured him that I not only remembered him but also thought of him often. Mike said he was living in Pennsylvania with his lover of twenty-five years and that they were getting ready to retire. He was calling to say how sorry he was about his suicide attempt and that he hoped I didn't think too badly of him.

"Of course not," I responded. "I've got only good memories. In fact, you still rate high among the best sex partners I've ever had." We both laughed.

"That makes me feel better," Mike said. "But I should never have done what I did to you. You were so young, and I'm sorry."

"It's really OK. You know, I think of you every time I hear Mahler's 'Kindertotenleider.' The recording you gave me, I played it to death just a few years ago. I can't tell you how glad I am that you found the courage to call me."

We promised to keep in touch. I hung up the phone, and Ron insisted I tell him the whole story. I was touched by Mike's unexpected call. It was as if a loose string had been tied. Is this a part of aging? Little unfinished life stories brought to conclusions?

The following week, I received a small envelope in the mail containing a tape of "Kindertotenleider." No card attached.

In less than a year Mike's lover called to tell me he had died of a heart attack. He added that he was grateful that Mike and I were able to renew our affections for each other. I hung up the phone, put on the tape he sent, and thought about Mike.

I had been home about two weeks when I started to make plans for my return to New York. I regretted the wasted year, but it was no worse than what most kids do their freshman year at college: parties, beer, and lots of sex. Chalk it up to experience. If I had to spend time in Jacksonville, I was going to make it count.

I began teaching class for any dancing school in town that would have me. I worked with the Ballet Guild of Jacksonville and was dancing six days a week. Betty Ogilvie, an ex-Balanchine dancer, had a studio on the southside. She was an excellent teacher and assured me that I could become a ballet dancer. I worked hard. Soon after, Edward Caton, a world-famous choreographer, came to Jacksonville to teach master classes. One of the best teachers in New York, he offered me a scholarship to the Ballet Russe School and suggested I come to New York as soon as possible.

I had saved my money, studied hard, and learned some good—and difficult—lessons. I was also in the best shape of my life, and my technique was developing nicely. Once again I packed my bags, said my farewells, and left for fame and fortune in the big city.

A bit older and wiser, I arrived in New York in fall 1956. My old friend, Tony Bianchino, needed a roommate, so my timing was perfect. He had a one-bedroom garden apartment right off the park.

Right away I applied at the Hotel St. George in Brooklyn Heights, and to my amazement I got a job as the night cashier and auditor, working from eleven P.M. until eight A.M., six days a week. My salary was enough to pay for food and rent, with a bit left over. One problem solved.

When I arrived at the Ballet Russe School, I found out Eddie Caton was in South America teaching classes and choreographing a new ballet. The administration told me they knew nothing about me or my promised scholarship. Frederick Franklin, one of the teachers, heard about my troubles and immediately came to my aid, suggesting that I take his class. Eddie was a bit of a character, and Freddy must have realized that he had forgotten to mention my arrival. I took Freddy's class, and later he apologized for the mix-up and assured me that he would take care of everything. He spoke to the head of the school, and soon after I was given a full scholarship.

The schedule I had set for myself was taxing, to say the least. I would go to work at midnight, get off at eight, sleep for three hours, then attend my first class at noon. I took four classes a day, the last ending at six. Then I'd go home to sleep for a few hours before the whole thing started over again. By the time Sunday came around, I could never get out of bed. It was the best sleep I've ever had, those Sundays.

I had little, if any, time for sexual activities. But over the next ten months, this schedule I was living gave me the confidence I needed to get me through my audition to become a member of the Ballet Russe de Monte Carlo. I had worked hard to become a professional ballet dancer, and this was the final obstacle. Pass this audition, and my dream could come true.

The audition was incredibly difficult. First, Freddy gave a short ballet class, then Leon Danielian led a character class, and finally Madame Swaboda conducted a pas de deux class. We were judged in all these classes by a panel of our instructors. To add to the pressure, the company had just returned from touring and filled the sides of the class room to capacity. All these dancers watching their future competition. It was harder than any performance I'd ever done. I was extremely nervous, but after a few minutes my nerves vanished and were replaced by pure energy. This transformation is what makes performing so pleasurable.

I was offered a contract for the coming season.

A few days after the audition, I was taking class from Igor Schwezoff at the Ballet Theater School. Igor was a wonderful teacher, and his class allowed me to enjoy dance for the sake of dance. Sonny, his lover, played piano for all of Igor's classes. After class, Lucia Chase, director of Ballet Theater, asked if I would be interested in joining her company. I was flabbergasted. I did a lot of soul-searching and out of loyalty chose to stay with Ballet Russe.

Rehearsals went better than I could have imagined. We spent four weeks rehearsing *Swan Lake*, *The Nutcracker*, *Gaîté Parisienne*, *Scheherazade*, *Coppélia*, *Le Beau Danube*, *Les Sylphides*, *Giselle*, and *Raymonda*, which provided the basics for all the programs we would perform on tour.

After we learned all the elements, we started to put entire ballets together. The last week of rehearsal, Alicia Alonso and Igor Youskevich, one of the great partnerships in ballet, appeared. Their personal relationship, which was well known, only enhanced their already electrifying performances. Unfortunately, they only performed in seven of the 110 cities we played over a ten-month period.

Whenever Alicia and Igor danced, the theater wings were packed to capacity with all the dancers who weren't onstage. When the corps de ballet stands in the wings watching, instead of resting in the dressing room or preparing for the next ballet, you know something special is taking place. I never missed a chance to watch and learn.

To this day, I have never seen a better *Black Swan* pas de deux than Alicia's and Igor's—or a more erotic one. On more than one occasion Alicia would exit the stage with little bite marks on her neck. Then, the very next night, I'd see their *Giselle*, and the innocence she conveyed was even more astonishing. If only we'd had them to watch every night.

We opened our tour with ten days in San Juan, Puerto Rico, the first and longest stand we played during the entire tour. After we had performed all the ballets in our repertoire, we began our U.S. tour. Since most of the dates were one-night stands, the company traveled in two buses. Every day we piled into the buses by eight A.M., and at about four in the afternoon, we'd arrive at our hotel. Our schedule was always the same: drop off our bags, get a bite to eat, go to the theater for rehearsal, put on our makeup, perform, have something to eat again, then get to bed at about two A.M. It was not the life I had imagined. I thought there would be some artistic direction, some period of learning. Instead it became a job.

We played everywhere from opera houses to school auditoriums, and even the Grand Ole Opry. Sometimes we got dressed in the scenery trucks that had been backed up to a connecting door in the building. Sometimes we put on our makeup outdoors before the sun went down because the dressing rooms had no lights other than a fluorescent tube in the ceiling.

It hadn't taken Ballet Russe long to make a name for itself, taking dance to an array of venues. I had even seen them perform in Jacksonville when I was twelve. We had no time for continued learning, and seldom did we even have time for class. All our effort was put into performing. Almost always we did one-night stands, which eliminated repertoire rehearsals, and the same scenery could be loaded on and off the trucks.

Our U.S. tour started in the South and worked its way indirectly north. One of the highlights for me, of course, was our engagement in Jacksonville. Because of the demand for tickets, we did three performances, two evenings and a matinee. Everyone wanted to see the hometown boy turned professional dancer. It meant a lot to me to have my proud parents see me accomplish my dream to be in a ballet company.

Contrary to the myth that all ballet dancers are gay, most of our male dancers were straight and married. At that time, word of mouth was the only way to find out if there was even a gay bar in the town where we were staying. Usually, Denny Lamont, one of the few gay dancers in the troupe, would walk around the city looking for people who were obviously gay, sometimes even drag queens, and ask them where to go for fun. Believe me, this led to some wild adventures. One time it landed us at a whorehouse in Juarez, Mexico, where we watched some porno movies. When the madam shut off the projector and started to produce her wares, we ran out the door. We laughed all the way back to the States.

That year, the troupe got a week off at Christmas, so I spent a few days at home, then checked into the West Side YMCA in New York. Soon after, I was waiting for the elevator when an attractive young man asked me where I had bought my rehearsal bag. We talked for a bit then made a date for coffee. “Pay me a compliment, tell me you want me, and I’m yours” should have been my motto, because before I left to join the troupe, I had fallen in love...again.

His name was Ed Manaresi, a teacher who lived in Morristown, N.J. He was five foot seven, with short brown hair, brown eyes, and an Ivy League look. He was also kind, intelligent, and, most of all, had a wonderful sense of humor. We’d only had a few days together, but that was enough for us to make a commitment.

On the whole, touring is a celibate affair. Our troupe had six months of traveling left, so my new romance was sustained mostly through the U.S. Postal Service and an occasional phone call.

After a while I started to become dissatisfied with my life as a ballet dancer. I loved performing, but we didn’t have a company class, and the rehearsals dealt mostly with adjusting to the differences in stage size, location of dressing rooms, and other logistics. We were neither motivated nor inspired by any discernible artistic direction. In fact, we had no artistic leadership whatsoever. Mostly I missed the thrill that comes with acquiring knowledge and making the body respond to almost impossible tasks. On this tour the only challenge was trying to get some sleep on the bus.

I think things would have been different if we hadn’t played mostly one-nighters. This was the late ’50s, and ballet was just starting to take its place in American culture. One-night stands made it possible for us to fill out a complete season, but they also had a way of running together. Some nights we didn’t even know what city we were in, only what ballet we were performing. The only magic left by the end of our tour was *Swan Lake*. We only performed an Act II version, and though I did little but stand and pose with my partner while the principals danced, there was no denying then that I was a dancer in a major ballet company performing in one of the greatest ballets ever choreographed—a fantasy fulfilled.

At the end of the season, I left the company with no immediate plans, but I knew I needed more than Ballet Russe could supply. Fortunately, that spring I received an offer from Betty Ogilvie in Jacksonville to take over her school for the summer while she did summer stock in Sacramento. The one thing that persuaded me to accept was knowing I could choreograph as many ballets as I chose. Ed, excited about spending the summer in Florida, came with me. In August, Betty asked if I would stay on a while longer, through the year, and I accepted. I enjoyed teaching almost as much as dancing. Ed secured a teaching job at one of the high schools, and we settled in. My family was glad to have me home, and they asked no questions about the young man I had brought home. In fact, they liked him a lot.

After the spring Ballet Guild performances, Betty decided she was ready to come home. I returned to New York alone, since Ed's teaching contract wouldn't end until after summer school was over.

I stayed with Ben Cenerino, a friend of Ed's, in an apartment on 69th Street, right off Central Park West. Soon after, an apartment became available in Ben's building. A large studio, it had originally been the library of the house and all the paneling had been retained. It was perfect, and Ben was right upstairs.

I started taking classes and auditioning for Broadway shows. At every audition I'd get down to the very end and for some reason I'd be the last one cut. I was five foot eight and could usually fit into either group, tall or short, but inevitably I was cut each time.

In one audition Michael Kidd, the choreographer, asked for anyone who could do acrobatics and aerials to stand in one group. Remembering my acrobatic experience at Miss Bagaley's, I gingerly joined the group. First, continuous cartwheels. I got through those. Then handsprings. Again success. Next he asked for a round-off flip-flop. I did a perfect round-off, went into the back flip, and landed flat on my head. My arms folded like an umbrella, leaving all that force nowhere to go but down. I wasn't knocked out cold—but almost.

Michael was concerned for my well-being, but after he realized I was all right, we had a good laugh. I couldn't stop rubbing my head, though. The more I rubbed, the more we laughed. All of us, about a hundred guys, laughing. I was mortified but laughing.

I didn't get the job.

One night after an evening class, I heard that Rod Alexander, the choreographer of *The Show of Shows*, needed dancers for an industrial show. Evening auditions were rare, but it was right around the corner, so I took a chance.

The audition lasted three hours, and we did every imaginable kind of dancing. Suddenly I noticed only eight of us were left. We took turns singing for the musical director, and when we were finished we stood in a line for what seemed another hour. Finally, at about midnight, Lou Kristopher, Rod's assistant, walked over and asked if we were all available for the summer. My God, I got a job!

Although they hired me for a Ford industrial show in Detroit, it turned into three jobs. We made a film for Ford to be sent to all their dealers over the world, we performed in a stage production presenting all the new model cars to dealers who traveled to Detroit, and we simultaneously rehearsed a dance concert for a tour of the Orient. It was quite a summer in Detroit. Industrial shows usually traveled to major cities, but Ford decided to bring its top salesmen to Detroit instead. This was the year the company was going to introduce the Ford Falcon, so they wanted the show to be something special...and it was.

We shot the film first, as some parts were also to be used in the stage production. Starring in the film were Jack Parr, Walter Pidgeon, and Janis Paige. Jack was quite shy, Walter quite large, and Janis was something else.

On her first entrance into the rehearsal hall, Janis exclaimed, "Hi, everybody. I'm Janis! Which of you guys are the titty lifters?" Three of us were to do a number with her, and she was raring to go. She was a joy to work with in the number and kept us all laughing, telling us at one point that Walter was notorious for having one of the largest dicks in Hollywood. At that time I could still be shocked, and I was—a little. It was the first time I'd ever heard a woman discuss penis size. "Cocks are like diamonds," she said. "They're all wonderful, but I prefer the bigger ones." I liked her a lot, but four days later she finished her part and left. It was a major production, and I was amazed at the amount of money corporations spent on these shows. Although I loved it, this would be the only film in which I'd perform.

After finishing the film, we started rehearsing for the live production. Ray Bolger and Jane Powell had been brought in for the show. The dancers, though, didn't have any numbers with them except for a finale. Ray sang his classic "Once in Love With Amy," and Jane performed an incredible medley from *Porgy and Bess*. We were to do only two shows a week for six weeks, as Ford was bringing its people to Detroit in shifts. Between shows, ten of us were to rehearse our show, *Dance Jubilee*, for a tour to the Orient.

Ray was nice, but his wife was a lot nicer. He only wanted to play golf and drink vodka, so we saw little of him. Jane, on the other hand, was quite friendly. She was alone and missed her husband, so she spent a lot of time at our rehearsals for the tour. I was starstruck by her. Just a few years before, I had sat in the movie theater watching *A Date With Judy*, *Two Weeks With Love*, and my favorite, *Royal Wedding*, with Fred Astaire. I grew up on MGM musicals, and Jane mesmerized me.

The stage production, held at the Ford Auditorium, was just as spectacular as our film had been. The highlight of the show occurred when the orchestra pit parted in the middle and up from the basement on a platform rose the shiny new Falcon. When it reached the desired height, about five feet above the conductor's head, the lights flashed and the Falcon revolved, an exciting moment as this car was the big new hope for Ford.

At the technical rehearsal everything had gone beautifully until this moment. Someone backstage pressed the wrong button and the car rose up before the orchestra pit opened, thus smashing the only existing prototype of the car. There was no motor inside, just the frame and interior, but without a doubt it was flattened. We finished the rehearsal anyway, and as we left the theater for the night, about thirty white-coated men arrived, each with a trusty mallet. By the time we arrived the next day, these same men were polishing and refining the edges of the newly restored Falcon. Power, fear, and a hell of a lot of money played their part in getting the car back together. Humpty Dumpty could have been put back together just as easily—all he'd need was a little corporate funding.

Has anyone ever spent a great summer in Detroit? I did. I made good money, worked hard, learned a lot, ate well, and even won third-place prize in a fishing tournament: dinner for six at Little Harry's.

When we finished the Ford show, it was back to New York to rehearse and prepare for our nine-month tour. *Dance Jubilee* was sponsored by the President's Special Program for International Cultural Presentations and featured ten dancers, five musicians, five technicians, and a singer, Dale Monroe. Along with Rod Alexander and his dance partner, Gemze de Lappe, there was Rod's lover, Lou Kristopher, with his dance partner, Carmen Gutierrez. Carol D'Andrea was paired with Pat Heim, Audrey Deckmann with Pat Cummings, and Bella Shalom was my partner. The ten of us performed a two-hour cavalcade of American dance. We started with an 1880s minstrel show—all of us playing banjos—and proceeded through the Cakewalk, castle walk, black bottom, the lindy, a hoedown, movie dances of the 1930s, an Agnes de Mille-style western ballet, and finished with a Gershwin jazz finale incorporating all forms of theater dance. It was a difficult show to dance, made even harder by quick costume changes.

During rehearsals in late September, I got a call from Jane.

"Jane, who?" I asked.

"Powell," she laughed. "Did you forget me so soon?"

I was so embarrassed. In Detroit she had asked for my number, but I never imagined she would use it. She was in town to do *The Garry Moore Show* and invited me to see the show and have dinner afterward. We had a wonderful evening. I was with Jane Powell, the movie star, and it was like being with an old friend.

I was happier than ever, but Ed and I were still apart. He was still teaching in Florida, and I was going to be out of the country for at least six months. It seemed to be our lot not to be together, so we parted ways. I wanted sex to be an extension of some deeper feeling, but for now sex would have to remain something apart from love. Don't get me wrong. I loved sex, all kinds, but I wanted it to be a part of something larger, and it didn't look like it was ever going to be. I wasn't sexually attracted to other dancers, and if I kept traveling with shows, sex inevitably was going to lose some of its importance.

Our company traveled mostly by two chartered DC-4 planes, one for the personnel and one for our four tons of equipment. We left New York on October 2, 1959, and arrived in Athens, Greece, seventeen hours later, at four A.M. This was my first trip abroad, so I wasn't about to go to sleep. After checking into my room, I spent the remaining dark hours staring out my window in disbelief at the view of the Acropolis. Our rehearsal was set for four P.M., so I had a few hours to take in everything and adjust to the excitement of being on foreign shores.

We went through our first dress rehearsal without many problems.

Our greatest challenge was getting out of our sweat-soaked costumes and into the next outfit. With so few in the cast, we had to dance continuously. We sweated so profusely that the new costumes were wet as soon as we put them on. When we had finished our first dress rehearsal, we were all lying flat on the stage trying to regain our normal breathing.

"OK, let's take ten minutes, then start again from the top, with costumes," announced Rod, barely able to get the words out between his own gasps for breath. We did it again and again and again.

We opened the next evening. The performance started at ten P.M. so that everyone could have a leisurely dinner and a short rest before going to the theater. Our first show went without a hitch, and we were grateful for all those rehearsals. It was a huge success.

The next afternoon, I was looking at some Greek vases with male figures on them in a store window. They were almost pornographic; I had never seen figures with erections so publicly displayed. Even though they were classic designs, I was amazed to find them out in the open. Then I realized a man was standing alongside me. We struck up a conversation. He must have paid me a compliment because we made a date for after the show that night. I met him for a drink, then we went to my hotel. He told me his name was Willy Dermont, that he was Dutch, and that he owned the Hotel Unique, the most notorious gay hotel in the world, in Amsterdam. He said that if I visited there, I'd have a place to stay.

We had a good time that night. But it would be the last sex for me until our troupe reached Thailand, months later—that is, with the exception of one strange incident in Thessalonica the following week.

We had originally been booked in a hotel on the waterfront, but it was so loud and commercial that I decided to move to the Villa Ritz, a small hotel on the side of a mountain, overlooking the entire city and the Aegean Sea. Gemze, the lead dancer, and John Carresi, our trumpet player, had fallen in love and wanted something a bit quieter as well. Since it was the off-season, the hotel was not full. Besides Carol, Audrey, and the three of us, the hotel's only other guests were a young Italian man and his two children. They were in the room across the hall from mine.

I became intrigued with this man and his children, whom I often saw dining in the hotel. Where was his wife? Would she join them later? Was he a widower? You didn't see many European men traveling alone with children. My interest wasn't at all sexual, at least not consciously. I didn't ogle, but several times our eyes met. He'd smile and go back to adjusting the napkin under his son's chin. It all seemed innocent, so I was more than surprised one night when he knocked on my door at one A.M.

I had returned from the theater and was in the bath when I heard the knock. I stepped out of the tub, put on a towel, and opened the door. The Italian man was standing there with his robe open, revealing his naked body and a fully erect penis that would make even Janis Paige's jaw drop. I stood speechless. I didn't understand what was happening. We had only exchanged glances. I'd never even spoken with him, but he was standing there in all his glory. I just love surprises! I opened the door a little wider. He walked in, took off his robe, and got into my bed. I quickly followed, not even taking the time to dry off. We never spoke until he whispered "Good night," put on his robe, and left. The next day, I discovered he had checked out.

On October 20 we opened at the Rajh Shaw Stadium in Tehran. At a reception after the performance, we were invited by the Shah to come to the royal palace the next day.

It was unbelievable. I've never seen so much mosaic work in my life. When we went into the main chamber to see the Peacock Throne, Danny Gordon, our conductor, asked if it was for sale. We didn't laugh. Danny was quite a shopper.

Wherever we went in Iran, there were always people following us, amazed at the blond and beautiful young American girls with uncovered heads.

Next we traveled to Kabul, Afghanistan, where we opened at the Kabul Theater, still under construction. For the first time, women were allowed to attend the theater. Just a month before, women had been told they could break their purdah and abandon their *chaudri*, veils worn head to toe, and wear black coats and white scarves instead. The audience was filled with black and white that night. The sounds that came from the theater during that performance were like no other I can remember. The spectators were as excited as children, and when they began to learn the ritual connected with the theater, such as clapping, laughing, and even crying, they indulged themselves to the fullest.

The greatest reaction of the evening came in the "Johnny Guitar" number, an Agnes de Mille-type ballet. Carmen Gutierrez, dressed in only a corset, removed her robe and danced a pas de deux with Rod. When her robe dropped to the floor, there was a gasp of such proportion that it echoed through the hall. Imagine never having seen a bare female ankle and then seeing a woman half-naked. By the time the performance ended, the audience was a mass of smiling faces. Several years later, I remember reading with great sadness that the women of Afghanistan had been forced back into their purdah, and the memory of those joyful faces popped back into my mind.

We moved on to Pakistan. First to Lahore and then to Karachi. In mid November we arrived in Bangalore, India. Our first night there, Carol, Audrey, and I decided to see a performance of the dance company of Uday Shankar, the brother of Ravi Shankar. To get there, we had to take trishaws, which are similar to rickshaws except the driver pedals a bike. By the time we arrived at the concert hall, both Carol and Audrey were in tears. They had such compassion for the tubercular-looking driver that I had to restrain them from giving him all their rupees. In less than a month, in another city, in another trishaw, on the way to rehearsal, I heard Carol say, "Can't he go any faster? We're going to be late." Instantly, we both remembered the other incident and began to laugh in embarrassment that our compassion had been so dulled in such a short time.

For the next six weeks we traveled all over India. In Madras it was so hot that between performances we had to dry our costumes with electric fans.

We jumped up to Nagpur, a part of India not seen by many tourists. The quality of the food was poor, and we lived mostly on tea, oranges, and toast. The curries were tasty but so spicy that eating them at every meal began to take its toll. We all began to suffer Montezuma's revenge, and we weren't even in Mexico. He must have followed us to India.

One night Morty, our flutist, asked everyone to come to his room for a drink after the performance. When we all had drinks Morty said that he and John had something to help our dysentery. He took a joint out of a box, lit it, and passed it around. It was the first of many times I'd practice this ritual, and it immediately stopped our diarrhea. Just what the doctor ordered. We were to the point where we didn't know if we were going to make it through our performances. Pot made it possible.

We arrived in New Delhi a few days before Christmas. The city reminded me of Washington, D.C., with all its monuments and government buildings, and the cool climate was a welcome relief after the 115-degree days in the south.

One evening after rehearsal, several of us piled into two taxis to take the three-hour trip to Agra and the Taj Mahal. We arrived after midnight, and the gates were already closed. We remained in the car while the driver approached the main gate. A small door, set into the big doors, opened slightly. After a minute or two the driver walked back to the car and asked for some rupees for the guard. I handed him fifty or so. He pulled just a few rupees from the bunch and smiled as gave me the rest back.

"We don't want him to retire. We just want him to open the gate," our driver laughed.

We all approached a tiny door. The moon was full, and when it was my turn to step inside, I lost my breath at the sight. Glowing in the distance beyond the reflecting pool stood the Taj Mahal. I don't think the finest of poets can captured the quality and beauty of this wonder. The building, a monument to Shah Jahan's love for his wife, took thirty years (1628–1658) to build. Jade, emeralds, rubies, and other precious and semiprecious stones are inlaid in flower patterns in marble walls. Two tombs stand under the main dome; one is for show and the other, the burial tomb of the shah and his wife, is not open to the public. The main dome itself has a chamber in which an echo lasts fifteen seconds.

The guards leading our private tour were quite hospitable and shared their dinner with us. We all sat on the floor under the main dome consuming warm curry, fruit, and tea. Morty took his flute from his case, which was always under his arm, and began to play arpeggios of notes that, because of the echo, came out as a chord. A few years later a famous jazz flutist would take advantage of the building's acoustics and record an album there. It was a magical night.

At eight A.M., when the Taj Mahal doors opened to the public, the first people in were the Yugoslavian National Ballet. As a special treat, our hosts turned on the fountains, and as Morty played his flute, we all danced together. What an experience—and all for a few rupees. Our driver, whom we named Barney, turned out to be a good friend for the remainder of our time in Delhi. On Christmas Day he invited us to his home for dinner with his family—an evening of songs, stories, and talk. Gemze even took a turn and improvised a dance for our pleasure.

We continued through India, then to Burma. In Rangoon and Mandalay we performed mostly on makeshift outdoor stages for crowds numbering fifteen to twenty thousand. Our piano was brought in by oxcart. The audience was made up mostly of Buddhist monks, all in saffron and red tunics. And we were being paid to do this! No matter how remote the location, audiences were always stunned by our performance. Most had never seen theater at all.

We arrived in Bangkok at the end of January, where our first show was a command performance for the King Bhumibol Adulyadej of Thailand, His Rama the ninth, and his wife, Princess Sirikit. The king was also quite a musician and invited our musicians to a jam session, which took place at a buffet dinner. They played some of the king's compositions as well as some by our trumpet player. The king was charming and humorous. "If I'm ever out of a job," he said, "I think I'd like to go to New York, drive a cab by day, and play in a band at night." And he could easily find work, as he was an accomplished clarinetist.

At this party we met Jim Thompson, who founded and owned the Thai Silk Industry. He invited us to supper the next evening at his magnificent home located on a *clung* (canal) directly across from the factory. He invited the Royal Thai Ballet to perform for us in his garden. We even witnessed the dancers being sewn into their costumes. The event was beautifully arranged.

David Sheffield, Jim's partner, asked me to stay the night in his guest house. He was staggeringly handsome, so I slept with him. It was my first sex in three months—how could it be anything but great? It seems, though, to me, every time is the best and that every show I do is the best show I've ever done.

At the end of January 1960, we arrived in Cambodia. We were told that if we missed Angkor Wat, we'd never forgive ourselves. But there were so many receptions, rehearsals, and performances, we thought we wouldn't have time. But where there's a will, there's a way. Two of the men assigned to our embassy were pilots, and they took leave to fly us there.

We didn't realize how immense Angkor Wat was until we saw it from the air. This place, an area of more than sixty square miles, is a wonderland of ornamental monuments, temples, and palaces, some with two-hundred-foot towers. Khmer warrior kings built it more than a thousand years ago when the Hindu-Buddhist civilization flourished. Hidden by jungle growth, the ruins were only discovered within the twentieth century and were still being restored.

The bas reliefs around the walls of the main temple showed the warriors' entire way of life: the royal courts, their warfare, forms of torture, their forms of love and social structures. This was a fantastic trip, and, luckily, we got back in time for the performance.

In Taipei. Taiwan, we were honored at a luncheon given by the Andaggression League and were honored with the presence of Madame Chiang Kai-Shek. The luncheon consisted of twelve courses, and after each course she moved to another table, giving each of us a chance to speak with her. By the fifth course, when she reached our table, she seemed relaxed. She was most gracious and quite a conversationalist. Speaking of an orphanage she had founded several years earlier, she mentioned how nice it would be if the children could see our performance.

Unfortunately, that would be impossible since our shows were completely sold out, but I suggested that the company might agree to do a special performance for them. She didn't waste a minute, and by the eighth course we were scheduled to perform for the children and some of the armed forces of Formosa. We were a generous company and did many things like this to spread American goodwill.

Next it was on to Korea. The most exciting thing I saw there was a man's head on the hood of a Turkish squad's jeep, in the style of a hood ornament. The Turks had found the man stealing from their garden and had beheaded him, placed the head on the jeep, and were driving it through the streets as a warning for others.

We went to Pusan, South Korea, and Saigon, Vietnam, before ending our tour in the Philippines in Manila. It was the tour of a lifetime, transforming us all with the things we saw and did. Apparently, we left our mark—and a few memories as well—in the places we visited.

Wakefield Poole's solo in *Rod Alexander's Dance Jubilee*, a dance show sponsored by the United States Information Service. The troupe traveled around through Europe, the Middle East, and Asia in 1959 and 1960.

Dance Jubilee members Josie Zampedri and Wakefield Poole sleep on the plane during the tour, 1959.

Wakefield Poole backstage during the Broadway run of *Tenderloin* (1960).

Chapter Four

Broadway at Last

New York City, 1960

After a short visit with my family, I returned to New York. I had no prospects for work, but in early April, Gemze called about an audition for a Broadway revival of *Finian's Rainbow*. She had spoken to Herb Ross, the director-choreographer, and he said I should audition—meaning, if he liked me, I'd get the job.

When I arrived at the City Center, I was surprised to see Gemze, who said, "Just relax and have a good time." Good advice. If you can follow it, even if you don't get the job, you've at least had a good time. You win either way.

Peter Conlow, the co-choreographer, ran the audition. I sensed right away that he didn't like me. I almost lost the job, but Herb liked me as much as Peter disliked me, so he hired me.

Knowing Peter disliked me, I found it difficult to work with him, but I was determined. We were working at the City Center, basically doing summer stock in the city. The productions were quite good, and our cast was great: Bobby Howes, Howard Morris, Jeanne Carson, Biff McGuire, Sorrell Booke, and Robert Guillaume. I loved the score, which contains one of my favorite songs, "Look to the Rainbow," and the show was loaded with dancing. When we opened April 27, 1960, reviews were so favorable that after the run the show was moved to Broadway.

We had a week off and opened at the 46th Street Theater. I loved to stare out the window of my dressing room, which overlooked the Variety Arts Rehearsal Studios across the street. The third-floor front studio was often used by Bob Fosse and Gwen Verdon. They'd work for weeks on pre-production, just the two of them, and I'd arrive at the theater early just to watch them work. Once in a while I could hear the sound of the piano from their studio, or over the din of traffic noises on 46th Street, I'd hear Bob counting. I heard them laugh and I heard him yell.

It was wonderful to be a fly on the wall. The magic of being part of the theater filled me; for just an instant, some energy force rises and fills your entire soul. I was in the dressing room of my first Broadway show, and I was secretly watching and listening to two of the most famous theater personalities work and create. I hoped that one day I'd get to work with them. They were also my neighbors on 69th Street, so I saw them a lot, going to the market or getting in a cab, but this was different.

Near the end of the show's run, I invited Ed (my ex-lover), Ben Cenerino, and Nick Proccacino to see the last matinee before the pending actors' strike and to have dinner after the show. We were seated at our table in Fornos, a popular Spanish restaurant on 52nd Street. It was a favorite spot on matinee days and was always full of celebrities who were appearing on Broadway. Zero Mostel was a regular.

We were having our drinks, and they were stroking my ego, telling me how impressed they were to see me on the Broadway stage, when Ed stopped mid sentence.

"My God," he said. "Look who just walked in! Carol Burnett! Holy shit, she's walking right toward us." Sure as could be, he was right.

"Excuse me, aren't you Wakefield Poole?" she asked.

"Yes," I managed. "Aren't you Carol Burnett?" We both laughed, and my friends sat stunned.

"Do you mind if I join you for a moment?" she asked. "I'm supposed to meet Joe Bova for dinner, and he's late." Joe was co-starring in *Once Upon a Mattress*.

Still in the dark as to how she knew my name, I stood up, pulled over an extra chair, and asked her to sit.

"I should explain," she said, putting her hand to her mouth, then resting it on my arm. "I'm a friend of Lou Christopher's, and last night

I saw photos and movies of your trip to the Orient. I recognized you when I walked in the door. I hope you don't mind my butting in like this."

"Mind?" I answered. "You just made our day."

We had a few laughs, and when Joe arrived we were having such a good time that he pulled up another chair and we finished the meal together. My friends were impressed. She was so real. The last time I saw her, many years later, she was still the same way.

On June 1, because of the Actors' Equity strike, our show closed. I had just become an Equity member and now I was on strike. One minute you're on Broadway, the next, you're on unemployment. After the strike ended, the fall shows started to cast, and I went to my first Equity audition, for *Tenderloin* at the 46th Street Theater. It was just the same, except now there was more competition—better and more experienced dancers. Since I had just played there, I felt comfortable on the stage and less nervous than I'd felt at other auditions.

Joe Layton, the choreographer, was gangly and looked just like Jerry Lewis. He moved awkwardly, and his choreography reflected this. Strangely enough, the movement felt comfortable on my body. I gave a wonderful audition and was called back to the finals at the end of the week. We were told to bring sheet music, dance clothes, and to be prepared for a long stay. About sixty-five men were trying out for eight spots. I was pretty nervous.

On my way to the finals, I met Ron Lee, one of the dancers from *Finian's Rainbow*. He knew Joe personally and told me I was going to get the job. Joe had told him I was one of the best dancers he had ever auditioned and that if I could sing at all, I'd have a spot in the show. But I had just been through this.

Before *Finian's Rainbow* I had auditioned for a replacement role in *West Side Story*. Lee Becker and Howard Geofreys both told me I had the part, but after six auditions over a period of two weeks, I was told I looked too old. Who knows if that's the real reason.

The audition was long. At five P.M. I was still there when they brought back all the women. Then we stood in lines while from the audience the production team whispered about us. I was moved around from one group to another, asked to stand with this woman and that woman.

Even with my limited experience, I knew there was a problem and that I might not get the job. Then a striking older man stepped up from the house and crossed over to stand right in front of me. He reached up, touched my hair, and said, "Nice color," as his hand felt my stubble of a beard. "Grow a mustache." He winked and turned out to face the house. "I think he'll be fine now," he announced to the group as he moved to rejoin them. He was Cecil Beaton, and I learned later that he had gotten me the job. Joe had wanted me, but there was opposition from the producers, Bobby Griffith and Hal Prince, who thought I was too young looking to play the part of a John in a whorehouse.

Incidentally, these were the same producers who, a few months earlier, had found me too old for *West Side Story*. Mr. Beaton had solved the problem by simply asking me to grow a little facial hair.

The rehearsal process was completely different from *Finian's*. This was a brand-new show, and changes were to be expected. In the middle of rehearsing a scene, Mr. Abbott often stopped to turn out to the audience. "Give me a funny line here," he would quietly demand into the darkness. If he turned around and kept rehearsing, on the next break a new line would appear for the scene. If he just stood there, it would be no more than a few seconds before the line could be heard coming from the back of the house, where William and James Goldman were observing and writing additional dialogue.

Mr. Abbott was quiet and never for an instant appeared unsure about what he was doing. I had heard how brilliant he was, so I was surprised when some of the choices he made seemed, even to me, wrong for a show about a minister and his efforts to shut down whorehouses in the Tenderloin of New York.

Our first performance was in New Haven, Conn., and after the technical rehearsal I went out to dinner with Pat Turner. Pat and I had become friends since the first day of rehearsal, when she had come over to me during a break.

"Take it easy, will ya? You're making us all look bad," she advised. "Just mark a little once in a while. You know how to mark, don't you? Dance more with your mind and less with your body. Give me a cigarette, will ya? Want a sip of coffee?"

I don't think she ever wanted any answers to her questions. I gave her a cigarette and took a sip of her cold coffee, soaking my newly grown handlebar mustache in the process. I was still learning to adapt to this itchy monstrosity I had growing on my lip. Pat was the first true "gypsy" I had met. A gypsy is a chorus dancer who's done a lot of shows, has a lot of experience, and has a certain attitude about everything. They're not negative necessarily, just overly realistic.

We were just about to order our food when Joe Layton joined us. After dinner he asked me to take a walk. I hadn't seen the town, so I accepted. We walked to the campus and around the outskirts of the town, talking about everything. During rehearsals I realized that we often thought alike. Sometimes I'd know what he was going to do before he did it. I liked his dances, but most of all I liked his mind. An hour or so later, we arrived at our hotel and got into the elevator. My room was on the third floor and his on the fourth.

As he pressed the "up" button, he asked what my room was like. I answered, not really knowing the correct response. I mean, it had a bed, a table, a chair, and a bathroom. What else could I say about it? The elevator door opened, and I was about to say good night when he asked to see my room.

I led the way, and when we got inside Joe plopped onto one of the beds as I fixed us a nightcap. We must have talked for another hour or so. My mustache was beginning to itch again, and I made some remark about it.

"I've always wondered what it would be like to kiss someone with a mustache," Joe said. Then there were a few moments of silence. Joe finished his drink and said he'd better go. I said good night and showed him to the door.

I had just finished my shower and was putting on my pajamas when the phone rang. It was Joe. "Look, I'd like you to come up and sleep with me tonight," he said quietly. "I don't want to be alone. OK?"

"Well, I'm all ready for bed and I—"

"Just slip on a robe and come up the stairs," he interrupted. I could tell from his tone that no matter what I said, he would have a comeback.

"Give me a few minutes."

"Great. I'm going to soak in the tub, but I'll leave the door unlocked. Just come on in. Room 403."

I hung up the phone, put on my robe, closed the door, and made my way up the stairs to Joe's room. The door was slightly ajar. I opened it slowly. His room was a little bigger than mine, but everything else was the same. The television was playing softly and splashing noises were coming from the bath.

"Hello," I sang out quietly.

"Hi! I'll be out in a minute or two. Just hop into bed and make yourself at home." There were two double beds in the room. The one closest to the door was turned down, so I moved to the far bed, turned back the covers, and hopped in. Soon after, Joe emerged from the bath.

"There," he said buttoning his pajamas. "I feel better." Then he looked at me and started to smile. "What are you doing over there? I asked you to come up and sleep with *me*." He got into his bed and opened the covers to me. "Come on over here!"

Talk about a ton of bricks. Talk about being naïve. My mind raced back. "I always wondered what it would be like to kiss someone with a mustache." He had said that! Why didn't I hear it? *But he's married; he can't want me.* All this was flashing in my head as I crossed the great divide between the two beds.

Joe was holding the covers open in such a way that when I got into the bed, I was also getting into his arms. He kissed me gently and held me close. I was just beginning to relax and catch up to the present circumstances when the phone rang. It was Evelyn Russell, Joe's wife. As they talked I began to feel like "the other woman." How many movies had I seen this in? I wasn't really listening to his conversation—I was having one with myself—when I heard my name.

"No, I'm all right," he explained. "Wake's going to stay with me tonight and keep me company."

He was telling his wife about me! Now I was really confused. I finally told my mind to shut up and stop thinking so much.

Joe and I had sex that night, and I don't remember a thing about it except that it wasn't the most passionate sex I'd ever had. Under the circumstances I had a hard time getting an erection—just too many surprises. In all the years I would work with Joe, our relationship would never be defined. We loved each other, and our friendship continued to grow and develop. When I first met Evelyn it was like meeting another piece of Joe. She was a severe but attractive woman who was always perfectly groomed and made-up. She usually pulled her dark red hair into a tight French twist, and her clothes were always well-tailored. She smoked incessantly, and the lavish cigarette holder she used was the finishing touch. I loved her instantly. She was a wonderful woman who always made me laugh and never made me feel anything but pride for my feelings for her husband. Indeed, she was secure and not at all threatened by my relationship with Joe.

After mixed reviews in New Haven, we continued to make changes to *Tenderloin*. Mr. Abbott was clearly not up to par with this show. He always said that the way to get him to do a show was to tell him what a great job he'd do and that no one else could do it. Evidently, that's what Bobby and Hal had done. They were wrong!

Bad decisions were made. They cut everything that was the least bit racy, which included anything humorous. Slowly, other good things began to go. They did make a few smart changes, though. And we did have a lot of fun backstage. Jerri Archer, for example, played the madam of the whorehouse. She wasn't very funny in the part, but she had these enormous breasts. One night I went to the makeup room to get some wax for my mustache. Cecil Beaton was standing, making slight makeup and hair adjustments. Jerri was sitting in the chair, and Ronnie DeMann had just finished working on her. Jerri, dressed in her sheer dressing gown, got up, walked over to Beaton, grabbed him by the neck, and pulled him to her breasts.

"Thanks, Cecil, darling," she said. "I feel much sexier, now." She kissed him on the forehead, turned, flared her robe, and exited the room—and I mean *exited.*

"If that woman puts her breasts in my face one more time, I'll not be held responsible for my actions," Beaton said, wiping his forehead with a silk handkerchief from his breast pocket. It was a hilarious episode, but none of us laughed. He was that upset.

It wasn't long before Christine Norden, a British actress, was brought in to replace Jerri. She was beautiful, funny, and also well-endowed. The role of the madam started to work. Unfortunately, the show had wonderful possibilities that were never realized because of poor direction.

The show opened in New York on October 17, 1960, at the 46th Street Theater. I was so excited—a real opening night. Before the curtain went up Mr. Abbott called the company onstage for the proverbial pep talk. Then, Eddie Phillips received the gypsy robe, which is usually given to the person who has done the most shows and is a minor celebrity among his peers. The recipient is almost always a chorus member, but in this case Eddie was the perfect choice, so an exception was made. It had been a tradition for years and continues to this day.

The show went well that night, and afterward we all dressed up for the party at Sardi's. This was my first opening-night party, and I had many expectations. Unfortunately, I was totally disappointed.

When we arrived, there was no place to sit. All the tables were filled with strange people. Backers. We had to stand between the tables, dodging waiters with drinks in one hand, platters of food in the other. By the time the first review was passed around, everyone was ready to leave. TENDERLOIN UNDONE, one headline read. The other reviews were about the same, but because of theater parties the show ran for nearly a year. So now I had learned what it was like to do a show from the beginning and also that opening-night parties are for backers.

I loved doing the show, and being on Broadway was exciting. Sometimes in the dressing room, if the circumstances were right, we could hear Ethel Merman blasting away in *Gypsy* at the Imperial. Our stages were back-to-back, with only a brick wall between. Each night our show ended first, and some nights I'd slip into the side doors to watch their bows. The ushers would always open the doors early, and I could catch the bows then cut through the parking lot on the way to Ralph's, the local watering hole, for a nightcap.

In early November Joe was getting ready to do a TV special for Leland Hayward called *The Gershwin Years*, and he asked most of us to work on it with him. All rehearsals would be arranged so as not to interfere with *Tenderloin* matinees. The schedule would be difficult for about four weeks, but the money would be great.

A star-studded affair, the show featured performances by Ethel Merman, Frank Sinatra, Richard Rodgers, Florence Henderson, and Julie London, to name a few. Joe choreographed two huge ballets, one for Grover Dale to *The Second Rhapsody*, and one for Alvin Ailey, Carmen DeLavalade, and Harold Pierson to the *Porgy and Bess* suite.

The Second Rhapsody, a full-company affair, was technically innovative, almost science fiction. Grover appeared in negative while the rest of the cast appeared in positive. The entire number centered around his trying to get in with the rest of us but always hitting a barrier. Even though it was an abstract piece, I know Joe was making a subtle, heartfelt statement about racism and discrimination. Considering it was 1960, something like this was daring for network TV.

The *Porgy* piece was shot on a Long Island wharf where we had dirt, nails, splinters from the old wood, and inclement weather to contend with. Despite all these hardships, it was a wonderful experience. But during the editing and transferring of the tape, one of the technicians accidentally erased the entire number. There was such a row that the editor was fired and *The New York Times* even did a story on it.

As it was now winter, we couldn't go back to Long Island, so the crew, Alvin, Carmen, and Harold, all went to Florida to reshoot, and it turned out even better. Now we really were in the South, on a wharf, and wanting to get on that boat for ol' New York.

Working with Ethel Merman proved to be the most exciting part of the job. Skipper Damon (Cathryn Damon, who later would gain fame as Mary on the TV show *Soap*) was Merman's stand-in at the beginning. Joe set the numbers with her, and we rehearsed to get everything perfect before Merman even appeared.

Only once did she come to the rehearsal studio. At the beginning she popped in to go over the music and set keys with Jay Blackton. But that was it until we were ready to shoot the numbers. In that respect, the entire show was shot like a movie. She walked in, watched the number with Skipper doing her part, then said, "Let's shoot it!"

The first number was "Lola Lo," and four of us played "stage-door Johnny" to her Broadway star. She had only watched the number two times, never rehearsed it, and did it perfectly in one take. Her second big number was "Wintergreen for President," a big production number. The same thing happened. It was pages long, but she sang through the number with Jay at the piano, put down her score, and went through the staging once with Joe and Skipper. Then into costumes and makeup. Bam, it was done. I have never in my life seen anything as amazing.

A friend of mine, Billy Weslow, a dancer with New York City Ballet, was an assistant to Merman, and they had become real pals. On one of many long breaks, he took me in to see her. I had done a number with her—she had sat on my knee—and yet I had not really talked to her. Merman was friendly and joked with us constantly. I mentioned that I had seen films of her Broadway performance in *Panama Hattie* as well as *Annie Get Your Gun*. She was surprised and unaware that any films of these shows existed. I explained that a friend of mine in Jacksonville, Ray Knight, a newspaper theater critic, had been taking movies of Broadway shows, illegally, for years. Before I left her dressing room, I promised to put her in touch with Ray. Of course, I wasted no time doing so. He made her copies of everything he had and sent them to her.

Ray's films were wonderful. They were silent, of course, but he tracked them with original cast recordings whenever possible. He'd only film during the loud numbers so as not to be heard by the theater staff. After his death some years later, his films were donated to Theater on Film and Tape in Los Angeles. Recently, I saw some of his footage in a Richard Rodgers's TV documentary and was happy to learn that all of his amazing footage was being used and seen.

In late February, Joe Calvin, a stage manager, offered me a job to tour Europe with *West Side Story*. He said I wouldn't even have to audition, that my name was on record and that all my grades were fours. Howard Geofreys, Jerome Robbins's assistant, kept score cards from all his auditions. Now they were casting an entire production from his lists. I thought about it for a few days, consulted Joe Layton, who approved my decision to go, and accepted the job. Joe then called Jerry Robbins on my behalf. A few days later I signed for the six-month tour.

Robbins rehearsed us for a few days. After the first day, however, he called me aside and told me he didn't think I was right for the show. I was flabbergasted, I had just given notice at *Tenderloin* and now I was losing this job. He explained that he was putting together a company, Ballets USA, in a few months and that he would love for me to join them for a European tour. Where I got the nerve for what came next, I don't know, but I looked at him and said, "I just quit my job in *Tenderloin*, and I've signed a six-month contract. And unless you want to buy me out of it, I'm going on this tour."

The next day at rehearsal, I was made a Shark, a Puerto Rican. They needed stronger dancers on that side, so I'd have to wear light Egyptian makeup and dye my hair. The latter, I refused to do. So I became this very dark Shark with light brown hair who ended up doing every bit of dancing a Shark can do in the show.

In early March we left for Israel, where we were to do final rehearsals and open our tour at the Habima Theater in Tel Aviv. Our first night there, we were invited to see the National Theater's performance of *The Miracle Worker* at the Habima. I had just seen the play the night before on Broadway with Anne Bancroft and Patty Duke. Although the Habima production was in Hebrew, it was still mesmerizing.

After a week of technical and dress rehearsals, we opened for a two-week run, then went to Haifa for a week. The show went extremely well. The choreography seemed to come naturally from our bodies, and the score moved the cast's emotions, as well as the audience's, along with the story.

We spent most of our time in Israel at sidewalk cafés in Dusseldorf Square drinking coffee and cognac. Some of us had taken up knitting, so we caused a few heads to turn. During the run we went to a kibbutz to do a performance. Our bus was shot at on the way, but the driver said the Arabs weren't trying to hit us, just frighten us a bit. They succeeded. The remainder of our time in Israel was quiet.

In no time we were aboard a ship on the Mediterranean bound for France. From Marseilles we went to Paris. What could be better than Paris in April? We opened at the Alhambra Theater with no advance sales, but after rave reviews people lined up for blocks to buy tickets. Suddenly, we were the rage of Paris. Along with the Kirov Ballet and a young dancer named Nureyev, we were the thing to see. We were booked to return to Paris for another month, later in the summer.

Stan Papich and I decided to room together. Stan played Diesel in the company and was very Charles Bronson in looks and attitude. We found rooms at the Hotel Crystal, a quaint little place frequented by musicians, on the left bank, and around the corner from the Café Flore, where we spent a great deal of time drinking cognac.

At that café one afternoon I met Michel Babouhot. A tall, handsome Frenchman with dark curly hair, he displayed the charm and grace of an ambassador. I instantly fell in love. It was Paris, it was April, and I was merely following the rules.

Michel managed Pierre Faviret, a men's clothing shop on rue St-Honore. We met every day for lunch. Most nights, he picked me up after the show and we went to some club or a private party. On one of these occasions I met George Reich, the choreographer at the Olympia. By the end of the evening, he asked me to work on a TV special for Maurice Chevalier. I could hardly believe it.

Working on television in Paris proved to be quite different from my experience in New York. There they took two-hour lunches in the Bois de Boulogne, then went back for an hour or two of rehearsals. What a life! Michel had a lot of friends in the film industry, and we spent many of our nights in their company. Annie Girardot and my all-time favorite, Jean Marais, were among them. During most of these evenings, only French was spoken. Fortunately, my four years of high school French had paid off. I had no trouble understanding and in no time at all was conversing with the best of them. I felt like Paris was at my fingertips, and my hands were empty and eager. Michel was an incredible lover, so I was getting little sleep but having the time of my life.

One night Stan asked me to have dinner with his friend from the States, Ralph Burns, a composer and arranger. He was a small man but attractive and compelling, with a wonderful sense of humor. I liked him immediately. After dinner we went for drinks at the Mars Club. He was meeting friends and thought I'd enjoy the music. Well, his friends turned out to be Lena Horne and her husband, Lennie Heyton.

Who needed to drink? I was high just watching her hold on to Lennie's arm, look into his eyes, and ask, "Daddy, can I have another gin?" The love between them was evident, and they still acted like newlyweds. It was a special night and ended, as did so many nights in Paris, at Les Halles for oysters, onion soup, and strong French coffee.

A few years later I was dancing on *The Perry Como Show*, where Lena was guest starring. Lennie had died, and she was just starting to work again. At one point I went into the makeup room. Again, Ronnie DeMann was there doing Lena's hair. Ron introduced us, but I said we had already met in Paris. I reminded her of our night at the Mars Club. For an instant, she got a faraway look in her eyes, like she was replaying the moment. Then a faint smile appeared on her face, and she said, quietly, "Oh, yes, you were with Ralph and Stanley. That was a nice evening, wasn't it?" I smiled and agreed.

On Saturday nights Michel and a friend, Philippe Goodable, would pick me up at the theater and we'd take off to his country house in

Vernon, which stood next door to the home of the French actress Michele Morgan. I kept teasing Michel about going next door to borrow a cup of sugar, but I never got to meet her. She was on location filming.

We would get up early in the morning and immediately go to the strawberry fields to pick our breakfast. Then we'd head back to the house to spend a few hours over coffee, papers, and beautiful French strawberries before going back to bed. All we did for two days was eat, sleep, and fuck. Except for the fucking, this was really a time of rest, which we didn't get much of during the week. Was this the European lifestyle I always heard about? During the week, work hard and play hard. During the weekend, rest and fuck. In America we work hard during the week, play hard on the weekends, and never get enough rest or sleep.

The month was over, and before we knew it we were off to Italy. We would be in Turin for a few weeks, then in Florence. Michel and Philippe came to visit in Florence, and by mid June we returned to Paris.

Hal Prince and Arthur Laurents came to the opening. The audience, this time, was star studded and included both Anna Magnani and Ingrid Bergman. Rumor had it that this was the first time they'd appeared in the same place since their big feud. Bergman came backstage to say hello and to thank us. She was dressed in an ankle-length gown under an evening coat that looked like it had been designed for royalty. She was quite gracious. Magnani sent us a note that was posted on the call board. It seemed she was taking no chance of running into Bergman.

After the performance Bob Avian and I were taking off our makeup when we heard a knock on the door.

"Come in," I said. As the door flew open, Jean Marais entered the room, followed by Michel, George Reich, and Annie Girardot. I can't possibly remember what Jean was saying. It was mostly just words: *formidable* and *magnifique* with a few *Ah, Poole*'s tossed in here and there. He got a kick out of calling me Poole, since it means *whore* in French.

What I'll never forget, though, is the look on Bob's face when he saw who was at the door. He was usually so cool, but this time our jaws dropped open. We were sitting there in our dance belts entertaining two of the biggest stars in France. We finished off the night at Los Calavados with a wonderful late supper and too much champagne.

The month flew by quickly. By the time we were to leave for Germany, I had decided to return to Paris at the end of the tour. George Reich had offered me a job working with him, and I was still crazy for Michel. I wanted some sort of commitment, but it never came. Stan and I both felt that perhaps Michel was being kept. But Michel did encourage me to come back to Paris to give it a try. When I left at the end of July, I left with the intention of returning to Paris to work and pursue my relationship with Michel.

Munich was fun, and Stan and I continued to room together. We were compatible and had no trouble being honest with each other. I can't remember our ever having a disagreement.

One night after the show, we went to the Grunne Gans for a late supper. Stan had been making eyes at our waiter all through dinner, so I wasn't surprised that when we'd finished, our waiter suggested we move to the bar for a drink. The bartender, an attractive woman in her late twenties, began flirting with me, and after a drink or two we were deep in conversation. Stan decided to wait around for the waiter to get off work, so I went back to the hotel.

Sometime after four A.M. I felt a nude body crawl in bed next to me. It took me a second to come out of my stupor. I wasn't feeling much at the moment, but I clearly felt a woman's breast. Soon I realized it was Gretchen, the bartender. It turned out Stan had to bring her along or his waiter wouldn't come home with him. Fortunately, I found her attractive, and she wanted me. So there we were, Stan in his bed with his waiter and I, in mine, with the female bartender. When we talked about it later, I couldn't stop laughing long enough to really get mad at him.

"What if I had trouble making love to her?" I asked. "Did that even enter your mind?"

"You'll go to bed with anyone if they tell you they want you, and you'd fuck a snake if someone held its head," Stan laughed. As I said, we were honest with each other.

Our next stop was Amsterdam. Remembering Willie Dermont's offer to stay at his hotel, the Unique, I had written for a reservation. I received a sweet note saying that he not only remembered me but also that he often thought about our time together. He would have it no other way; I should be his guest during my stay in Amsterdam.

After the final curtain on our opening night in Amsterdam, there was no applause. But suddenly there was a deafening sound like none other I'd heard in the theater. The audience was stamping its feet so fast, it sounded like a stampede. I lost count of the number of bows we took that night.

A few days later I became quite ill. I was running a high fever and couldn't keep down any food. Willie's staff at the hotel was wonderful, all beautiful young men who would fulfill any desire expressed to them. In my case, Willie told them that I was not to be left alone and that I should always have hot tea beside my bed. After a few days of this care, I still hadn't improved, so Willie sent for his personal doctor, who informed me that I was having a relapse of hepatitis. (I'd had a bad case when I was seventeen.) As soon as he told me, I recognized the symptoms, especially the headaches.

Ah, Paris! The rich food, the wine, and all those nights with no sleep had taken their toll, so I decided to leave the company and return to the States.

After a few weeks of rest and care, my health returned, and I was ready to go back to work. I made a few calls to New York. Vito Durante, a good friend and the dance captain of *The Unsinkable Molly Brown*, offered me a job. In three days I was back in New York rehearsing. The following week, I joined the show.

Being a replacement in a Broadway show is not an easy task. The most important thing is that you fit into the costumes with minimal alterations. After working alone all week with the dance captain, the company is called in. Then it's time to fit your little piece into the big puzzle. Producers like to put in replacements on matinees. That way, you have two performances to make minor adjustments, and any major mistake can be corrected between shows.

My first scene with Tammy Grimes was a big number, "Belly Up to the Bar." She walked in from the wings, straight toward me with her hand held out. "Hello, Wakefield," she said, looking me directly in the eyes. "Welcome." Then she turned to Vito. "Let's do it," she said as she took her place for the start of the number. I didn't even get a chance to say hello. The rehearsal went as well as they usually do, and I made no outrageous mistakes.

My first performance was another matter all together. During "Belly Up to the Bar," I popped a contact lens. At that time contacts were expensive, and I wasn't about to lose it. I dropped to my knees, took off my miner's hat, and began looking for my lost lens as Tammy continued the song. There I was on all fours, feeling about for something almost impossible to see even under the best of conditions. I played a drunken miner in the scene, so it wasn't out of character for me to be crawling around on the floor. As Tammy crossed over to my side of the stage, her follow spot caught the edge of my lens lying on the floor right in her path. I scooped it up, put it in my mouth for safe keeping, took her by the arm, and continued the dance, never missing a step.

One night after the show I met Joe and Evelyn Layton for dinner. We caught up on things since *Tenderloin* and had a few laughs, which was always the case when Evelyn was around. She had this wonderful ability to ferret out truths and to voice her observations in a wry, witty, hilarious manner. Therein lay her art. She knew exactly how much volume to use to reach her intended audience, so she was never coarse or common. She always reminded me of Kay Thompson or Eve Arden.

After dessert, Joe asked me to work with him on the new Richard Rodgers musical, *No Strings*. We would rehearse for six weeks, then go on the road for two months before opening in New York. Immediately after, we would start on the TV version of *Once Upon a Mattress*. Not only was I going to assist Joe, but I was also going to work with Carol Burnett and Richard Rodgers. I was on my way again.

A Richard Rodgers show was guaranteed to run at least a year, so performers clamored to be in it. We auditioned more than five hundred dancers for just twenty parts. We would have no singing chorus at all, but because the show was about Paris fashion, we needed girls who could dance and who looked like models. It was a concept show in which the dancers moved the scenery, a technique now used in all major shows. Movie techniques, including cross fades and dissolves, were also used in the production.

This show was ground breaking for many other reasons. Richard Rodgers wrote his own lyrics for the first time, and he included no strings in the orchestra, which was located backstage rather than in the pit. This made the music sound recorded, like a movie sound track—just what they wanted. Also, for the first time in any musical, each principal had his own body microphone.

Joe was at the peak of his creativity, and Richard Rodgers completely supported him. Every decision about every detail was made only after much thought and discussion, and Joe's concept of the show extended into every department from Donald Brooks's gowns for Diahann Carroll to the orchestrations by my old friend Ralph Burns.

One day during a break I was sitting on the piano bench having a cup of soup. Mr. Rodgers sat down next to me and started to pick out a simple tune. Just like in the movies, everyone in the room gravitated to the piano. I got up to let Peter Matz, the conductor, slip in next to Mr. Rodgers. He added some frills as they both sang, "La La La La La," the title of the new song for the French star Nicole Adam. In less than ten minutes Mr. Rodgers had composed a song.

Once the show opened I would be the resident director. I had to know the show like the back of my hand, so I was rehearsing fourteen or fifteen hours a day and loving every minute of it. Joe was wonderful; his mind and imagination totally seduced me.

On January 2, 1962, we left for Detroit. The following Sunday, we were onstage rehearsing the casino ballet, when from the back of the house I heard, "Oh, my God, the show must be in trouble! The dancers are rehearsing!" It was Evelyn. She walked down the aisle like Bette Davis does in *All About Eve*, when she arrives at the theater to read with the understudy. When she reached the front row, she stopped and sighed, "Ah, Detroit! If God wanted to give the world an enema, this is where he'd stick the nozzle."

We all laughed as Joe went over to greet her. She took Joe's coffee cup out of his hand, drained it dry, then gave him a big kiss as they sat down in the audience to grab a few minutes of time together.

The show had only one major problem. The love affair between Diahann and Dick Kiley seemed to lose strength at the end of the show. She tells him to go home and get himself together and that she'll wait for him in Paris, her safe and beautiful world. Since she's black and he's white, she can't live with him in Maine. "She's the heroine in this story," said Mr. Rodgers. "*She* has to have the strength, not him. She has to tell him to go home."

One night in New Haven I was having dinner with Diahann, Dick Kiley, and Noel Adam and her husband, Sydney Chaplin. Sydney had just seen the show and was saying that something didn't feel right about the ending. Dick thought the main characters both weak and afraid, and at the end the love affair had no meaning. Love, evidently in this case, could not conquer all. But during that discussion, things got mixed up and lines were switched by mistake. Suddenly, it worked. Richard got so excited. It all came together.

In this new version David says, "I must go home to find myself and write." (This shows his strength and proves he will do it.)

Then Barbara says, "Yes, I'll come with you." (This proves she loves him enough to risk being subjected to bigotry.)

Finally, David says, "No. You should stay here, in your safe and beautiful world. I'll come back when I've done what I have to do. Until then, the sweetest sounds are still inside my head." It really worked. It was perfect and not a word had to be rewritten.

By the time dinner was over, I had promised to speak with Joe, which I did. He, in turn brought the idea to Sam Taylor and Mr. Rodgers, who thought it would be a mistake to make a change so late. We were to open in New York in less than a week and the show had been frozen. What a shame! It would have made quite a difference in the New York reviews, as most critics had trouble with the love affair. It was a very courageous show as far as racial issues were concerned, but it could have gone further. We opened at the 54th Street Theater to mostly good reviews and settled in for a nice run. This was 1962, and racism was still rearing its ugly face publicly. During each performance we had about two or three walkouts. Some quietly walked up the aisle, while others muttered obscenities all the way to the exit.

One night, however, we could not ignore the disturbances. After storming up the aisle, wife in tow, a man turned back toward the stage and screamed, "Nigger lovers!" Diahann, dumbstruck, fumbled through the scene and couldn't find her way back. Dick Kiley, always the perfect gentleman, stepped forward and spoke quietly to the audience.

"We're very sorry for this interruption," he said politely. "With your permission we would like to start the scene over where Miss Carroll enters." He stepped back, took Diahann's hand, walked her to the side of the stage where she was to make her entrance, and the audience burst into applause.

My first replacement audition for *No Strings* coincided with Bob Fosse's auditions for *Little Me*. Equity arranged for Fosse to audition girls in the morning and boys in the afternoon and for me to do the opposite.

The turnout was overwhelming. That afternoon I was sitting in the orchestra waiting for the girls' audition to start. We had an enormous turnout for the boys' audition that morning, so we were expecting a large crowd. I asked to see the girls, then jumped onstage. I faced into the audience to speak with Fred Smith, the stage manager, and when I turned back toward the stage, I couldn't move an inch. The entire stage was packed with girls. I let out a little sound of surprise, and everyone laughed.

I welcomed everyone, apologized, and explained that I would have to eliminate some of them before we could even start to learn some steps. I asked the girls to do grand jets, a running, jumping step across the stage, and I judged them in turn saying "Thank you" or "Stay." If I said "Stay," Harry would give them a number.

We were moving quickly, and I had positioned myself in the audience. There was no orchestra pit for the show, so I was only a foot from the stage. Suddenly, one of the girls whom I had just excused was standing in front of me. She looked down, put both hands on her hips, stamped her foot, and screamed. "Is that all I get for ten fuckin' years of training? A thank-you? Who the fuck do you think you are, talking to me like that? This is fair?" She continued to scream obscenities as Fred picked her up and carried her off the stage. "I'm sorry, let's start again, with...you," I said pointing to one of the girls. "I have no idea what that was all about."

"You were lucky," a tiny voice spoke out. "This morning at Bob Fosse's audition, she hit him with her rehearsal bag and knocked him into the orchestra pit."

Later, in the film *All That Jazz*, Fosse would use that audition, all those girls jammed into such a tight space, as inspiration. He did an overhead shot of all the girls waiting on the stage and you couldn't see an inch of stage anywhere in the frame. That one image showed how competitive being a dancer can be.

My sex life was almost nonexistent at this time. Every night after the show, I'd meet my old pals at Ralph's for a few drinks. One night, however, I didn't feel like going all the way down to 45th Street, so I dropped by to see who was at Confucius, a hangout for the casts of shows playing uptown theaters. I spotted Eddie Phillips from *Tenderloin* at the bar sitting with Ken Porter, a stage manager, and someone I didn't recognize. As I turned toward them, all I could see was this beautiful ass in tight pants clinging seductively to the bar stool. It was attached to a small waist that led up to broad shoulders, which led to the back of a nicely shaped head topped off with straight, silky brown hair. As I approached them the mystery man turned to face me. Then Eddie took my hand and pulled me into the space between their stools. "How the hell are you?" he asked, patting my cheek. "What are you drinking? Do you know Dick Colacino?"

All these questions! I couldn't possibly answer since I was much too busy falling in love and I was much too close to take it all in. I ordered a drink and took a step back so that my eyes could focus. "No, I don't think I do know—what was your name?" I asked turning to face him.

"Dick," he said with a smile that told me he enjoyed saying his name. "Dick Colacino."

To this day I can't look at Bruce Willis without thinking about Dick. They look so much alike, and they give off the same sexual energy.

Thoughts spun in my head: *I don't even know if this guy is gay. He's with Eddie, who's straight and married, but on the other side is Ken, who's gay, so it's anybody's guess. But those tight pants....* My mind was racing, and I thought Dick would get away if I didn't make a decision and ask him to spend the rest of his life with me. The chemical reaction was overwhelming. My drink arrived and snapped me out of my fantasy long enough to hear Dick say he was a dancer in *My Fair Lady*. I wasn't usually attracted to dancers, but something definitely was happening here. My speculation kept up for half an hour or so. I kept waiting for some sign, a pin to drop, anything.... Nothing. I was intrigued.

Eddie got up to leave, and Ken eventually followed. I couldn't think of a legitimate reason to ask Dick home without opening myself up to embarrassment. I lived uptown, and it made no sense to ask him to go all that way for a cup of coffee. I was just about to take off when he turned and asked if I'd like to stay the night with him. I gulped down my drink, stood up, held out my hand, and in that "after-you" fashion, followed him out the door.

Dick had a small but comfortable apartment in the theater district. We sat at his kitchen table drinking coffee, talking for what seemed hours, during which he got up to do a few minor chores. I kept waiting for something sexual to happen. At one point he took off his shirt, revealing well-developed arms and prominent nipples that seemed to be trying to escape his sleeveless undershirt. I could think of nothing but sex. Was it all wishful thinking? Usually when I went home with someone, it wasn't long before clothes and inhibitions went flying. But that wasn't the case here. I didn't know what was going on, but it was still exciting.

Suddenly Dick was standing by my chair. His hand went to the back of my head, and as he lightly rubbed the nape of my neck, he pulled me toward him. I turned around and wrapped my arms around his waist. He drew me in until my cheek rested against his stomach. We just held each other like that for a few moments. Then he took a step back and unzipped his fly. His dick was large, even in its flaccid state, but it began to grow, and then it just kept growing. It was beautiful! Again, it embarrassed me that I would find a dick beautiful. But it was. Some people have beautiful eyes or beautiful hair. Why shouldn't some have beautiful dicks? Dick did his name proud. No wonder he liked saying it, and no wonder he smiled faintly whenever he did.

Dick bent down and gave me a tender kiss, helped me from the chair, and led me into the bedroom. When I left the next morning, we made plans to meet again that night. Dick had been totally "trade" during our sex, so I still wasn't sure about his sexual preference.

Trade used to be a gay expression for someone who's totally passive sexually. Guys who are trade are supposed to be straight, but at the same time they enjoy a good blow job, no matter who's giving it. Most trade is found in men's rooms and public places. There's generally no tenderness, and usually it's a spur-of-the-moment thing. A trade doesn't reciprocate and, other than holding the back of your head, rarely touches you. I've known guys who only liked trade and who seldom, if ever, had mutual sex. These men also had a little saying that holds a bit of truth: "This year's trade is next year's competition."

I had never been into trade, but Dick changed my mind that night. It was a new experience for me: I was like his whore, and yet at the same time I felt very masculine. Sex with Dick was different, exciting. He held me in his arms, we kissed, and although we made love passionately, love was not a part of our relationship. At least in my head it wasn't. We became the ultimate fuck buddies. I was happy—and I was busy.

When Joe returned after a short vacation, we started to work on the TV production of *Once Upon a Mattress*. The cast was terrific: Carol Burnett, Jane White, Bill Hayes, Shanee Wallace, Jack Gilford, Joe Bova, and Elliot Gould. I was still doing *No Strings* every night. Having two jobs is difficult in any situation, but I worked best under pressure. We retained some of the choreography from the original production, but most was restaged for TV.

I had an idea for the credits: to print them on mattresses and do a comedy ballet with the cast running around holding them. Giving me the reins for the first time, Joe said, "Do it!" I featured Michael Bennett in the number. When he got back from Europe, he stayed with me for a few days. I was casting dancers, so he got not only a bed for a few nights but also his first TV job, a principal dancer contract, and his union card from the American Federation of Television and Radio Artists. This was the first of many times Michael and I would help each other.

I spent a lot of time with Elliot Gould working on his "Very Soft Shoes" number. He's a large man, like a basketball player, but when he danced he was something else. We got along well, and he needed to talk to someone. He was married to Barbra Streisand at the time, and they were having problems. Barbra's career was riding the crest of newfound stardom with her CBS special *My Name Is Barbra*, while Elliot's was on the wane. He had hoped *Mattress* would jump-start his career, but it didn't happen and he'd have to wait a few years to attain star status with *M*A*S*H* and, later, total respect as an actor for his performance in *The Long Goodbye*.

Elliot was starring in *I Can Get It for You Wholesale*, in which Barbra played a supporting role. I saw the show opening night, and I'll never forget her amazing performance. The critics felt the same way. It's funny, but with our ties to Joe Layton, I only met Barbra once. We shared a limo and boat ride to Fire Island one Saturday night after the show. Fred Smith and I from *No Strings* and Harold Lang, Barbra, and Elliot from *Wholesale*. I don't remember much about that trip except that we drank Black Russians, which is why I don't remember much about that trip.

I was working so many hours that I have a lot of hazy memories of this period, mostly fragments. Bill Hayes in white tights, I'll never get out of my mind—gorgeous and everyone wanted him. I remember Shanee Wallace's raspy but delicate soprano voice and her bawdy laugh, Jack Gilford's wonderful animal imitations, Jane White's full, rounded tones, and Carol Burnett's talent, energy, and her being so fucking real. I was, am, and forever will be, an admirer.

I also have fond memories of my friendship with Mary Rodgers. I had met her during rehearsals for *No Strings* but didn't get to know her until I worked with her on *Mattress*. I respected her direct approach and ability to adapt to situations while still proving her point. She's a survivor.

Around this time I obtained my first agent, Bruce Savan, who'd approached me at the dress rehearsal of *Mattress*. From then on he represented me and got me a lot of work.

I also choreographed a local ABC program called *Show Street*, hosted by Phyllis Diller. She'd fly in Sunday mornings from whatever city she'd played Saturday night, arrive at the theater, eat a hamburger with lots of raw onion, and proceed to tape three shows before calling it a day. It was a nice first choreography job, not demanding enough but fun.

Another job I picked up at this time was choreographing shows at the Peppermint Lounge. I did a new show there every six months for more than two years. On each opening night the manager, Sam, would walk over, shake my hand, tell me "Good show," and slip me five hundred dollars in cash, usually in twenties and tens. When I left I'd walk down 45th Street with a big wad of money bulging in my front pocket. It's a wonder I was never mugged (probably because 45th Street was a hustler area and almost everyone had a big bulge in the front of his pants).

Marvin Shulman became my business manager and made it his job to go by the lounge every Saturday night to pick up my hundred-dollar royalty payment, always in cash. He'd walk past the bouncer, through the crowd, and into the kitchen, where Sam would welcome him with a handshake and a folded hundred-dollar bill. After Marvin had eyed the crowd, he'd leave and go a few steps east to the Wagon Wheel, a hustler bar (just to "check it out," he'd say). I teased him about this constantly.

Around this time David Hayes, the set designer, arranged for me to present a sample of my choreography to George Balanchine. David and his wife, Elenore, and I had become good friends on *No Strings*, and they were both supportive. I could hardly believe this was happening.

I called Paula Tennyson, Susan May, and Jimmy Brussock, all good friends from my Ballet Russe days, to dance the ballet for me. They agreed, and when we were ready the date was set. At the last minute Jimmy pulled out and I had to dance the part myself. I wasn't prepared physically, but I certainly knew the steps and had no other option. We arrived at the American School of Ballet just as the company class was finishing. There would be a little break before rehearsal, so Mr. Balanchine invited them all to watch. Helio played the piano for us. It went well, and we got a nice hand from the company. Balanchine spoke to Susan and Paula before turning to me, then took my hand. "Very nice," he said, looking straight into my eyes. "Thank you for coming to dance for us."

He released my hand, turned away, and prepared to hold his rehearsal. I was blown away. I had just danced one of my own ballets for George Balanchine. And he was right. It was a nice ballet.

I was still seeing Dick on a regular basis, but things were getting a bit edgy. I had hired him as a replacement in the show, and now we were constantly together. We got so close, I became scared of my feelings. When this had happened before, I always withdrew and ended the affair. This was to be no exception.

Our sex was still mostly one-sided, and it frightened me that I cared more about satisfying him than myself. This must have really confused him. We had great sex, no doubt about it, yet I held back. Eventually, I suggested we stop seeing each other.

Dick took the news in stride, or so it seemed, until that evening at the theater. He failed to make his first entrance in the show and couldn't be found. He never showed up. When I returned to my dressing room, I opened the door and found him on the floor, fully dressed in his costume, lying in a pool of blood. He had gotten into my dressing room and had cut his wrists. He was still alive but barely. Someone called an ambulance, and before the next act started he was gone. I finished the show in a state of shock, carefully watched by the cast. This was a very public incident. The sirens and the presence of the paramedics made the entire cast as well as the audience aware of the situation.

After the show was over, Alan Johnson and Sandy Leeds took me out for a drink so that I wouldn't be alone. All I could think of was Mike Bayens's attempted suicide and now Dick's. What was wrong with me? I was preoccupied when we entered Confucius. On his usual stool sat Eddie Phillips, and I realized that this was where Dick and I had met.

"Hey, Wakefield. What's new?" Eddie asked with that twinkle in his eye, and I knew word had gotten out. Of course, Dick would lose his job, which didn't ease my guilt.

The next day, I went to see Dick at Bellevue Hospital. Within a month he'd moved into my apartment, and we became lovers again. I finally made a commitment but for the wrong reason. I still hadn't fully embraced my homosexuality.

No Strings wasn't a fun show to perform, so we had a lot of cast replacements. Some shows are like that—effective but a lot of hard work. I was constantly putting new people into the show.

When Pat Heim, who'd been on the Orient tour with me, decided to leave *No Strings*, I planned a bit of fun for his last show. Even offstage, we could pass for twin brothers, and people would constantly get us mixed up. Pat was straight, but guys were always touching his ass, thinking it was me—or so he said. And I always told him I was "Madge, the pretty one" and that he was just plain, so how could there be any confusion!

I received permission from Mr. Rodgers to play a trick during Pat's last performance. In the party scene the chorus is spread across the entire stage in a single line. They're frozen in exaggerated poses for about three minutes, then they begin to waltz with their partners. When Pat turned to take his partner in his arms, she was gone. Instead, I was there in all her glory, replacing her in full drag.

"I told you I was Madge, the pretty one!" I said. He exploded with laughter and swept me into his arms as we finished the number, high heels and all. I danced pretty well in heels, but I was sure everyone's eyes in the audience were on me—that homely girl with the large nose, mixed in with all the beauties.

As I came offstage at the intermission, I was immediately called to the stage door. Bobby Morse, from backstage at *How to Succeed in Business*, was on the phone. I had been instrumental in getting Carole D'Andrea, his wife, to marry him, so we were old buddies. He had heard about my drag performance.

"You didn't really, did you?"

"Uh-huh," I answered.

We laughed. Little did he know that in a few years he and Larry Kert would be doing the same thing every night in *Sugar*, a musical version of *Some Like It Hot*. Once again, his call showed me how fast the grapevine works. My reputation was growing by leaps and bounds. I was becoming notorious!

Dick and I maintained our relationship for more than a year. The sex was still incredible, but I had doubts about the future. Since our relationship had become public, I was troubled by my growing "homosexual reputation." For the first time in my life, I was embarrassed by what I was. It was the strangest relationship I would ever have.

Dick could not get a job, and it seemed no one would give him a second chance. Finally, Bob Hergert hired him for a revival of *The Boys From Syracuse*. I spoke with Mr. Rodgers, and with the help of director Christopher Hewett (later to become TV's *Mr. Belvedere*), persuaded him to allow Dick to join the cast.

Opening off Broadway in April 1963, the show was an enormous hit. After a good month's run and when things began to settle down, I asked Dick to move out since he was working and could support himself now. It was not a pleasant experience, but he did leave. Despite all the ugliness we went through, I continued to have sex with him periodically during the next year, until he moved to Las Vegas.

I had been seeing a therapist at this time, and he influenced me more than I realized, encouraging me to seek out heterosexual relationships. I wanted a relationship, but there was always something that wasn't right. I was sophisticated sexually but not emotionally. So I decided to date women again. This was not an all-out effort to go straight but simply to try something else. I wanted to find out what I was looking for.

I began seeing Ellen Halpin. We'd met during *Finian's Rainbow* and were attracted to each other. Now we were working together again in *No Strings*. I needed a vacation, so I asked her along. We both left the show for a five-day trip to San Juan, Puerto Rico, and by the end of the trip we were having an affair. After we returned we spent several nights a week together.

Ellen and I continued to see each other through the summer of 1963. We had fun together, and our sex stayed fresh and exciting, which was encouraging. And my feelings for her kept developing. Marriage was not out of the question.

I drank a lot during this period, but Ellen could drink me under the table and show no signs of its effect. As a matter of fact, all my friends at this time drank a lot. When we finished our shows each night there wasn't much else to do.

In June 1963 we started pre-production on Noël Coward's *The Girl Who Came to Supper*, a musical version of Terence Rattigan's *The Sleeping Prince* (A.K.A. *The Prince and the Showgirl*).

Joe Layton had worked with Noël on *Sail Away* a few seasons earlier, and they had become great friends. Wanting to remain so, Joe informed me that besides being his associate, I would act as a go-between for him and Noël. That way, he said, tempers could be kept at a minimum.

Noël and I hit it off tremendously. During run-throughs I'd sit with him in the orchestra, take notes for him, and give them to Joe. If a disagreement arose, I would take Joe's response back to Noël...and on and on. It was fun but far from easy. I always had to sit on Noël's right side so that I could write with my right hand. I had to because Noël always held one of my hands in his lap. But he never made a pass and, remarkably, neither did I. But to people who noticed, it looked shocking. Need I say, Noël lived to shock.

Once Joe passed us on his way to the stage and announced, without changing his gait, "If you two don't cut it out, you're going to wind up in Louis Sobel's column."

"My dear boy," Noël whispered in my ear, "you must be more careful where you put your hand. Reputations are at stake!" He squeezed my hand a little tighter. Instantly, Noël became a giggling boy in his teens, losing all traces of sophistication and then, just as suddenly, his seriousness returned. Even Noël Coward couldn't be Noël Coward all the time.

Rehearsals had been a pleasure. We had a wonderful cast led by José Ferrer and Florence Henderson. Besides Noël and his charm, we had Harry Kurnitz and his humor, as well as Oliver Smith and Irene Sharaff with their taste and elegance. To top it all off, Harry's assistant, Mae Murray, had just come from Hollywood. She had been Marilyn Monroe's housekeeper and secretary and had actually found her body.

I had been a Marilyn Monroe fan since I first saw her, and I recognized her talent immediately. The fact that I didn't think about fucking her while watching her act had a lot to do with my seeing her talent. Anyway, no amount of prodding would get Mae to betray any confidences. Although she told me many stories, none were of a personal nature. Even after Marilyn's death, she remained a faithful friend.

During a break from costume fittings one day, Joe and I had the distinct pleasure of having lunch with Irene Sharaff at Pearl's, a chic Chinese restaurant in the theater district. Irene was one of the most famous designers in Hollywood. She was at MGM during its peak period, designing for all the major musicals and winning Academy Awards for *An American in Paris* and *The King and I*. Pearl was a friend of hers, so Irene had designed the interior of the restaurant.

Irene wanted to discuss the possibility of doing a show about Isadora Duncan. She had this pet project in the back of her head, and after watching Joe and me work together, she thought we would be right for the project. It was a lovely lunch but nothing ever came of it.

We opened the show in Boston. The day we arrived, we held the first orchestra reading in the Bradford Hotel ballroom. This is always my favorite time in the rehearsal process, when you first hear the orchestrations and get the true feelings and shades of the score.

Jay Blackton, the conductor, began to read through the score. Noël,

Joe, John Smolka, and I were there as well as Jerry Adler, the stage manager. At one point I went downstairs to get some coffee.

The coffee shop and the bar were divided by the entrance to the hotel, a sort of arcade, with glass doors leading to each. As I was waiting for my order, I glanced toward the bar and saw a woman standing with her back to me and talking to two gentlemen. All I could see, besides the back of her head, was an incredible pair of legs. Even through two glass doors, and before she turned around, I knew it was Marlene Dietrich. She was performing her one-woman show in Framingham, not far from Boston. It was also matinee day and intermission next door at the Shubert Theater, where Robert Horton was starring in *110 in the Shade*.

When I went back upstairs I mentioned to Noël and Joe that I had seen Marlene in the bar. Noël jumped to his feet, took me by the arm, and nudged me toward the exit, all the while saying, "Run, dear boy, find her, bring her to me. Hurry."

Well, I ran down the flight of stairs and through the lobby. I could see through the glass door that the bar had emptied and that the second act had started. I assumed she had gone back with the other theatergoers, but I still had the good sense to go inside and make sure. Thank God I did. There she was, with her friends, sitting at a corner table. I took a deep breath and approached them.

"Excuse me, Miss Dietrich. Mr. Coward is upstairs in the ballroom, and he's requested that I bring you to him. We are—"

Before I could finish she squealed, stood up, took me by the arm, and whisked me out the door. She didn't even say a word to the two men with her. She just left them. When we entered the room she dropped my arm and flew into Noël's.

He twirled her about like they were in their twenties. Right before my eyes, they became two school kids, and for the next few hours I watched and listened. It was here that I learned that age is only a way to mark time, not a state of mind. At this moment they were two twenty year olds in sixty-year-old bodies. It was also here that I learned that when you're around legends, stay quiet, listen, and let the memories pile up.

They exchanged compliments as to how wonderful each looked, all the while touching each other as if to make sure the other was really there. They also agreed with the other's compliments. To illustrate a point, Marlene would lift her skirt and show her legs, all the while laughing, playing with her scarf, and tossing her hair. She had been at the matinee and had not wanted to go back after the first act. She kept saying to Noël how grateful she was that the show was so dreadful, otherwise she would have missed him. Noël had seen the show the night before and voiced his opinion.

"Robert Horton's idea of acting the cowboy," he demonstrated, "is to push his pelvis forward and swagger. I wanted to shout, 'Show us your cock and get on with it!'"

They laughed, and I just felt lucky to be where I was at that exact moment. Noël's music was background for this whole incredible scene because the orchestra rehearsal continued through it all. I don't know how the musicians could concentrate with these two right there in front of them. Just before the break, she said her good-byes, and Noël escorted her out of the room. I looked at Joe and we smiled.

After the Boston opening, even with the great reviews, the work continued. Noël wrote a new number for José Ferrer called "Middle Age," a vaudeville-style number, with hat and cane. But instead of a cane, he took a fencing sword off the wall.

I staged and rehearsed the number in two days, showed it to Joe, and after a few minor adjustments, Robert Russell Bennett came in to view the number before doing the orchestrations.

The next day, we rehearsed José with the orchestra before putting in the number that night. Joe didn't show up so that he wouldn't have to deal with Noël. Well, Noël hated the number. He told me to simplify the staging so that he could understand every lyric.

A half-hour before the performance, I told Joe about Noël's objections and that he said not to add the number that night.

Joe responded, "Fuck, Noël! The number goes in tonight. I'll take care of it."

I was used to this. It was part of my job, so I believed he would talk to Noël. I went to José's dressing room right before the performance. He was putting on his mike and trying to stuff the battery pack down the front of his dance belt. He was notorious for being well-hung—and not shy about showing it. He stuck his hand down the front of his dance belt, brought out two hands full, and rearranged it.

"Just what I need, something else stuffed in this confounded thing," he complained, pushing the battery into an already crowded dance belt. I wished him luck and left him to his stuffing.

I watched the number from the wings. José performed wonderfully and took special care with his diction. After the number was over I went to the dancers' dressing room to have a cigarette. In less than a minute the door flew open and in raged Noël, screaming. I stood there fighting back the tears as he ranted on about my incompetence, how I let him down, and that next time, if there was a next time, I should do what he told me. The dancers were all there, so I felt embarrassed and humiliated. The tears finally flowed down my cheeks as Noël turned and left the room.

Joe had forgotten to speak to him.

The men's dressing room had never been so quiet. I took a deep breath and lit another cigarette. The other had burned away in my hand. When I was just about finished, the door swung open again and Noël reappeared. He hurriedly crossed to me, and I was about to duck when he put his arms around me. He found out that I had spoken to Joe and that Joe decided to ignore his request. He apologized, calling me his "dear sweet boy," and to my amazement he turned to the dancers, who were still trying hard not to listen, and apologized. Somehow it didn't make me feel much better. Noël had turned on me so quickly, and in the time it took to smoke a cigarette, I had gone from friend to foe and back again. In show business things can change quickly.

The show went well until we arrived in Philadelphia, our last stop, before opening on Broadway. I was to leave the show at the end of the Philly run, then go to London to start staging *No Strings*. Joe was to join me there after *The Girl Who Came to Supper* opened on Broadway.

Suddenly, though, Joe became ill. He was so tired that he couldn't get out of bed, so Noël and I had to take over the rehearsals. We called in a doctor. Hepatitis. Within hours he was in a limo bound for a New York hospital.

We froze the show and let it play. When the time came for me to leave, the show was in great shape. I left for New York after the Wednesday matinee to prepare for my trip to London the following Saturday. As

I was ironing some shirts to take on my trip, the TV announced that President Kennedy had been shot. I didn't do much more that day than listen to the news reports. On the phone several times, however, I did speak with Noël, who was trying everything he could to get me to delay my trip for a few days.

Our opening number, "God Save the King, If He Can" was about assassination. Sung by José, the song defined his character and set up the conflict with his young son. Now, as a matter of good taste, it had to be changed. Noël even spoke with Mr. Rodgers to try to postpone my departure, but there was no way I could leave an entire company waiting in London. At this time it wasn't even certain Joe would be able to join me there, so I needed every minute of rehearsal time I could get. Noël was left to write, direct, and stage a new opening number. Now it was all his show.

I arrived in London and went straight to the Pastoria Hotel. José Ferrer had recommended the hotel and had written a note to their chef, an old friend of his, instructing him to take care of me, which he did.

I met Jerome Whyte, Mr. Rodgers's friend and London producer, for lunch at the Savoy, after which he was to take me to see the Her Majesty's Theater where we were to open. On the way he stopped by the Palace Theater where *The Sound of Music* was still playing. I went in with him, and as we walked out on to the stage, I saw that we were not alone. Margot Fonteyn and Rudolf Nureyev, who were using the theater for a gala benefit, had stopped by to check out the space. Jerome introduced us, and they went into a discussion about the gala.

After a few minutes they said their farewells to Jerry, shook my hand, and departed. I was a little groggy from lack of sleep, so I hoped I hadn't stared too much. Would I ever get over being starstruck? Hell, I was in London, directing a Richard Rodgers show, and I was still reacting like a hick.

That night, Jerry had tickets for me to see *Hamlet* with Peter O'Toole. He had arranged for David Holiday, who was to play the role of Mike Robinson in *Strings*, to be my date. How strange, come to think of it, that Jerry would fix me up with a male date. Even after Dick's suicide attempt, no comments were ever made about my sexual preference.

Rehearsals began the next morning. The cast included Beverly Todd, Art Lund, Hy Hazel, Ferdy Mayne, Erica Rogers, David Haliday, and Marti Stevens as Comfort O'Connell. Joe told me that Marti was a close friend and that I should get to know her. We got along well and dined together three or four times a week. If we didn't go to the New Friend, her favorite Chinese restaurant in the East End, she would join me at the Pastoria.

The rehearsals for the London company of *No Strings* were the most pleasant I've ever had in the theater. I love rehearsing out of town because there are no distractions, only work. By the time Mr. Rodgers and Sam Taylor arrived, I was doing run-throughs with scenery and lights, and we still had a week before previews. We were in great shape, and Mr. Rodgers let me know how pleased he was.

With this in mind I made one more attempt to get him to change the final scene, which I had typed out. I gave copies to him and Sam Taylor.

After a few minutes the real truth behind not making the change in New York emerged. Mr. Rodgers did not want to lose a reprise of "Maine," the character David's song about his home. But this time Barbara, Diahann Carroll's character, would sing it. It wasn't one of the better songs in the score, but Mr. Rodgers said that if Barbara didn't tell David to go home, she couldn't sing his song. In this reprise she uses his own words, so to speak, to get him to go home and write again. Rodgers wouldn't budge, and even Sam, whom I had almost convinced, backed down under pressure. I guess Mr. Rodgers thought "Maine" could become another popular state song, like "Oklahoma." It didn't happen.

The day before our first complete dress rehearsal, Marti took me aside. "My friend would like to come to the dress rehearsal tomorrow, and I was wondering if she could sit in the mezzanine with you. She doesn't want to cause a fuss or be a distraction."

I knew her friend was Marlene Dietrich because we had been to Marlene's flat for drinks one night. Only Jane (the lighting designer) and I were allowed in the balcony, so it would be private. I agreed. I was to meet her at the stage door five minutes before curtain.

When I got there at the appointed time, Marlene walked in the door. She was dressed in a gray suit and coat with a beautiful silk scarf tied under her chin. She took my hand, kissed me on the cheek—my God, she really did—and followed me through the twisting corridors and up the stairs to the mezzanine. She sat next to me with her arm through mine. I didn't take one note. I wasn't about to move a muscle.

After the first act she leaned over and whispered in my ear, "You have trouble with Marti, no?"

She was right. In the show Marti's character, Comfort O'Connell, was a Texas millionaire who also happened to be a nymphomaniac. Marti was having a hard time being crude. She understood the role but couldn't produce the desired effect. It was the only problem with her performance—and a major one.

"Don't worry, I'll fix for you," Marlene said, and she did. When the second act ended we stood and she took my hand.

"Come," she demanded, leading me through the row of seats. "Take me downstairs to see Sam and Dick. The performance is over. Now I would like to say hello." She had a way of ordering you around that didn't seem like ordering and a way of taking your help while she was demanding it. She was...Marlene.

By the time we opened, Marti had it down. There were no subtleties written into the part. Comfort was loud and brash and now so was Marti, thanks to Marlene. I don't know what she did, but she did it.

Beverly Todd was splendid as Barbara, and Art Lund, the nicest man in the world, equally good as David. The show opened to the best reviews a Rodgers show ever received in London, yet it ran for less than a year.

Joe didn't make it to London, so it was agreed that I would receive half his fee and royalty payments for directing the show. But it never happened. Joe said that payment was the responsibility of the Rodgers's office and they claimed it was his. Other than my assistant salary and a ten pound raise in my per diem, I never received a penny for directing the show. Joe told me once that the only way to make a lot of money was to do something that continues making money for you while you're doing something else. Well, I wasn't going to find that out this time.

The most valuable thing I got out of the experience was a note from Mr. Rodgers, thanking me for my work, signed *Dick*. Jerry Whyte told me it was now OK for me to call Mr. Rodgers "Dick."

I returned to New York in January 1964. Now, after three months abroad, I was alone, had no job, no money coming in, and no work prospects. Talk about the ups and downs of show biz—I was experiencing it big time. It was the end of the season, and nothing would be happening until the summer. Fortunately, with Marvin as my manager, my rent and bills would be paid, and I would get a small allowance, but I hated being out of work.

Soon, however, I got a call to replace one of the dancers on *The Garry Moore Show*. It was a great job and came at a perfect time. Ernie Flatt was the choreographer, but after several months he left, turning over his chores to Kevin Carlisle. I knew most of the dancers, Randy, Eddie, Carl, Jayne, Marie, Dru, and a pretty blond named Nancy Van Rijn.

Nancy and I had met several times and, even though Paul Jasmin was a good friend to each of us, we had never spent any time together. I was drawn to her immediately. She was tall, thin, soft-spoken, and independent. After a couple of weeks on the show, I invited her home for dinner.

We had a few drinks while I prepared veal marsala. Nancy was amazed and would later say that she fell in love watching me peel and flute mushrooms. We had a romantic evening, and she stayed the night. As a matter of fact, after that she never went back to her own apartment for any length of time except to pick up clothes and personal belongings. She had been having an affair with Hilly Elkins, a Broadway agent and producer, for some time, but there was something magical in the way Nancy and I hit it off. I felt at ease with her and asked her to marry me after only a few weeks. She declined, but I kept asking. Then I didn't ask anymore.

One night after sex, we were lying in the bed and she said, "You haven't asked me to marry you lately."

"Well," I said. "Would your answer be any different?"

"Yes. It would."

"Then let's do it," I said, taking her in my arms.

We both had some wild times, yet we didn't talk about our past affairs. For whatever reasons, we both wanted to slow down from our fast-paced lives.

We made all the arrangements, and on May 18, 1964, we were married in Yonkers, N.Y. Jayne Turner and Tom Porter stood up for us.

Jennifer West, Jere Admire, and Paul Jasmin also attended. When we returned to the city, we met the rest of our friends at Sardi's for our wedding supper.

After dinner we went to the Peppermint Lounge. My show was still playing there, so we received the royal treatment. We danced and drank champagne. A wedding breakfast at Larry Fuller and Michael Bennett's apartment was followed by a trip to Coney Island to watch the sunrise and then home. Nancy took a shower and went to rehearsal. My call wasn't until after lunch, so I went to bed. That was our wedding.

We shared so many close friends that our life settled into a nice place. We both continued to work on *The Garry Moore Show* through the end of the season. Nancy then took a job in the DuPont show at the World's Fair in New York, while I continued to freelance.

Paul Jasmin arranged for me to stage a number for two friends of his, Peter and Chris, who were going to appear on *The Tonight Show*. It was a fun job, paid well, and Peter and I became good buddies. Peter would later strike out on his own, writing songs and performing them under the name Peter Allen.

Also around this time I got my first job for Music Fairs, an organization of five theaters in the round, choreographing *The Pajama Game*, starring Liza Minnelli. She was supposed to do *Mattress*, which is probably why I was hired for the job, but at the last minute a change was made. It was not a good role for Liza, not enough for her to sing. She was terrific in the show, but after the bows she would do her nightclub act, *Liza With a Z*, so that the audience could hear her sing some more.

Liza and I hung out together and by the time we opened had grown quite close. Show business encourages fast friendships. Holding on to them is another matter. One afternoon, driving Liza to the theater, she asked for advice. She was seriously considering marrying Peter Allen. I remember her saying, "Things seem to be working so well for you and Nancy that I thought I'd ask about me and Peter...."

As her voice trailed off, I knew what she was asking or, I should say, not asking. I took a second, then answered.

"Do you love him? Does he make you happy? Does he fuck you good? If the answer is yes to all three, then do it. If the answer ever becomes no to any of them, get out."

She took my advice, all of it. I'd also bet she has no regrets about any of it.

I first met Liza while she was in *Best Foot Forward.* Mary Ann Niles, Broadway's most famous gypsy and Bob Fosse's first wife, brought her to my apartment one night after the show. We drank and listened to music until the sun rose. I remember at one point Liza standing in front of the fireplace with her hands firmly gripping the mantel. She leaned back and, looking up toward some unknown God, announced, "I want to sing just like Mama!" Whoever heard, I think her wish was granted.

I did a few episodes of *The Ed Sullivan Show*, and Ernie Flatt asked me to do *The Entertainers*, with Carol Burnett, John Davidson, Katarina Valente, and Tessie O'Shea. It was an odd group. After one season, though, Carol would move to California, CBS would premiere *The Carol Burnett Show*, and I'd get to look for another job.

I didn't have to wait long. During the camera rehearsal for the last show of the series, I received a phone call from my agent. The Rodgers's office wanted me to do the musical staging for his new Broadway show *Do I Hear a Waltz?*

I couldn't believe my ears. They were offering me my own show. Nancy and I were happy, and everything I wanted was within reach. I was going to work with Richard Rodgers, Arthur Laurents, Stephen Sondheim, and the new hot director on the international scene, John Dexter from the Royal Court. I knew this would be one of the great learning experiences of my life. I was right, but I was also wrong.

Chapter Five

Do I Hear a Waltz?

New York City, 1964

The first meeting of the production staff was scheduled at the Rodgers and Hammerstein office on Madison Avenue. Eddie Blum, the casting director, asked that I meet with him an hour before to go over a few things. I had worked with him closely during the casting of *No Strings*, so we were friends. He was a direct individual, always as polite as he was honest.

I arrived on time and took a seat in his office. Eddie gave me a script and said he wanted to talk about my duties, telling me the show would include no dancing but that some heavy staging would be required. John Dexter, the director, would stage all the musical numbers, relying heavily on my assistance. Since there would be no choreography, my newly created title would be choreographic associate. Eddie let me know I was also there to support to Mr. Rodgers, to be on his side. *What a strange comment*, I mentally noted. I thought we were doing a Broadway show, not waging a war.

Rodgers had wanted Joe Layton to direct, and Arthur Laurents had wanted John. Arthur got his way, and I was part of the compromise. It was to be Dick, Jerry Whyte, and me opposing Arthur, Steve, and John. The sides were even, at least in number.

This compromise affected how Steve and Arthur treated me. I never felt part of their team. So, of course, that's what I wanted more than anything. When Eddie and I finished talking, John was brought in to meet me. He was a strange little man, resembling Phil Collins. Eddie introduced us and left the room.

"I've heard about you from Dick. He holds you in high regard," John said, taking Eddie's chair. "I saw *No Strings* in London." He stopped talking and lit a cigarette.

"I've heard about you too," I said, "but unfortunately I haven't had the opportunity to see any of your work." For some reason I found myself hiding my enthusiasm, but I continued, "I'm looking forward to this very much."

"Now let's get something straight," John said. "You know that there's to be no dancing, but when I need some movement, I'll turn things over to you. I would prefer, if you have any ideas or anything to say, that you wait until a break to speak with me in private. This is the way I like to work. Clear?" His voice was hard-edged and surprisingly threatening. He didn't wait for an answer. He stood and motioned for me to follow him. "Let's go in to join the others," he said. "I think they want to take some photographs."

His lack of warmth stunned me, but I followed him out of the office. On the way he placed his hand on my shoulder and spoke to me once more. "Would you make up a list of the characters you want for the opening number in the Piazza San Marco and get them to me tomorrow?" he said, finishing just as we arrived at Dick's office. I quickly realized there would be little or no discussion about anything—and no spontaneity whatsoever.

Jerome Whyte approached me as I entered the room, giving me a big hug. I had felt so unwelcome. That hug was just what I needed. Jerome introduced Arthur Laurents, whom I'd already met in Paris, and Stephen Sondheim, whom I hadn't yet met.

My initial reaction to Stephen was quite sensual. I found him extremely attractive, even though he was slightly overweight, his suit was slightly wrinkled, cigarette ashes trailed down the front of his shirt, and his hair was a little mussed. In the middle of all this tension, I still had room for sexual fantasies. I was withdrawing to a place where I was much more secure.

Beni Montresor, the set and costume designer, came in late. After a few minutes of small talk, we gathered around a table, looking at sketches for the show, while a photographer snapped away. When he had the shots he needed, we all left. That's about all we accomplished during that initial meeting. The guarded and not-so-friendly atmosphere of this first encounter would become the norm.

Nancy and I had been married for more than a year. We had so many mutual friends that our social life didn't change much. We loved to play bridge, and many nights we'd play until dawn. Our sex life was still pretty good, but neither of us made it our priority. When it happened, it happened.

We went into rehearsal, and it wasn't long before personality conflicts at the top started to affect everyone in the cast. Many times John would wave me off, motioning behind his back, preventing me from even listening to creative discussions among him, Arthur, and Stephen. Why this treatment? Hell, I wasn't a spy; I was supposed to be a comrade.

Mr. Rodgers had a reputation of being a little homophobic, and here he was collaborating with homosexuals. I could see his discomfort, and most of the time he was on the defensive. On this show he was the producer as well as the composer. He had a lot of power, but it was always a "majority rules" situation.

John was blatant about his homosexuality. That didn't bother me, of course. As a matter of fact, it's the only thing I liked about him. The top names in the theater, all these great minds, all this talent, and no one was communicating. Throw into this mix a social façade of friendliness, and you have the recipe for disaster.

Elizabeth Allen and Sergio Franchi starred in the show, supported by Madeline Sherwood, Julienne Marie, Stuart Damon, Jack Manning, and Carol Bruce. Surprisingly, the cast got along well. Most of the trouble lay at the top. The two factions had completely different visions of the show.

The decision not to include dancing was the biggest mistake. The show was called *Do I Hear a Waltz?*, for God's sake. Without dancing, it was like bad sex: It didn't satisfy on any level. I know Arthur envisioned a small, musicalized version of his play, not a large, dancing musical comedy, but that wasn't what we were doing.

We somehow got through the rehearsal period without any major bloodshed, but on the last day in New York before going to New Haven, that all changed.

After the morning rehearsal John informed the cast that we would do an afternoon run-through. He said that everyone could invite four people to watch. Elizabeth Allen immediately spoke out against any such plan. Unfortunately, she did it in front of the entire company.

"No, I don't think so!" she announced. "I don't feel secure enough yet to perform in front of an audience. Also, look at me—I'm a mess." John walked over to her. They spoke softly for a few seconds, and then out of the silence, he screamed, "Fuck you, you pig!" A shouting match ensued in front of the whole cast. John stormed off the stage, picked up his jacket, and charged out of the theater.

We went ahead with the run-through with an audience that afternoon, and Elizabeth performed with the fevered pitch of Ethel Merman in *Gypsy* rather than showing any of the vulnerable characteristics of Leona. John and Elizabeth didn't speak to each other for weeks afterward.

In New Haven the technical rehearsals didn't turn out much better. Beni was known mostly for his opera costumes. The concept for the show was "Venice Remembered." Beni translated that into scrims and chiffon costumes. Everything would have a light, wispy feel to it, faint, like a memory. Great idea on paper, but it didn't translate. The costumes just looked cheap.

We played the show without changes that week. But the minute we arrived in Boston, Mary and Dorothy Rodgers took the cast members shopping at Filene's for new costumes. Even the men's suits had been soft fabrics and pastel colors. They all had to go.

We opened, and although the show ran smoothly, it was still a disaster. Talk had begun about replacing Elizabeth with Gwen Verdon, and panic was setting in. After the second performance in Boston, Jerry Whyte took me aside and informed me that choreography would be added and that Herb Ross was to become the show's choreographer, replacing me. He would also take over the direction. John, according to contract, could not be fired, so I was to take the blame for this fiasco.

"That's foolish," I said, hiding my disappointment that I wasn't even given a chance. "There's no reason for me to be the victim here. You don't need one. The show never had a choreographer—I'm a choreographic associate. Herb will welcome my assistance. Ask him. I've been paid already, so it doesn't make any sense for me to leave." The next day he called me to say Herb would love for me to stay on.

We began to add dancing to the show. Herb, his wife Nora Kaye, and I worked on the new numbers in the Bradford Hotel ballroom at night while the cast was performing the show. We worked quickly, and as we put pieces into the show, the cast began to feel much better. Herb and Nora brought a little sanity into the mix. The two factions became less noticeable as Herb took over most of the responsibility (at least in front of the company). Morale improved.

John, however, became less visible as the days went by. His growing absence was a relief. He had done nothing to dispel my first impression that he was a nasty, insensitive man.

One night during rehearsal I finished dancing one of the variations we had choreographed for the "Two by Two" number. "That works really well," Herb said as I sat down on the floor to catch my breath. "Maybe you should dance it in the show!"

"You're a terrific dancer, Wake. Are you sure you're ready to give up performing?" Nora added.

The two of them continued to pursue the subject, and before long they asked me to work with them and dance in Herb's next show, *On a Clear Day You Can See Forever*. I was flattered but on my way to becoming a choreographer. Why would I want to dance in a new show?

I didn't understand. I should have realized that they were trying to tell me I wasn't ready to meet the challenge of my opportunities. They knew I was in for a rough time, and they liked me well enough to try to guide my future. Now that I see what they were trying to do for me, my ignorance of the situation only supported their belief.

On the other hand, if they'd been more direct and simply stated the truth—that I was not yet experienced enough—I might have understood. I knew I was a good dancer, but that's not what I wanted anymore. I wanted to choreograph, and I thought I had a choice. They should have told me I didn't. Not yet, anyway.

The show got better. I befriended Arthur and Steven, and things generally became more pleasant. One night after the show, Arthur invited us to a little party in his suite for all the principals.

Midway through the evening, we began to hear voices from Helen Blount's room next door. The understudies were at her party, and evidently they were drinking more than we were. We could hear every word they said, and they were speaking mostly about all of us and how bad everything was.

One by one, we all got raked over the coals. We laughed, and when we'd heard enough, Arthur opened his door and knocked on Helen's. When she opened the door Arthur put his finger to his lips. "Ssshh," he said, "We're trying to talk in here. Could you keep it down just a bit? We can hear every word you say." He closed the door as we all burst into laughter. They would have a few anxious moments the next day for sure.

That night on the phone, I told this story to Marvin, my manager. He, in turn, told Tom Porter, and the next afternoon the incident appeared in Dorothy Kilgallen's column in the *Journal American*. I questioned Tom. He finally admitted that for years he had supplied items for her column. I should have guessed.

Several times I'd noticed that little pieces of gossip, incidents that I had observed, would appear in her column. Now I knew. It was Tom! My good friend, Tom! My best man, Tom, had sold these little stories to her for a hundred bucks a week. Tom, a production stage manager, had access to a lot of dirt. He made me swear not to tell our friends. I realized that if I did, he would lose all his sources, so I kept his secret until Kilgallen's death.

The show opened on Broadway March 18, 1965, to mostly tepid reviews, but because of advance bookings it would run six months. The only totally positive thing I took away from this experience was that Nancy and I grew close to Mary Rodgers and her husband, Henry Guettel. We often played bridge with them, and once the show opened in New York, we spent many good times at their home in Monticello. Mary and Henry were generous with their friendship, and we began to feel like an extension of their family. They were great parents, so naturally they had great children—all so individual, bright, and inquisitive. One of our great thrills was taking them to see the Beatles at

Shea Stadium. We went in a limo and sat in box seats, ten rows from the front. Now, that's seeing the Beatles! Nobody *heard* the Beatles at Shea Stadium. You merely saw them and heard screaming. Still, being witness to such controlled mass hysteria is not an everyday occurrence. Unbelievable.

About three months into the run, someone called from the Society of Stage Directors and Choreographers. In New Haven I was told I had to join. "I'm calling to inquire why we haven't received our portion of your royalty payments for *Do I Hear a Waltz?*" a voice announced.

I told her I'd received a flat fee, no royalties.

"Then the producers have violated the agreement we have with the League of Broadway Theater Producers. You, as choreographer, are entitled to a minimum of one half of one percent of the gross, and we are entitled to a percentage of your royalty."

Before I knew it the society was suing the Rodgers's office, on my behalf, for unpaid royalties. Two numbers originally staged by me remained in the show untouched: "No Understand" and "What Do We Do, We Fly," so they felt I was entitled to the royalty no matter what credit I received by contract.

I spoke with Dick Rodgers about the situation, explaining that I hadn't initiated the suit and that I had no choice in the matter. At the end of our talk he walked me to the door, thanked me for coming in, patted me on the shoulder, and told me not to worry.

"Everything will be fine, just fine," he assured me.

Several months later at the arbitration, he entered the room and shook his finger at me like he was scolding a schoolboy. Later, during his testimony, I would stare in disbelief as he took out a piece of paper and read the *Webster's Dictionary* definition of choreography.

"Design of ballet, dancing movement," he read. "There was no ballet or dancing movement in the show until Herb Ross joined the production." He folded his paper and placed it into his pocket. He was finished. Herb, Steven, Arthur, no one from the production staff was available to testify. Danny Daniels, who had absolutely no connection with the show, testified on my behalf, stating that any set movement to music was choreography.

The arbitrator decided in Rodgers's favor and we lost. I thought it would be a simple case, that I would receive my small check and that would be it. We were not talking about a great amount of money, so I'd figured it would be no contest. It seemed that no matter what, fate was determined to cast me as the victim, and this time it took a total of fifteen minutes. No matter what you call it, I had staged two numbers in the show. They remained in the show for the entire Broadway run. It was only a matter of semantics.

Once again, I was totally naïve and had put my fate into someone else's hands. I had trusted Mr. Rodgers when he told me that everything would be "Just fine." He didn't lie to me. It *was* just fine—for him. He saved himself a few thousand dollars. Of course, results of the suit made all the papers, even *Variety*.

At this point everything began to take a ugly turn. Gossip started that my marriage was a career move on my part and that I got married to ward off any rumors about my being gay. Rumors? After the scandal of my affair with Dick, there weren't any rumors! Everyone on Broadway knew the facts, so what doubt was left in anyone's mind as to my sexual behavior?

Interestingly, after that, work became hard to find. Most of the TV shows were starting to transfer to California, but Kevin Carlisle hired me again to dance on an NBC variety series called *Coliseum*, with guests ranging from Woody Allen to Leslie Uggams. It was a bad show, but it helped pay the bills. Nancy, however, continued to work on a few TV shows and landed a Final Touch detergent commercial. Fortunately, between the two of us we were able to manage during this tough period. There was always stock. I choreographed *I Married An Angel* with Don Ameche, Margaret Whitting, and Tania Elg, and now I was going to direct and choreograph *No Strings* starring Diahann Carroll.

It turned out to be a terrific production and made more money than any other show in the history of Music Fairs. But best of all, I finally got to do my version of the show, and it worked like I knew it would. Diahann said the revised script made all the difference and should have been that way all along.

Mr. Rodgers went to see the show at Westbury and never mentioned the changes to me. Either he didn't notice or was embarrassed that it had worked so well.

Nancy and I took a house on Fire Island for the summer with Paul "Jazz" Jasmin and Marvin. For the first time, the four of us spent time together. It was an exceptional summer. We must have made quite a picture because midsummer, along with Jazz's basset hound, Dorothy, we were made into life-size cutout figures and placed in Bendel's windows to sell children's clothes. B.B. Boucher, the window dresser and a friend, drew caricatures of each of us, cut them out, and pinned clothes on them—a big thrill for all of us.

About this time my sex drive began to ebb. My self-esteem was in the basement and manifested itself in the usual manner—no erection. Our sex life had become practically nonexistent. I realized that Nancy must have been feeling the same things I was, all the "uns": unattractive, undesirable, unsexy, unhappy. Mine all stemmed from my lack of desire not only for her but for anyone.

This period has been hard to reconstruct in my mind. It was all so negative. Since I was unable to get work, my self-esteem continued its downward spiral. This, along with Nancy's working more than I did and Marvin's paying my bills, led to a complete breakdown of my confidence. For the first time in my life, I had no direction, no dreams, and a lot of time on my hands. I also missed being wanted by men. I'd never realized how much I needed to be wanted. Promiscuity had been a wonderful way to build my confidence. And that was gone now too. Other dogs snapping at my heels: My mother was dying of cancer, and my father had to have a major heart operation. This was a dark time, and it reared its ugly head through depression and impotence.

I also started to watch TV. I'd never had the time to watch more than an occasional late show, but now I found the real power of the box. You can totally lose yourself, forget your troubles, find an escape that is usually only found in drugs, and you can do it in your own living room. For me, TV replaced sex and became my drug in the '60s.

I hadn't done any real drugs since my time in India. In fact, there was still an ounce of pot and a pipe in the desk drawer that Bob Bishop from *Waltz* had given us on our first anniversary. We never smoked it. Maybe we should have!

It wasn't all doom and gloom, though. Socially, we were invited to many parties. We went to all the opening nights. We played games with Stephen Sondheim, Tony Perkins, Lee Remick, Jerry Robbins, Sherry Lewis, Ken and Mitzie Welch, Herb and Nora, and Mary and Henry. It was actually pretty glamorous. For all appearances, Nancy and I were another up-and-coming young Broadway couple.

I remember one Christmas party at the Rodgers's home. I'd never been in a room so brimming with famous people. Dorothy Rodgers had injured her leg and had to sit in a chair the whole time. Everyone went to her at some point during the evening. Even in a chair, with her foot propped on a stool, she was a most gracious hostess. A true lady.

Danny Kaye and I spent most of the evening watching the chef make omelets. Danny was getting all his secrets out of him and must have eaten four or five throughout the night. I had three myself. Since it was before the cholesterol scare, we felt no guilt about having eaten so many eggs.

Shortly before the party ended, Nancy and I were sitting on the sofa with Burt Shevelove and Stephen Sondheim. I looked at a painting over the mantel and realized I'd never been in a home decorated with so much fine art—museum-quality art, at that.

Nancy landed a job working on *Showboat*, which was performed at Lincoln Center during the summer and went on tour in the fall. Before they left, Margaret Hamilton threw a dinner party and invited Nancy and me to her house on Gramercy Park. I was excited to be with the "Wicked Witch of the West," but I contained myself enough not to embarrass her. Now I had met both witches from *The Wizard of Oz*. She was a gracious hostess, a wonderful cook, and had taken a big fancy to Nancy. She kept telling me how lovely Nancy was and that I should take great care to treat her right.

I wished I could have done just that. Our sex life at this point was nonexistent. I simply had no desire and an awful amount of guilt. I was actually relieved that Nancy was going on tour. I could stop pressuring myself to perform sexually and maybe, in her absence, get my act together. I loved her but doubted I'd ever have another erection.

I still find it strange that a little thing like an erection, or the lack of one, can cause such huge emotional problems. I should have followed the advice I'd given to Liza. I was no longer fucking Nancy good. I was no longer fucking Nancy, period, so I should have ended it. Neither of us were ready to face reality, so we ignored our physical life and made do with what we had. I don't know which was worse, my not being able to find a job or my not being able to get it up. In either case, this began the worst period of my life.

I was under the misconception that agents get work for you. Again I was naïve. They merely field offers and negotiate. Friends tried to support me as best they could, but word of mouth about my abilities had been bad lately.

In October 1965 Robert Viharo got me into the Actors Studio as an observer in the directors' unit. He was dating our friend, Jennifer West, and one night suggested I use my free time to learn. I jumped at the chance, and after extensive interviews I was accepted.

Other friends helped. Henry Guettel called in a few favors to set up a few interviews for me, including one for *A Joyful Noise* starring John Raitt. I came pretty close, but they hired Michael Bennett instead. This was to be his first show, his big break. We spoke about it, and I told him I was envious but happy for him and that he could always count on me if he needed anything.

With Nancy working, and my picking up odd jobs dancing, we managed to get through another winter.

In summer 1967 I was hired to choreograph *Half a Sixpence*, with Lesley Gore and Tony Tanner, for Music Fairs. The director, Bob Hergert, was terrific to work with. My confidence began to return, and I did some really excellent work. But three days before we were to open, I became deliriously ill in the middle of the night. I had a fever of 104 degrees and shook throughout the night. Bob never left my side. About five or six in the morning, my fever broke, and I finally dropped off to sleep.

I was a little weak the next morning but still managed to make it to rehearsal. At about eleven A.M. I received a long-distance phone call from my father. My mother had died early that morning, about the time my fever had broken.

Later, I would make a connection between my illness and my mom's death. We always had a sort of ESP with one another. I'd call her and she would pick up her phone to call me before it rang. Things like that.

I believe I physically experienced my mother's death. She wanted me to be there, so I was there. Simple as that. The funeral was scheduled for the next day.

"I can't possibly get home, Dad," I said, trying not to panic over the phone. "The show opens in three days, I have two numbers to finish, and there's no one to replace me. What can I do?"

My father answered with his usual wisdom. "Wake, your mother always worried about you when you weren't working, so I know she'd understand why you can't be here. So do I. It's everybody else in the family who might not see it our way, but don't worry about them. I love you. Come home when you can."

"I love you too, Dad." I hung up the phone. Bob asked if I needed to take a little time off. I didn't. I wanted to get on with it. I didn't have time to fall apart.

I finished the show and in a week was on my way to Florida to be with my dad. It was perfect that I arrived when I did because everything was slowly slipping back to normal. My sisters and their families were getting back to their routines, which meant that my dad was left to his, which now was nonexistent. Except for his work, his routine had disappeared with my mother's death. Naturally, he needed me, and thank God, this time I was there for him. In less than a year my father remarried a woman named Myrtice who had two daughters and a grandchild. They all moved into our home. My dad had someone to be with, someone to love, a whole new family.

I found a positive side to living in New York and not being able to share all my family's experiences. I have very few memories of my mom's illness and did not witness any of her severe pain. Most of my memories are good ones, uninterrupted by horrific incidents that occur with terminal illness. I was spared those memories that I'm sure, to this day, haunt my sister Pat.

Nancy was on the road with *Sherry*, a musical version of *The Man Who Came to Dinner*. While they were in Philadelphia I went down for a weekend, but it was strained since we had been apart so much. Absence does not always make the heart grow fonder. A month or so later, Nancy and I admitted failure, and soon after, she found an apartment and moved out. There were no tears, no ranting, no anger—just sadness. On May 18, 1968, our fourth anniversary, Nancy and I kissed good-bye at the front door of our apartment, and she got onto the elevator and left my life. I didn't stop loving Nancy. I just stopped being able to make love to her.

Chapter Six

Good Drugs, Good Times

New York City, 1968

For the first time in four years, I was alone. I had two floors and seven rooms to roam around, one of those apartments you only hear about. The living room measured eighteen feet by twenty-four feet and had a twenty-four foot ceiling. Three huge windows faced north on 72nd Street, which opened it up even more. Upstairs was the bathroom and a master bedroom with French windows that opened into the living room. The den, guest room, kitchen, guest bath, and dining hall were all on the bottom floor. You just don't give up apartments like that in New York. So I asked my old friend Shelly DeSatnick to share the space with me, and he agreed. After a little affair in 1959, he and I had become good friends.

Shelly began teaching bridge to Mary, Henry, Jerry Robbins, Joe Nelson, and me, and we had become fanatical players. Michael Stewart and Stephen Sondheim joined occasionally so that we could play two tables of duplicate bridge. We had whole weekends where all we did was eat and play bridge.

I had begun to have sex again, mostly anonymous, mostly at the baths, and mostly forgettable. Then I met Steve Kirk. He owned and operated an answering service for actors and professionals. I met him at a movie theater, and he drove me home on his motorcycle. When we got there I offered him a beer, and he offered me some grass. That night I didn't have any sexual problems. I truly relaxed. The chatterbox in the back of my head must have passed out from the weed because I felt truly comfortable, sexually, for the first time in years. Steve and I became fuck buddies, and I became a pothead. If grass wasn't the answer to my problems, it was a great Band-Aid. Gradually, my sex drive returned.

I managed to get through another winter doing a few episodes of *The Ed Sullivan Show*, a couple of Perry Como specials, and a few industrial shows. My first job that summer was directing *South Pacific*, with Howard Keel, and then *Oklahoma*, with Gordon MacRae. I had worked with Howard when I put him into the road company of *No Strings*. He was still fun.

Gordon was another experience. He was the most theatrical singer I'd ever worked with. He knew exactly what he had to do and did it—and that voice! He knew the character so well that there was an ease about him, matched by the quality of his voice, which was mellow and sweet but masculine. He was so secure that he was able to give so much support to his fellow actors.

On that show I became friendly with Carol Bishop, a dancer in the chorus. She had looks, a great body, and could really dance. She had it all, but she didn't audition well. She got the job only because Jack Beber, a choreographer, had recommended her. She should have been dancing on Broadway—she was that good. When the summer was over, I called Ron Field, who was getting ready to do *Golden Rainbow*, with Steve Lawrence and Eydie Gorme. I explained that Carol was talented and right for his show, even though she couldn't audition well, but that he should hire her anyway. He was receptive and asked her to come see him. If he liked her looks and body, as a favor to me, she could have the job. No audition required.

Shortly after, she was in for the run of the show. An interesting note: Nancy ended up assisting Ron Field on that show. George Thorn, who would become Nancy's new husband, was the production stage manager, and Tom Porter, my best man, was the stage manager. Talk about six degrees of separation.

A few years later Carol would win the Tony Award for best supporting actress in a musical, playing Sheila in *A Chorus Line*, a girl who also auditioned badly. She was no longer Carol; she was Tony Award-winning Kelly Bishop. Of course, she didn't thank me in her acceptance speech. She probably doesn't even remember that I called Ron on her behalf, but I know I had a part in shaping her life, helping her get her first job on Broadway. It still amazes me how such a small action can change the direction of someone's life. Most of us aren't aware of the power we possess to alter the lives of others with just a few words or a simple action.

Joe was doing a new show with Michael Stewart, and they both wanted me to work with them. They said the show would have no chorus, and I cringed. Was it going to be another *Waltz*? That concept certainly hadn't worked. How would this be any different?

They should have said "no principals," because everyone in the show would do multiple roles as well as chorus work, in an episodic telling of the life of George M. Cohan. The show was to be called *George M!* and would star Joel Grey. I had four months before rehearsals started, but at least I had a job to look forward to. Joe wanted me to be in charge of the show as I'd done with *No Strings*.

Early in the fall, Fred Ebb called to see if I was available to stage the number "If They Could See Me Now" for Liza's act. I'd never worked with Fred, so I knew that the offer had come by way of Liza, Peter, or even Ron Field, who staged the act originally but was not available to do a new number. So the task came to me. The number turned out OK but was nothing special. The concept was pretty cliché—trunk with props: feather boa, top hat, cane, etc. Fred was not at his best here. Liza was only an average dancer, with limited dance vocabulary, but we got the job done.

A few months later when Ron Field became available, they asked him to redo the number. Once again, my work wasn't satisfactory. Upset, I started to doubt my ability.

I was seeing a lot of Peter Allen. Liza was busy, and Peter's career was just beginning to take off, so he had some free time. We would meet in Central Park, at the restaurant by the fountain, drink Sangria, have a little lunch, smoke ourselves silly, and laugh. We had a great time together. I remember one afternoon, I decided to ask them both to dinner. I called Shelly and said I was bringing Liza and Peter home. He offered to cook the meal and still remembers to this day what he cooked.

A couple of months later at the opening night of *George M!* Liza didn't remember Shelly or that he had cooked this wonderful meal for them. She was polite, but it was obvious to him that she really didn't remember. Shelly was devastated.

We started pre-production on *George M!* and Michael Stewart decided that at the end of the show when George has a fight with the actors' union, he'd take the baton out of the conductor's hand, break it, and walk offstage. Since there would be no music until the finale, we'd do a sound ballet and everything would be performed to speeches or sound effects. We did make one compromise. We used Guy Lombardo's New Year's broadcasts several times in the montage to clarify time frames and in the background played "Auld Lang Syne." We worked hard on it, and the ballet ran about ten minutes. In essence, it was our eleven-o'clock number.

We performed the ballet only once, on opening night in Detroit, and it was never seen again. I was stunned that all our effort could be thrown out after only one performance.

Years later, in 1978, interviewing Michael on Emerald City, a gay TV show in New York, I asked him why he took out the ballet after only one performance. His answer: "I knew it would never work and couldn't stand feeling the wave of hate that came from the audience even one more time. It was hopeless. Besides, we had more important problems."

It still amazes me to this day, but Michael was the first completely out-of-the-closet writer I knew in the theater, which was unheard of at that time. Even Noël Coward had a veil, no matter how thin, over his personal life. I guess if everyone had Michael's success, there would be more courageous people. He had so much money that he even gave his royalties from *Hello, Dolly!* to Yale's drama department. He later told me he had made a mistake and should have given it to aid writers instead of actors. Michael had to answer to no one but himself, and his standards were high. He was a tough cookie and had a mouth as loose as mine. I guess that's why we got along so well. He once told me that I was truly crazed, the most certifiable person he knew. I laughed, but I should have realized he wasn't kidding.

Joe and I did the best work we'd ever done together, and the show began to take shape despite our bad beginnings in Detroit. We had twenty minutes to add, and we began a new montage that would include many of the most well-known Cohan songs and end with "You're a Grand Old Flag." Now this was around the time of Vietnam and waving the U.S. flag was not fashionable. If this show had been done at another time, it probably would have run for years. At that time people were not proud to be Americans. It was the year of *Hair* and a time of protest.

Jerry Dodge and I became close during rehearsal. He was Joel Grey's understudy and a terrific tap dancer. Joel, on the other hand, was not. But he was one of the hardest workers I've ever known. The company hired a personal tap trainer, and between the two of us, we worked Joel until he could dance every step with full confidence. In the end, he received a Tony nomination.

The entire cast was filled with up-and-comers, young hopefuls looking for their big break, which made for a fiercely competitive rehearsal period. Besides Joel and Jerry, we had Betty Ann Rhodes; Bernadette Peters, fresh from her success in *Dames at Sea*; Jill O'Hara from the original *Hair*; and Jamie Donnelly. Everyone else was signed to chorus contracts, but they all wanted their moment in the show. It was a volatile rehearsal period.

One night at the end of rehearsal, I was alone onstage, looking for my tap shoes, when I found a small notebook. Upon reading a few entries, I discovered it belonged to Bernadette. I couldn't stop reading it. It was fascinating! Michael's book for the show was very episodic, and nothing was fleshed out or complete. Bernadette, outside of the musical numbers, had maybe thirty lines of dialogue in the whole show, so she had written things down to help her. There were huge jumps in time in the show, so she needed to find bridges for herself that were not in the script.

She had made up an entire scene where George comes into her room late one night and sits on her bed. He talks about his ambition and his love for his family. It continued, expanding her every moment in the show to help her overcome the brevity of her scenes. She'd done this on her own, and once again her hard work paid off. She was terrific. I knew that with her talent, brains, ambition, and her mother's help, she would become a star. Her mother, as I remember her, was a real stage mother. Bernadette was everything to her. I never found her to be overbearing because she did everything for her daughter, not for herself. And she did it with such love that it never came off negatively. When Bernadette accepted her 1999 Tony Award for *Annie Get Your Gun* she spoke about her mother, now deceased, and thanked her for her part in making her career a success.

My sex life continued to improve and was aided no doubt by my new commitment to smoking grass. Straight married men were even coming on to me—and not just a few. Had I become so notoriously queer that they had no fear I might reject them? I'm not talking about men wanting a blow job—I'd known that type since I was nine—but men who wanted to experience love with the same sex. Suddenly I had a lot of these men around me. I'd meet them at the baths, the Everard Baths, and the Penn Post across from Penn Station, which was known for its "straight" clientele. The hottest time was between four and seven P.M. They would check in, have a quickie, then catch the train home to their families.

Shelly was still living with me, and between the two of us, something sexual occurred at our house daily. I had an affair with one man who had a wife and five or six children. He was tall, knockdown gorgeous, charming, intelligent, and rich. I could have fallen in love with him easily, but there was no hope of a relationship. At this point I was looking for someone to share my life, not just my bed.

I enjoyed the rehearsals for *George M!*, a difficult period and a lot of hard work, but we all communicated and never quit working. "Popularity" was a dance number that progressed from rehearsal into performance right onstage and led directly into the finale of the first act, "Give My Regards to Broadway." It stopped the show every night. I have no doubt that this number, although the show was loaded with dancing, was the reason Joe received the Tony Award that year for best choreography.

Right before the half-hour call on opening night, I was called to the stage manager's desk. Emergency! When I crossed the stage I saw the gypsy robe. All my years as a dancer, I'd avoided the honor, but this time they'd caught me. It was mine for the night, and I loved it. I had to wear it in front of the company before the curtain rose. I have only one regret about winning the robe. I painted my favorite tap shoes white, had everyone in the cast sign in red and blue ink, and added them to the all ready hundreds of items hanging from the robe. I missed those shoes for months and never got another pair to feel as good or make as good a sound.

The show opened on Joel's birthday, so the opening-night party served two purposes. It was, by the way, the best opening-night party I ever attended. Konrad Matthaei, David Black, and Lorin Price, the producers, spared no expense. Everyone had a seat at a table, and there was waiter service for everything. Unlike most opening-night parties, this one was a pleasure. The ballroom of the Plaza was beautifully decorated in red, white, and blue, with flags and flowers, and the food was exceptional. And one thing happened that night that I'll never forget.

When Jackie Alloway, my date, and I arrived at the Plaza, we went to take the elevator to the ballroom. Once we were inside, and just as the doors were about to close, a couple approached. Suddenly, out of a cloud of smoke from a foot-long cigarette holder, emerged Tallulah Bankhead accompanied by someone. Did anyone ever notice who Tallulah was with? I don't think so.

As she entered the elevator the attendant said, "Excuse me, Miss Bankhead, I'm sorry, but there's no smoking in the elevator. Would you mind putting out your cigarette?"

The car was deadly quiet as if someone had turned off the sound, and I'm not sure anyone was breathing. I know I wasn't. Suddenly, that laugh, her laugh, cut through the silence. She handed the cigarette to her companion to put out and said, in that voice that once you've heard you can't forget, "Of course not, dahling. I certainly wouldn't want to burn down the Plaza. It's one of the few good things left in New York."

We all laughed as the doors closed. Up we went, with Tallulah in an elevator filled with her secondhand smoke and the echo of that delicious laughter, to the ballroom and an evening that would fill me with wonderful memories.

The show received good notices, and Joel got raves. Michael Stewart didn't fare as well with the book.

The Sunday following the opening we made the cast recording. It went well until we got to "Give My Regards to Broadway," where we had trouble with Joel's tap section. We did two more takes and a couple of pickups, but Goddard Liberson, the producer, was not happy with what we'd recorded. Joel tapped like a fool in the show, but this was like a close-up, and his taps didn't record cleanly. We finally moved on to the next number.

Later in the session, when Joel wasn't around, at Goddard's request I put on my tap shoes and "tapped in" for Joel. I don't think they ever told Joel that it's not his tapping on the recording. He was so proud of his tap dancing that no one had the heart, including me, to tell him—until now. I think he can handle it. He can console himself with his Tony Award for *Cabaret* and knowing he beat out Al Pacino, James Caan, and Robert Duvall for his Oscar for *Cabaret*. We settled in for a nice run at the Palace Theater.

One day when I arrived at the theater, the stage manager told me President Nixon was coming to see the show and that two of his Secret Service agents wanted to speak with me. I met with them and discussed the content of the show and some of its effects. The agents came to the show that evening, and after one more meeting everything was set.

The night arrived, President Nixon arrived, and so did our worst show ever. All the places where laughs had been consistent became caverns of silence. There were no laughs, but when the numbers ended, the applause was deafening. The audience was being schizophrenic, and the pace of the show went right out the window. We later realized that the Secret Service agents who lined the aisles had intimidated the audience, sending out a touch of fear in the air just from their presence. After the show President Nixon came backstage to meet the cast. Along with the staff, I was personally introduced and shook his hand. He was as charming as he could be. Joel presented him with an original recording of Cohan singing "Over There." He thanked Joel, then turned to all of us.

"I would like for you all to visit us in Washington. We'll see what we can do about that. All right, David?" President Nixon said to David Black, one of our producers, who nodded in approval. As promised, a few weeks later we were asked to perform at the 1969 Inaugural Ball in Washington. The entire company came down to perform the montage that ended with "You're a Grand Old Flag." Several people in the show took this opportunity to flex their political muscle by refusing to perform. Harvey Evans and Scott Salmon were among the protesters of the Vietnam War who refused to perform for President Nixon and to carry the flag. I was sympathetic but upset that I had to perform in their place. But the show came off well, no one found out about the protest, and it turned out to be an exciting evening with Dinah Shore, Ed McMahon, and James Brown, the king of soul.

Right after we returned to New York, Joe was called in to doctor *Dear World*, a new show by Jerry Herman, starring Angela Lansbury. They were in previews at the Hellinger Theater and in trouble.

Jerry Herman was wonderful to work with, and Angela was something else. I'd loved her since seeing her sing "Goodbye Little Yellow Bird" in *The Picture of Dorian Gray* and didn't quite know how to deal with her. Joe forced my hand by asking me to restage "Each Tomorrow Morning," one of her numbers. The rehearsal was scheduled to take place before the matinee.

I was there extra early to prepare as much as possible before Angela arrived. When she did appear, I made the unpardonable mistake of gushing all over her like an idiot fan, ending with how difficult it was for me to forget who she was and how I hoped....I went on and on. It was disgusting!

She interrupted. "Well, Wakefield, get over it. Now call me Angela and let's get to work." She didn't mean to embarrass me with her comments. She meant to relax me. She did both, and by the time Joe arrived we'd finished the number, and I had learned not to gush over stars—they really don't like it. I'd been around many stars and never had a problem, but Angela, for some reason, evoked that response. It was the first and last time I would lose control around a celebrity.

We did as much as we could to salvage the show, but it wasn't very good. I blamed the set, which had a big fountain that never disappeared, no matter how they disguised it. It was like playing "find the fountain" each time a new scene appeared. Also, the audience wasn't ready to accept Angela in this role so soon after *Mame*. The score, however, was wonderful. The show opened, played its run, and Angela won her second Tony Award.

Professionally, this became one of the busiest periods of my life. I was still in charge of day-to-day operations of *George M!* but suddenly I was directing a lot of industrial shows. They were great fun, and I did some terrific work. For the next few years I worked for Prince Matchabelli, Quaker Oats, Nabisco, Lee's Carpets, and even did a Rheingold Beer industrial film. These shows became my bread and butter.

Joe asked me to choreograph *The Littlest Angel* for Hallmark Hall of Fame. He was going to direct this star-filled musical version using a process called Chromakey, which is now called blue screen. This was the first time it would be used for an entire production. Cab Calloway, Johnny Whitaker, Fred Gwynne, and James Coco starred. E.G. Marshall played God, and one of my favorites, Connie Stevens, played an angel.

Connie had just given birth to her daughter, Jolie, and I built a number around her, using a flying apparatus by Peter Foy, the same man who'd flown Mary Martin in *Peter Pan*. When I said "just given birth," I meant it. It was sheer torture for her to be strapped into the harness, but she managed beautifully. We got along well. I even met Eddie Fisher!

Walter Miller, the director, needed a choreographer for the Macy's parade that year and hired me. At seven A.M. on Thanksgiving I was on Central Park West putting people in position on the floats and doing last-minute changes in the choreography. Right after Christmas we went to Miami to do the Orange Bowl Parade, hosted by Joe Garagiola and Anita Bryant.

We were invited to Anita's house on Biscayne Bay for an outdoor barbecue. I met her husband and saw the house, complete with a prie-dieu at the foot of her bed. I wasn't comfortable with her, her husband was a jerk, and there was nothing real about either of them. The only good thing I remember about her was that she worked hard. That's probably how she got where she was; it certainly wasn't talent.

I was no longer sure of my own talent, so I relied on my energy and willingness to work. Things were turning around for me, and I wasn't about to relax for a minute. I started to prepare the road company of *George M!* Joel was going to do Los Angeles, San Francisco, and the Dallas State Fair, then be replaced by Darryl Hickman. Then Frank DeSal came into my life.

I met him one day when he and Raymond St. Jacques walked into Marvin's office wearing full-length mink coats. They were high as kites, but I didn't know that until later. We bonded immediately. Frank was also a Pisces, so I think we had experienced a lot of the same things in our lifetimes. Although Frank was an average dancer, he was a good character type. He could play a variety of roles believably, so I hired him to play the part of Sam Harris at the Papermill Playhouse and then to replace Bill Gerber in the road company. I was to put Darryl Hickman into the show at the same time.

One morning, right before we started rehearsals, Frank called. "What have you got planned for today?" he asked.

"Not a thing, really. Why?"

"We have a little surprise cooked up for you. Pull yourself together and come over in half an hour. You're going to spend the day with Heinz and me." Heinz, Frank's new lover, was tall, thin, blond, attractive, and German.

I didn't know it at the moment, but I was about to have another life-changing experience. I took a quick shower and arrived at Frank's apartment. It was an incredible spring day—you know, corny as it is, the kind that makes you glad to be alive. The sun was bright, the breeze was cool, and I had no idea what was in store. Whatever it was, it was the perfect day for it.

Heinz met me at the door, and we sat down for a cup of coffee. Frank came out of the bathroom, wrapped in towel, and dressed while making small talk. When he was done he came over to the table carrying a little wooden box. He fished out a piece of paper and unwrapped it.

"Here, take this." Frank handed me a small orange pill. "Sunshine, direct from Mr. Leary." He gave one to Heinz and kept one for himself, then rewrapped the paper to protect his stash.

"I wanted to do something for you. You know, for giving me the job. Heinz and I thought this was the right time for you to take a trip with us."

"Where are we going?" I asked.

"We don't know. Wherever it takes us!" Heinz laughed as he popped the pill in his mouth. Frank followed, and I, trustingly, did the same. I didn't know what to expect and I didn't ask.

We got some things together, and in a few minutes we were ringing Ray Chabeau's doorbell. Ray was a Bob Fosse dancer, a friend of Frank's, and also hired to dance at Papermill. When he opened the door Frank put his fingers in Ray's mouth, closed his jaw, and rubbed his throat. I realized he was giving Ray a hit of acid as well, and he gave it to him as you'd give a dog a pill.

"Well, hello to you too, and what have I just taken?" Ray asked, swallowing the pill dry.

"As if it matters. Get the dog and let's go," Frank said. "It's a great day, and we should get to the park before we start to come on."

In a few seconds we were all off to Central Park with Ray's huge Newfoundland in tow.

It had been about a half hour since we'd taken the pills, and now we were lying on the grass in the park. I don't remember feeling anything physical happening, but suddenly colors became more vivid—more vivid than I can ever remember. The ground had started to roll like ocean waves, and the skyscrapers had begun to hula in slow motion when I said out loud, "Oh, my God. What have I done?"

Every time you drop acid, there's that moment when you start to come on to the drug, when you have to take responsibility for your actions. It's too late to do anything about it. It's like getting on a roller coaster. The ride's not over till it's over. Each time I took the drug, I accepted all that from the start and never had a bad trip.

We spent the entire day doing ordinary things but reacting to and experiencing them as never before, like being in a movie and watching it at the same time. This was the first time I experienced multiple realities. Everything in the world wasn't how I perceived it but was many different things to different people. Frank and Heinz hadn't told me what to expect, so everything came from the drug, from me, and not from an imposed warning from someone else's insecurities and fears. I'd never had so many revelations before. It was like being given new sight.

We moved through the day, stopping to see friends, eating when we wanted, drinking herbal tea, and smoking lots of pot. Before I knew it we were at my house. There were now six of us, and I was cooking spaghetti carbonara for everyone. About nine o'clock that night, everyone was gone and I was alone. It had been some day, but it felt unfinished.

Frank, Heinz, and the others had gone home to fuck. I thought I'd do the same and go to the Continental Baths.

It was only two blocks away, so I'd have no trouble getting there. I needed someplace to hang my hat, as Frank put it, so I was off to the baths.

Chapter Seven

Peter

New York City, 1968

The bathhouse scene in New York was peaking. We had the old granddad, the Everard Baths on 28th Street, sometimes called the Black Foot Club because the floors were so dirty. I'd heard rumors that the Police Athletic League operated it. Although the police were purging gays on the streets, in movie theaters, and in bars, they weren't above making money off behavior that to them was "abnormal" and "obscene." Thank God for that!

We also had the St. Marks in the East Village, the Club Baths on Second Avenue, the Sauna on 57th Street, and the newly opened Continental Baths on 74th Street. Since the Continental was right around the corner from my house, newly decorated by Richard Orbach, the hot decorator of the moment, and thus, new and clean, I chose it for the night's adventure. Mr. Orbach took a lot of heat from some of his clients after doing the job, since most of their apartments turned out to look just like the baths—lots of plastic, color, and dramatic lighting. Michael Bennett was one of his clients, but he got off on the fact that his apartment looked like a miniature Continental Baths.

I'd been to the baths many times but never on acid. Still, I wasn't anxious at all. In fact, I'd never felt so secure in a sexual situation. Hell, I was real cool.

I had attached myself to Eric, a frequent sex mate from the baths. We were both insatiable that night, going from room to room engaging in whatever, with whomever attracted us. In general, we were sexual pigs, finally ending up in my room, smoking a joint, and resting up for the next onslaught. We left the door open so that we could watch the traffic pass in the hall. Even while resting you kept your eyes open so as not to miss, perhaps, the love of your life.

There was a lot of walking around at the baths. If you were lucky enough to have a room, you could leave your door open, and if you liked what you saw, you proceeded from there. Everyone handled this differently, and the way they did was either a turn-on or not. Sometimes a quick response of "No, thanks. Just resting!" would be heard before one foot entered the room. It was exciting, but it made you face rejection. And there was always a quest of some sort, so naturally it was always an adventure. Guys would be sitting on beds playing with themselves under their towel, some would have no towel, and some would lie on their stomach with their ass raised by a pillow. Some brought candles, leather goods, rubber sheets, and lures from home, anything to intrigue and help make the catch. There was no doubt as to what they wanted. No time could be wasted.

Eric and I both noticed one guy who kept walking by our door. He'd hesitate for a moment, give us the once-over, then move on. After about the third time he did this, we took off after him, then brought him back to the room. His name was Peter. We had a successful threesome, and after we split up I hit the showers. I was getting dressed when I heard a knock on my door. It was Peter. It was even better the second time. Around five A.M. I asked him home for breakfast. It's interesting that most of my affairs start with food. I made a killer breakfast, and after our last cup of coffee, we made love yet another time.

Peter was about six foot two, brown eyed, brunet, masculine, and his body, although you could tell he went to a gym, still appeared natural. He waddled when he walked, the result of obesity as a child, but it was a cute walk, so out of character with the overall image he projected. At the baths his attitude had been cool, almost hustler-like, but once I got him home he immediately revealed his real personality.

When you went to the baths you could be whatever you wanted to be: top, bottom, voyeur, trade, whatever. That was what was so terrific about the baths, any baths. It was like going to the analyst. You could chase any fantasy, play any role.

The night I met Peter, as with most of my visits to the baths, I had been all of the above and then some, but while we were with Eric, Peter had remained quiet and cautious. He was intriguing, and as I said, he was really good at sex. The more we talked, the more I liked him. He was filled with surprises. He told me his full name was Peter Schneckenburger and that he was a computer analyst, setting up the billing system for Roosevelt Hospital. He was also an opera buff and a rock fan. He loved Rossini, Strauss, and Janáček but was also a Doors fan. A gourmet, he also loved hot dogs and pizza. He was both a redneck from New Orleans and a sophisticated New Yorker aware of all the joys the city held for anyone with the time and energy to pursue them.

We were both Southern but had totally different childhoods. I was a self-centered exhibitionist, primarily motivated by ambition, and Peter was just the opposite. His two aunts, and sometimes his mother, raised him. He'd spent most of his youth studying everything he could get his hands on. I'd spent my time in dancing schools and public toilets. Peter was the most learned person I had ever met in my life, but for a reason I never discovered, he kept this a secret from most. He wasn't shy about expressing his opinion but hesitated in letting you know how informed that opinion was.

After a few hours of sleep, we awoke with new energy and, to my surprise, no drug hangover. By this time I was smitten, and Peter was just as intrigued by me. It was one of those times when both parties are aware of the enormous possibilities before them and enter into a relationship without hesitation. We didn't talk about it—we just did it.

We spent the day going to galleries on Madison Avenue and to the Whitney Museum, where we had a nice lunch between a Calder sculpture and a crushed automobile piece by Chamberlain. I had always enjoyed art, but this was the first of many times that we would spend the day seeing what was happening at that moment in the art world and not just looking at great paintings from another time. I was amazed by it all. So much had happened since the day before when Frank had put that little orange pill in my mouth. So much!

Peter soon left for Europe with his best friend, Bill Boyd, and his ex-lover Bruce Poulett. In the two weeks before they left, we had established our relationship. When Peter returned he gave up his apartment and moved in with me. We kept ourselves busy going to rock concerts, art galleries, operas, ballets, Broadway shows, and lots of movies. I stopped seeing my straight friends. I missed their friendship, but they seemed to be a part of another time, another life, and I was moving in a different direction, away from everything I thought I lived for.

In 1969 *George M!* was released to stock, and I was busy doing almost every production on the East Coast. Music Fairs produced the first and succeeded in getting Mickey Rooney to star. It was a difficult show to do in stock since rehearsal time had to be tightly scheduled.

On the third day of rehearsal I was already a day behind. Mickey had spent so much time telling stories that we weren't getting in much rehearsal. I couldn't control him. He was such a disappointment. He couldn't really tap dance. In fact, he tapped even less than Joel. At one point he confessed that during the MGM days neither he nor Judy ever really tapped. They would learn the movements, but the taps were all what he called "air taps." Their feet moved, but the taps never hit the floor. If you look closely the next time you're watching one of their movies, you can see it yourself.

Mickey always had a distraction to fall back on when he became insecure. Once, in his dressing room, just when I thought he was finally listening, he went into the bathroom. Leaving the door open, he sat on the toilet with his pants around his ankles. Unconcerned with my presence, he took care of his business. I made a decision right then. I called Lee Gueber, the producer, and explained that I could no longer guarantee having the show ready on time. After a pause Lee asked me to continue working through the day. He would come to Gaithersburg that night, and we would sort this out. I agreed.

Later that night we were all in Mickey's room trying to find a way to finish this show. Mickey wouldn't see that he had become a disruptive element and that all his energy was going into entertaining the cast rather than learning his role. Finally, Lee made a call and, after a minute or two, handed me the phone. Mickey was in the middle of yet another story as I put the receiver to my ear. A strange voice called me by name but didn't give me his.

"Wakefield, Lee tells me you're having trouble with Mick and want to leave the show." I had no earthly idea to whom I was talking. I assumed it was Mickey's manager. He continued.

"Well, I guarantee you that after tonight that'll all be history. You're the only one to do it, and I'm here to promise you that things will be different. You'll have everything you need to finish the job. No more about leaving. Now put Mick on the phone."

Mickey took the phone with his usual over-the-top energy. After a few seconds his whole attitude changed. His face became ashen, and his volume was cut by two thirds. I still don't know who was on the other end of the phone or what was said to him. I was told later by Mickey's bodyguard that Mickey was given a "choice." I'd heard he had gambling debts and that he needed this tour to make things right. Mere rumors? Who knows.

Whatever the situation, Mickey began to concentrate. Actually, my attitude changed when I saw the effect of that call. My heart went out to him, so I became patient and more understanding. We finished rehearsing and had two days to spare for technical and dress rehearsal.

The next morning, word came that Judy Garland had died from an overdose, and suddenly we had the press up to our ears. Mickey did several interviews and had to attend the funeral. To my surprise, he asked me to go with him, but that would have been impossible. If I couldn't leave a show to attend my own mother's funeral, I certainly couldn't leave to go to Judy Garland's. As it was, Mickey had to miss a whole day of rehearsal. I really regretted not being able to go. Imagine going to Judy Garland's funeral with Mickey Rooney.

We opened on time, and Mickey was wonderful, showing a spontaneity that made everything his own, like he was making it up on the spot. In front of an audience he became Mickey Rooney, movie star extraordinaire. He could do it all and break their hearts at the same time.

After the matinee I was in Mickey's dressing room giving him some notes. Suddenly we heard a knock at the door and in swept Debbie Reynolds. She was performing her act nearby and had come to the show.

"Mickey, dalhink," she said in her best Zsa Zsa as she kissed him on the forehead. "You were wonderful. You should do zis part on Broadway."

"Well, if it isn't my little Debbie," he said standing up and taking her in his arms. "What brings you here?" Remembering me, he added, "By the way, this is Wakefield Poole, my director."

"Oh, I know Wakefield," she smiled. "I was at a party last year at his apartment. Do you still have that big white ladder in your living room?

I had thrown a party for the original cast of *George M!* and in the heat of the party, Harvey Evans, phone in hand, called out and asked if he could invite Debbie Reynolds.

"Only if she brings Carlton Carpenter and sings 'AbbaDabba Honeymoon,'" I shouted. Carlton didn't show, but Debbie came anyway and sang it for us. We had a wonderful time, sitting in front of the fireplace, drinking brandy and talking till dawn. How nice of her to remember!

The next year Mickey asked me to stage another tour. It was easier the second time, and we had more fun. When Mickey was real he was wonderful. The only trouble is, even Mickey doesn't know when he's being real. It happens infrequently, but if you're lucky enough to catch one of those times, he's unforgettable. Otherwise, he's a big pain in the ass.

I did many productions of *George M!* during the next year. Bill Hayes from *Mattress* took over for Mickey on one of the tours. Bill Hayes—still hot! Even without his white tights.

I did another *George M!* with Danny Mehan, and Kenneth Nelson, the original Michael in *Boys in the Band*, starred in a production at the Papermill Playhouse, along with Bonnie Franklin and Beth Howland. Both would soon get their big breaks on national TV shows. Bonnie would do *One Day at a Time*, and Beth, after a stint as the bride in Stephen Sondheim's *Company*, would appear as Vera on *Alice*.

I'd begun to understand that directing was more than just telling actors where to stand and guiding them through the emotional events of a piece. The main task of a good director should be to give the actor all the confidence he needs to realize his concepts and goals of the role. I was learning.

I finally got to live out one of my fantasies: dancing with Gwen Verdon. Years before, I had danced with her on *The Garry Moore Show* when Randy Doney, Larry Fuller, Bill Guskee, and I performed "I'm Old Fashioned," staged by Kevin Carlisle. It was everything I had imagined and more, but I really got the full effect of Gwen Verdon when I danced with her on *The Jackie Gleason Show*.

We had to travel to Miami and spend five days together. I got to know her a little. Better still, she got to know me. We rehearsed at Gleason's complex in Miami, which housed numerous rehearsal studios. One, for the June Taylor dancers, even had an overhead camera to rehearse those great Busby Berkeley moments. There was a costume department and a music recording studio, all built around a golf course. Gleason even had a chef and a full-time caddie. Now that's star treatment.

All the rooms were equipped with hidden cameras that were fed into Gleason's personal office. He could punch up any of the rooms and watch the rehearsals without your even knowing. Common today but unheard of then.

While meeting with Gleason in his office, Gwen noticed the monitors all in a row. She returned from his office and told us about the hidden cameras. Then, with a bit of devilment in her eyes, she suggested we face the opposite way when we rehearsed so that Gleason would only be able to see our backsides. It was a fun experience, even though he never mentioned it.

Back in New York, Peter and I spent a lot of time with Jerry Dodge and Mark McCrary. We'd get together on weekends at our apartment, drop mescaline, play with slide projectors, eight-millimeter movies, colored lights, and anything we could find to aid our visuals. We also hung a huge mirrored ball and placed slide projectors in the upper corners of the living room. With the high ceiling, the white walls, and the mirrors, and with the help of one-inch lenses, we could turn the entire room into whatever we wanted. It could be a forest, it could be the New York skyline, or we could just project slides of famous paintings on the walls.

All this interest in visuals spurred Peter to give me a 16-millimeter camera, which I started using for things other than documenting vacations and parties, after seeing some of Stephen Sondheim's films. Stephen loves games, and he made movies like most people play games. He would call his friends and tell them they were going to shoot a film the next day. He'd tell them what they needed, where to be, and at what time.

I saw two films he'd made with Leonard and Felicia Bernstein and Phyllis Newman. *Whatever Happened to Felicia Montealegre?* was about a concert pianist (Felicia), her page-turning, jealous younger sister (Phyllis), and a rock star (Leonard), played à la Brando, complete with leather jacket. God, it was funny.

The other was made to the Callas recording of the second act of *Tosca*, starring Leonard Bernstein as Scarpia and Felicia as Tosca. Stephen himself did a walk-on as a servant. They all dressed the parts and lip-synched the entire second act. Incredibly hilarious.

There were no limitations. You could do exactly what you wanted. It was easy. The more we played around, the better I got. I took my camera everywhere. I tried everything. I'd film the reflection of the New York skyline in the Central Park lake by turning the camera upside down and shooting only the reflection. When projected, it became an unusual piece of film. As I became more familiar with film, the content became more complicated, while the technical aspects became simpler. Film had begun to be a means of creative expression for me, so when I was offered an off-Broadway show to direct and choreograph, the concept I came up with, naturally, included film.

Frank DeSal assisted me with the choreography. I was still grateful for my first acid trip, so before we started rehearsal I planned a surprise for him, Heinz, and Peter. I ordered tickets to a rock music festival to be held in Wallkill, N.Y. The location was eventually changed, and we now know it as Woodstock.

I rented a car and reserved rooms in Monticello. A rainstorm hit that Friday afternoon, so we chose not to go to the concert grounds until Saturday morning. After breakfast we drove in that bumper-to-bumper traffic they were showing on TV. When we thought we were close enough, we parked the car on the side of the road and walked the rest of the way. It turned out to be a five-mile walk. We kept meeting people coming toward us shouting "Woodstock sucks!" Probably the results of bad drugs. We paid them no mind and kept going. But we did make another bad choice. We'd left our basket of fruit, sausage, cheese, bread, and wine in the car. Unfortunately, we parked too far away to go back for it and didn't even entertain the idea of returning to the hotel room. It wouldn't be easy to leave and come back, so for two days we lived on Coca-Cola, mescaline, and marijuana. I've never in my life, before or since, felt so free. It wasn't just doing drugs in front of cops for the first time, but in public the four of us were shamelessly expressing our feelings for each other just like the "normal" people around us.

The only negative aspect I recall is that the long grass was so wet that after a few hours of sitting on a blanket, our asses were damp and itchy and would remain so for two days.

By sunset Saturday evening they finally completed the stage and the back curtain just in time for Janis Joplin. In the middle of her first song, the Joshua Light Show was projected on the backdrop. The show was the most famous psychedelic light show on the East Coast and was performed regularly at Fillmore East, but the lights were pure magic that night. The crowd went crazy. It was, by far, my favorite moment.

We returned from Woodstock, and Frank and I started rehearsals for *Look Where I'm At*, which opened in early 1970. An instant flop. The writing and score were both mediocre, but all the visual concepts worked. The *Times* review said, "Even the inventiveness of Wakefield Poole could not save this show." It closed after one night.

At the same time things were going a little better for Michael Bennett. In April he had his first big success with the Broadway opening of Stephen Sondheim's *Company*. Michael's choreography was extraordinary and he had a wonderful working relationship with Stephen as well as Hal Prince.

Mark McCrary and Roger Puckett, owners of Triton Gallery, a theater- and movie-poster shop, asked me to do a show there. Mark and Jerry Dodge, his lover, spent many nights with Peter and me playing with images, slides, and movie projectors. He knew I was onto something and wanted to support me. The gallery handled Vittorio, a Canadian poster artist, and wanted to honor him with a show. He used cartoon-type characters in his work, which all had serious themes, such as "Save the Trees." I accepted, and what evolved was a multimedia show, *Images in Motion*, much of which was an extension of the things we were doing in my living room on heavy drugs. I used eight projectors, and the show included a five-minute animated film I'd made using one of his cartoon characters. It was an ambitious project.

The show started with a simple image of Yvonne Adair, Roger's wife, standing under the Marquee of the New Amsterdam Theater. As Ruby Keeler sang "42nd Street," Yvonne danced into the middle of the street, tapping her way down to Eighth Avenue, in and out of buses and taxis, up to 45th Street and into the front door of Triton Gallery.

I staged the finale to Tina Turner's "Gonna Take You Higher," using three dancers, Joe Nelson, Alan Sobec, and Leslie Lahee, dressed in white so that projections would show up on them. I also filmed Leslie dancing nude against a black background. At the climax of the number, that film was projected on her so that Leslie would be "dancing on herself." Her costume had three-foot-long white fringe sewn on the arms, so when she held them out, it made a movie screen. The scene brought down the house with applause.

At the end there were images everywhere in the room, projectors mounted on turntables going in all directions at once. People didn't expect anything like this—it was so new and exciting. We did only eight performances, and they got better each time. In the short time we played, we developed a small following.

Peter and I kept busy by going to practically everything that caught our attention. We read in the paper about an organ concert at Radio City Music Hall featuring E. Power Biggs and all the special effects the music hall could offer. We envisioned a Joshua Light Show-type production done mainstream. Psychedelia at the music hall. We immediately ordered tickets for this one-time event.

When the night arrived we had an early dinner, donned our best hippie clothes—fringe jackets and jeans—dropped mescaline, and took off for the music hall. When we arrived we found an audience of organists from all over the world: church organists, theater organists, and other professional musicians, all dressed in suits, ties, and semiformal dresses. No druggies. When we took stock of the situation, we just laughed. There we were, two gay long-haired hippies in fringe jackets, tripping our brains out in the midst of the moral majority, and we were all waiting to have our minds blown by Mr. Biggs. Regardless, it ended up to be a wonderful evening, and the music hall really rocked that night. The concert ended with "Stars and Stripes Forever," complete with a light show and a flag that covered the entire back wall of the music hall stage.

Peter and I went out a lot, but we also liked nothing better than staying home. We loved dining on roasted chicken with a nice Montrachet and listening to music or watching Tom Jones or the Smothers Brothers. We also went to the baths at least once a week. We had threesomes, even foursomes sometimes, and we had sex with other partners. We always got separate rooms when we went to the baths, and we had no rules. Whatever happened happened.

I've always lived with the belief that monogamy is against nature and that nothing is taboo. I would never dream of inconveniencing my partner so that I could go to bed with another person. On the other hand, if you can't be together, what's wrong with being with someone else? The only negative thing about this choice is that both parties run the possibility of falling in love with someone new. That's life!

Peter and I both worked hard at our relationship. We talked about what we wanted together, what we needed to make us happy. Realizing that our expectations and fears were the same, we grew even closer and seldom lost sight of the other's feelings. When we did—and we did sometimes—we expressed our regrets, forgot about the incident, and moved on. We were trying to purge fear from our lives. Without fear, anything is possible, everything is attainable.

One evening we went to the Continental Baths, and as usual we went our own ways. I met a tall, thin, rather sexy guy named Tom in the hall. He had fine brown hair, vivid blue eyes, and a sensitive look. We clicked right away, so I went to his room. We had great sex, and afterward we just lay there and talked. He was there with his lover too. It seemed that Peter and I weren't so unique after all. Before long, we went to the pool.

There was a lot of activity going on, people rushing around preparing for some special event, so we sat at the edge of the pool talking and watching the parade of men. I saw Peter and an attractive young man walking toward us. They stopped. Everyone said hello at once. Peter introduced me to Michael and I introduced him to Tom. We didn't have to introduce them to each other because Michael was Tom's lover. We laughed and joked about our all having such good taste.

We were getting to know each other, but it became difficult to talk. Some broad was doing her club act in the place next to the pool area that had been set aside as the dance floor. Guys were sitting around, in their towels, on the floor, and in straight-back chairs, laughing, clapping, and having a blast. History was being made in that other room, but no one was aware of it. Bette Midler was making her first appearance at the baths. We also weren't aware that we were making a little gay history of our own. Tom Stribling and Michael Maletta would be directly responsible for my making *Boys in the Sand.* If we four hadn't met that night....

With the opening of the Continental Baths, all bathhouses became more social and almost clublike. In the summer they had Sunday barbecues on the roof. I would see some of the same people each time, so I began to form sexual relationships with some and purely platonic ones with others. Few people went to the baths to have sex with only one partner, so between bouts there was time to communicate.

I kept working by doing more industrial shows and stock. I don't know whether the Rodgers office had anything to do with it, but every summer I was offered Rodgers and Hammerstein shows to direct. This summer I was directing two different productions of *The Sound of Music*, the first with Shirley Jones. Her husband, Jack Cassidy, and their children were with her, and they lived in a big trailer on the theater grounds. Shirley and Steven Elliot, a veteran of the Actors Studio, were excellent together.

Directly after that I was off to Minneapolis to direct another *Sound of Music*, starring Dorothy Collins. Despite my calling her Shirley all the time, we developed a long-lasting friendship. She had worked with Joe Layton, so every time I called her Shirley, she called me Joe.

Dick Rodgers called before I left for Minneapolis and asked that I take out the song "Ordinary Couple" and replace it with "Something Right" from the movie, saying it was more direct. Dorothy disagreed and begged me to let her sing the old song for me. She did and she was right. She could break your heart with just one phrase and make you smile with the next. "Ordinary Couple" stayed in that production. Dorothy, an underrated actress, was brilliant in the show. I miss her.

Peter and I continued our weekly routine of attending galleries and museums. On one of our excursions to the Whitney Museum, I ventured into the permanent collection. Peter was lagging behind, lingering over some painting. As I rounded a corner I stopped abruptly and caught my breath.

"Oh, my God! Oh, my God! Peter, come here!" I called out. He came up behind me. There, hanging on the wall, was me, looking out at myself in a painting titled *The New Yorkers*. In the piece, seated and standing around a table were Stephen Sondheim, Arthur Laurents, Richard Rodgers, Jerome White, John Dexter, Beni Montresor, and me. It was a painting of a photograph taken that awful day in the Rodgers office, the day I met John Dexter. It was a hoot, my likeness in a painting in the Whitney. I only wish that the moment depicted evoked a more pleasant memory.

I was so taken by the Warhol retrospective at the Whitney that I decided to return with my 16-millimeter camera and film the exhibit. I filmed the entire show doing dissolves and in-camera double exposures. I couldn't bring a tripod into the museum, so it was a difficult task. Warhol had become my favorite artist, and this exhibit was one of the best installations I had ever seen. The walls of the museum were plastered with Andy's Purple Cow wallpaper, and the paintings were hung against the design. The combination of the colors in the wallpaper and the colors in the paintings and prints was staggering. In this instance, less was definitely not more. More was more!

After weeks of editing and scoring, the finished piece documented the most exciting exhibit I had ever seen. In less than ten minutes, with the aid of music and sound effects, I shared my understanding of Warhol's genius. I set the images to music to change the effect or add to the impact of each image.

Andy's *Portrait of Ethel Skull* consists of multiple enlarged silkscreens of twenty-four photos taken in a Woolworth's "four photos for 25 cents booth." He painted them, stacked them alongside and on top of each other into one frame, and created a complex portrait of the woman.

In the film I began with a long shot of the entire painting followed by quick flashes of the individual pictures in rapid succession, at varying speeds, ending with a zoom out to the complete painting. I tracked this piece of film to a section from Strauss's *Clytemnestra*. The soprano begins to laugh, as only a soprano can, in a downward glissando, over and over and finally ends in a loud scream. The two worked well together, and by the end the viewer is laughing too. I liked this abstract way of making sense of things.

Several months later, I gave a copy to Andy. Sylvia Miles asked me to a screening of *Heat*, Andy's takeoff on *Sunset Boulevard*, in which she starred with Joe Dallesandro. Andy was notorious for giving different dates of his birth to interviewers, so when I handed him the reel of film, I said "Happy birthday, Andy...whenever." He giggled, nodded, and took the film can. I never heard from him, but I'm sure he watched it. He was too curious a person not to. The print is now in the Warhol Museum in Pittsburgh, PA.

I was having fun and learning so much in the process. This was what life was all about.

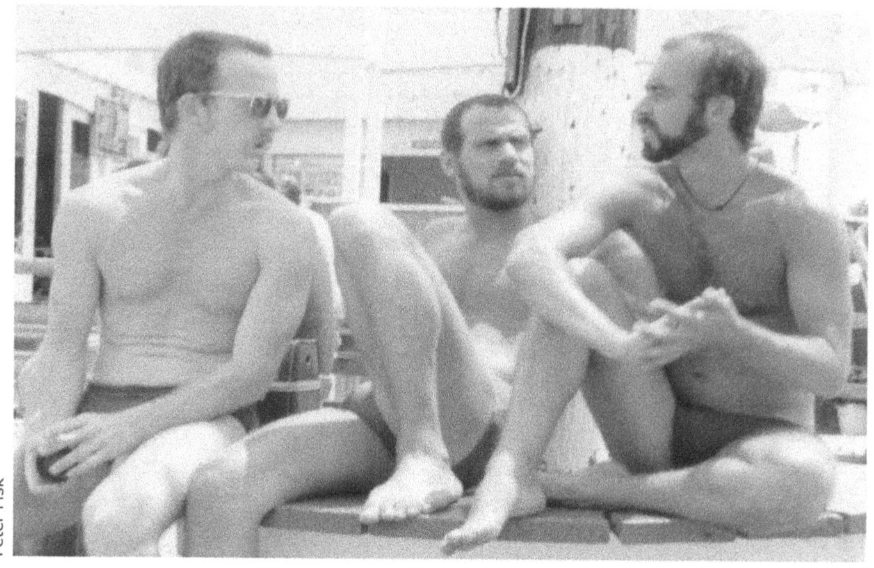
Peter Fisk

Wakefield Poole, Michael Maletta, and Ed Parente (left to right) enjoying summer in the Fire Island Pines, circa 1971.

Peter Fisk and Casey Donovan (Peter Schneckenburger and Cal Culver) share an intimate moment in Wakefield Poole's *Boys in the Sand* (1971).

Chapter Eight

Boys in the Sand

New York City, 1970

Michael Bennett was preparing to choreograph *Follies* on Broadway and asked if I would teach tap lessons to some of the cast members. Of course I would. I needed the money, and besides, Dorothy Collins would be one of my pupils. She finally got the Broadway show she'd deserved for so long.

The buzz was that *Follies* would surely be one of the hits of the season. I was creating another show at Triton Gallery for the artist David Byrd and had seen three posters for *Follies*, which he had submitted to Hal Prince's office. My favorite depicted a 1930s Gloria Swanson-type star dressed to the nines and standing in the rubble of the Roxy Theater. But they were all good, so I felt sure one would be accepted. Later, when I heard that Blaine Thompson Advertising said Hal had rejected them, I found it hard to believe. David was the perfect artist for the job. Something was wrong.

As fate would have it, a few days later while teaching my tap class, Hal Prince stopped by to say hello to some of the principals. In a moment of presumption I asked him why he didn't like David's submissions. Then, not even waiting for an answer, I proceeded to tell him what I thought of them. When I was done Hal looked confused and asked me to refresh his memory about the posters. The more I spoke, the more he realized he hadn't seen them. I suggested that if it wasn't too late, he should take a look. Hal asked me to have them sent to his office.

A few weeks later Hal showed up again during my tap classes. At the break he called me into one of the offices. "I'm so grateful that I wanted you to be the first to see this," he said, reaching into a large manila envelope. "It's the final draft and, God, it's good! Thank you."

There on the table was David Byrd's poster for *Follies*, a close-up of a Sphinx-like showgirl with a crack running down her cheek. Since the play was about the reunion of aging stars, it wasn't just good, it was perfect. And it would turn out to be the poster of the season!

I went with Robert Joffrey to the opening night of *Follies*—one of the most exciting evenings I ever spent in the theater. The concept of ghosts from the past wandering through the events of the evening, as well as having two actors for each leading role—one young and one old—was beautifully realized. The sets and costumes were visually astounding and the music, glorious. I was one of the few who didn't mind the thin book. I had just one criticism. Once in a while, in the dance numbers that were so inventive, I would see an ordinary step. One that was not put there for effect but just there for no reason. Perhaps Michael had been rushed.

When I saw Michael after the show, he asked me what I thought. I answered honestly. "I thought it was great. It's almost a perfect show."

Michael looked hurt for an instant, then pulled himself together and asked me to be specific. I had no reason to lie, so I voiced my criticisms.

Most of it was innovative, so new, and so different. Bob Fosse once said when accepting one of his Tony Awards, "Thank you, but I'll share this with the other nominees. We all use the same steps anyway." That certainly wasn't the case with Fosse's choreography and, mostly, it wasn't the case here. But, again, every now and then I'd see a familiar step that stood out. I probably shouldn't have brought it up, but Michael was insistent and eager to hear what I had to say. He was getting all this attention from the press, and still he was searching for perfection. He really wanted the truth. I liked that.

In March I was asked to direct a showcase for AFTRA, which every year produces a one-time-only performance, attended by producers, directors, agents, and casting directors. Larry Fuller was to choreograph.

When I walked into the first audition, the writers were already there. Ed Kresley, who was doing the music (I knew him by sight), had been Gower Champion's assistant on *Bye Bye Birdie*. The other two I had never met: Drey Shepperd, the lyricist, and Martin Sherman, who was writing the book. The show turned out well in that we accomplished our goal of showcasing young talent in an entertaining way. It also turned out to be four hours long...who to cut? I was so floored by the exceptional talent that I couldn't disappoint any of them by last-minute cuts. Some of the performers hoping for their big break included Billy Crystal, Kelly Bishop, Heather MacRae, Virginia Martin, Leta Galloway, and Dolph Sweet.

One night after rehearsal, Martin, Drey, Ed, Peter, and I went to the Park Miller, a legit theater that had been showing male films for a few months, to see some porno. Four years earlier, in this same theater, I'd seen Jennifer West do *Diamond Orchid*, a play about Eva Perón. The theater was huge, and the lights were so bright you could read a magazine in the audience. One customer was actually reading *The New York Times* that night. It was antiseptic looking, and no sex occurred because the police constantly walked in, subtly harassing the staff and anyone they thought was up to no good.

After about twenty minutes of loops, the main feature, *Highway Hustler*, came on. At one point the star of the movie is picked up, taken to a motel, and sodomized while a knife is held to his throat. It was not very erotic, to say the least.

Peter was sound asleep, Martin looked bored to death, and Drey and Ed were laughing. This whole scene was scored with an orchestral rendition of "June is Busting Out All Over." Later, we were all asking the same question: "Why can't someone make a good porno film that's not degrading?"

"Hell," I said, "I've got the camera Peter gave me. Maybe I should try. Just for the fun of it. Who wants to be in it?" We all laughed and continued to walk uptown. Not another word was mentioned about making a porno, but I put the thought on the back burner.

Tom and Michael invited us to their house on Fire Island for the weekend. They were sharing it with an artist, Ed Parente, and his lover, Fred Bricker. Ed was short, about five foot six, Italian, dark, and sensual in nature. Fred, on the other hand, was taller, fair, divorced, with children, and definitely the less experienced of the two. They made a good couple.

In the middle of the island with absolutely no view, their house was small and inviting, not one of the luxury homes located on the ocean or the bay. We all got along well, so well that we became their permanent house guests.

Ed and I became instant best friends. We were both Pisces, shared the same birthday, and thought alike about so many things. He was a working artist, so he lived on the island all summer, creating drawings and sculptures that were sold at Ballardo's on Christopher Street.

When I wasn't doing a show, I'd stay with him during the week. Ed and I gained a reputation for being strange, mainly because we were seen constantly with our butterfly nets, trying to capture butterflies for Ed's sculptures. He incorporated them, along with plaster body parts, into plastic boxes. A favorite of mine, done in multiples, was just a hand, palm up, fingers curved upward, with a monarch butterfly perched on the tip of one finger. We would go to the "Meat Rack" between the Grove and the Pines, take off our suits, sit on the ground bare-assed naked, and wait for our prey...monarchs. Guys looking for afternoon sex partners would pass and see two crazed, naked druggies with butterfly nets and not know what to make of us.

Our friend Michael Maletta cut hair for a living. Most of his clients were top models, and he was successful. He also wore a hair piece. But it was almost unnoticeable. Still, it affected the way he reacted to things, the rain, the wind, and he was constantly making sure that during sex you didn't touch his head. One weekend Peter and I decided to cut our hair with clippers. My hair was shoulder length, and I was ready for a change. I had been a hippie long enough. We'd been trimming our body hair with dog clippers, so we decided to do our heads, cutting our hair shorter than a crew cut. Before the weekend was over most of the guys in the Pines had followed suit. People actually came to our house and asked to use our clippers. I pleaded with Michael to let me do the same to him. I told him that his baldness was mostly in his head, not on it, so finally he let me cut his hair to a stubble. It looked great.

As soon as I finished we took a walk down the beach. Michael started to cry. He wasn't sobbing, but tears were running down his face. I asked if he was all right.

"I don't have to worry about which way the wind is blowing anymore," he said.

I started to laugh, and, in an instant, throwing his arms around me, he started to laugh too. We held on and laughed so hard, we fell down. We picked ourselves up, rushed into the ocean, and Michael got his head wet for the first time since I had known him. It was a great moment of friendship between us and one of my favorite memories of him.

I think it probably was the island, along with the ever-present sexual tension, that gave me an idea for a little film. The concept was simple.

A young man walks down the boardwalk, turns into the woods, and comes out on the bay side of the island. He spreads a blanket, takes off his clothes, and sits and waits, looking out over the water. A vision appears like Venus from the sea: a beautiful nude man who seems to walk on water as he approaches the waiting man. They immediately explore each other and eventually go into the woods. When they've finished fucking, the waiting man gets up, kisses the other, leaves, and disappears running into the bay. The man left on the blanket gets up, looks out over the water, puts on the clothes left by the other man, picks up the blanket, and walks down the shore as the scene fades.

One night we were sitting on the back deck smoking a joint. Fred and Ed were fucking in their room, and the noises filtered out of the window onto the deck. The mood was already sexual, so I told them about the movie I wanted to do. When I finished I asked Tom and Michael if they would like to do it. Knowing that it was just for us, they agreed and we set it up for the next week.

I bought some Kodak 16-millimeter film, cleaned the camera, and packed what I thought I'd need, which wasn't much. I was ready to go when Michael and Tom suddenly had second thoughts. This, I was to find out, was the normal course of events when someone agrees to perform sex acts on film. The desire is there, but the ego takes a second look, and fear takes over. Michael couldn't work through his fear. I was disappointed.

That afternoon at the Boatel, a combination hotel-restaurant-bar on the dock, Peter and I were talking with Dino, a good-looking Italian man who worked at the gift shop. The three of us had been flirting for weeks. I suddenly turned to him and asked if he'd like to make a film with Peter. They both looked a bit startled, but moments later we agreed to shoot the next day at six A.M. I spent the rest of the afternoon thinking about what I was going to do the following day. I rolled a few joints, loaded my camera, and I was ready.

The next morning, Peter and I met Dino at the dock. It took us fifteen minutes to walk to the end of the island, where I had scouted our location. The only things we brought besides our equipment were a blanket, grass, poppers, and some bottles of Pepsi.

We shot all the nonsexual scenes first, which took about an hour. Then we started on the sex scene. I had a hard time. From their first kiss, I felt a knot developing in the pit of my stomach. I had seen Peter in a lot of sexual situations, but this was different. I was, in essence, not even there. I had to deal with that. I was watching my partner make love with another man, and I was filming it. They were dealing with issues themselves. Besides the physical things—sand, heat, gnats, and keeping an erection—they were dealing with their decision to make this film, the effect it would have on their lives, if any, and with me personally as well. Peter was fucking Dino while I was recording it for others to see, and Dino was fucking my lover right in front of me. The tension was almost tangible.

But filming the sex scene fascinated me. I told them to experiment with each other as if it were the first time (and it was). I wanted them to do everything. No top, no bottom, just two men discovering each other. I had always been observant, but now I was able, with the help of the zoom lens, to actually see things I could never see with the naked eye. It was almost hypnotic, and at times the camera seemed to have a mind of its own. In that viewfinder I found a whole new private world. I was now an official voyeur and felt comfortable in my new role. I almost became invisible to the actors, and surprisingly, I was never tempted to enter into the action. The filming was my participation. I created my reality by selecting what would fill the small frame through which I looked.

In the middle of the sex scene, we were invaded by horseflies—anything but romantic. Somehow we managed, and we finished around eleven A.M. We went back to the house exhausted from all the mental stress as well as from the physical discomfort caused by the flies. Now all that was left was to find someone to develop the film. I had to go into town anyway the next week to prepare some backer auditions for a new show, *Delta Lady*, written by Drey and Martin, about a USO troop lost in the jungles of Vietnam. Sylvia Miles was to play the lead. But the show never happened. People weren't ready to see anything about the Vietnam experience. The wounds were still too fresh.

All during the summer, I'd been shooting material for the David Byrd show at Triton Gallery, which was scheduled for the fall. I had a complicated idea for the show: One end of the gallery would be covered with stretch fabric to form an abstract projection surface. Using twenty projectors, I wanted to visualize the progression of an idea, how it explodes and forms, goes off in diverse directions, and how it has to be reined in from time to time to keep the focus where it belongs.

For example, David had created the original poster for *Jesus Christ Superstar*, so during that section, using multiple images, I showed the entire life of Christ through famous paintings in rapid succession on one section of the screen. At the same time, in another section of the screen, I'd play a movie of David working on the poster while slides of details from the poster flashed around the entire surface. I projected a film of Christ riding into Jerusalem on a donkey, with supporting images of other well-known figures making entrances into cities—Marilyn Monroe getting off a plane in New York, Cleopatra riding into Rome, Hitler walking into Paris, Lindbergh's ticker-tape parade—playing simultaneously. The effect was mesmerizing.

David also created the posters for *Frank Merriwell*, *On the Town*, *Tommy at the Met*, *Lemon Sky*, and, of course, *Follies*. These, along with his many posters for Fillmore East, made up the content of the show.

It was true multimedia and was programmed and executed by hand. We took all the remotes from the slide projectors and mounted them on a plank so that we could play them like a keyboard. We had to memorize all the cues because there wasn't time to read a cue sheet. The 16-millimeter projectors and the Super 8s had to be manually turned on and off on cue. Nothing ran constantly, and the images appeared randomly over the surface.

The music acted as a blueprint for our cues. The score was eclectic, including classical, opera, show music, and rock and roll. The entire show ran forty minutes.

It was an ambitious project and would take more than six months to prepare. I had a small budget, most of which went to pay for film and developing, so there wasn't enough left to rent equipment; I had to borrow all the projectors.

While this was going on I found time to edit the film I did with Peter and Dino. I finished, ending up with a fifteen-minute movie tracked with Debussy's "Nocturnes" and "Afternoon of a Faun." I didn't put the sound on the film but merely played a tape, since I didn't know anything about sound tracks then.

We threw a little party on the island to show the film. About fifteen people attended. Ed and I had also done a shorter film. It was suppose to show Fred how much Ed loved him. At the end of the screening, everyone had tears in their eyes but Fred. He got up and left the house without a word. Ed didn't follow. Within a few weeks they separated and their affair ended.

The film of Peter and Dino fared much better. Everyone thought it was the best porno they had ever seen and suggested that I expand it to make a full-length movie. I'd made the movie with no money, just my American Express Card. If I wanted to pursue this project, I would need some financing.

I showed the film to Marvin, my business manager, and he flipped. In less than a minute we agreed that he would finance the movie and that we would become partners, fifty-fifty. I set out to think up two new sections for the film.

In the meantime, Dino wanted $2,000 for his participation. I couldn't afford to pay him that, so I decided to reshoot his section. As fate would have it, Joe Nelson was present when we were discussing the casting. Joe always seemed to stay in my life. He and his lover,

Randy, had been good friends to Nancy and me and remained so after our divorce.

"Hey, guys," he interrupted. "I've got the perfect person for you. He's blond, six feet tall, and handsome. He's got a nice dick, a beautiful ass, and he does everything. Want me to call him?"

That's how it happened. That easy!

A few days later Joe appeared at my door with Cal, A.K.A. Casey Donovan. When I opened the door the first thing I saw was this incredible smile on a very handsome face. His look was perfect—the type you see in magazine ads, not porno movies.

I showed him the section with Peter and Dino. When it was over, Cal stood up and said, "I want to do it! You just tell me what you want me to do and I'll do it. It's really great. When do we start?"

The next weekend we reshot the scene we called "Bayside." Peter said he wasn't really into Cal but that Cal was attractive enough to get him through it. I laughed and thanked him for his sacrifice.

The shoot went well and was quite intimate. Only the three of us were there except for some guy who was hiding in the bushes the whole time we were filming. I wonder what story he told his friends when he got back home.

After the first few minutes of shooting, I knew Cal was going to be terrific. The camera loved him. When we were done Cal came back to the house to discuss the other parts of the film. He mentioned a long-time fuck buddy he thought would be good for the last section. He was a bartender in the Grove, so Cal suggested we go for a drink.

On the walk to the Grove, Cal told me that Tommy Moore, the guy we were going to meet, was a black man. He hoped it wouldn't matter to me because he said they'd had great sex together. I had no problems with it. We got to the bar and met Tommy. He was hot, and after a few minutes he agreed. We made a schedule and planned to shoot his section, "Inside," in early August. Now we only had to find someone for the middle section.

On our way back to the Pines, we passed some men working on the roof of a new house.

"Look at that Italian guy on the roof," Cal said, drawing my attention to a pair of workers right out of a Quaintance drawing. "He's so fucking hot. He works out and has a great body and a smile to equal his Italian good looks. I've wanted to get him in bed the whole summer. It would be great if you could get him to do the movie. The hunky blond is his lover."

I don't know what got into me, but I said, "Let's ask."

I yelled up and asked if I could speak with them for a minute. They both came down the ladder and over to where we were standing.

"Excuse me, I know you're lovers, but I have a proposition."

They introduced themselves, and we sat down on the deck and smoked a joint. When we were done Danny DiCioccio, with his lover's approval, agreed to do "Poolside."

I needed a house for each of the next segments, so Cal asked two friends, Mel and Frank, if we could use theirs, a big beautiful house next to the Pines' Meat Rack, with a swimming pool and an adjacent guest house. They agreed to let us use the pool and guest house only. I accepted before they had a chance to reconsider, then set the filming for the next weekend.

On the morning of the shoot, we all met at Mel and Frank's. Ed had begged to come along, under the pretext of shooting stills. Good idea, so I agreed, if he would keep quiet. I'd found during the first segment that the less talking on the set, the better.

We filmed the sex scene first. I would film the exposition later. I found that shooting the sex scenes before the actors find any faults in their partner is the best road to take. This segment showed Cal relaxing around the island and by his pool. While reading the "wanton ads" in *Gay*, the newspaper, he comes across something of interest. He goes into the house, writes a note, mails it, and waits for a reply. A few days later he receives a small package, removes his clothes, and sits by the pool. He unwraps the package and finds a small plastic box containing a large white pill. He throws it into the pool. It bubbles and rolls until out of the water emerges an Italian Adonis. At this point the audience always laughs and claps. Imagine laughing and clapping during a porno movie. He swims over to Cal, at the edge of the pool, and after a look, takes Cal into his mouth, and instantly Cal has a raging erection. Later, he lifts Danny out of the water, lies back, and guides Danny's cock into his mouth.

What follows is an athletic love scene in which the action finally spills into the pool. I shot through shrubs and furniture, resulting in a voyeuristic feel. They exit the pool, dry off, put on clothes, and leave the house to walk down to the dock. There they pass a young man (Ed Parente), sitting on the fence by the dock, with the same issue of *Gay* under his arm. He slips off the fence, and, taking the paper, walks away to send off for a stud of his own as the film fades out.

It took less than two hours to shoot the sex scene. Danny was frenetic. He had made softcore films for Colt Studios. Colt only did the action up to the penetration, then edited to another angle. Danny brought his experience in porno with him, and it worked for that scene, but it was difficult to edit into a cohesive segment. After the shoot I asked Ed for the film he had shot. He had been wonderful and stayed totally in the background while getting his photos. Only one problem: He had forgotten to put film in the camera. We laughed. Now I had two sections finished and not one still photograph.

There was still the problem of finding a house for the third segment. Ed and I both had been aware of an elderly man whom we called "the count" because he reminded us of Dracula. He was European, about six foot six inches tall, thin but well-toned, and elegant. He was also hot and had a knockdown gorgeous young stud lover. To top it all off, he had a modern house, designed by Frank Gehry, after an Aztec temple. All the walls were wood paneled. Again, fearlessly, I just went up, knocked on the door, and asked if I could use his home to shoot a porno movie.

Much to my surprise, he was interested, so much so that I thought I might have trouble with his wanting to watch the filming. But that was not the case. He was so generous that when we arrived for our shoot at eight A.M., he showed us around the house, pointed out a large container of cocaine, another of grass, and a box of poppers. "Help yourself to whatever you need, and I'll be back around sundown," he said before taking his leave. Now that's what I call a good host.

This section is much more sophisticated than the other two. The first centers on dreams, hero worship, and innocence. The second, about coming out, includes the attainment of love and finding a partner. Now this last section would introduce hedonistic pleasures. The whole film features high-profile homosexuality with no guilt—and includes an interracial cast.

The segment starts with Cal waking up with the bright sun streaming into his bedroom window. As he opens the house to the morning breeze, he eyes a telephone repairman, Tommy, on the walk outside, checking the poles. He cruises him blatantly, but the repairman is hesitant. When Cal pulls aside the drape to reveal a raging pole of his own, the man shows interest but turns abruptly and walks away. Tommy looks over his shoulder several times, but Cal realizes he's just lost the big fish.

Cal wanders around the house and imagines having sex with the phone man in every room and hallway. Finally he reaches into the drawer by his bed and takes out a large black dildo. He impales himself and masturbates while imagining sex with the one that got away. When he finishes he walks downstairs and suddenly at the front door stands the phone man. Cal smiles and opens the screen door for him to enter as the picture fades out.

It was an easy shoot, just the three of us. Cal and Tommy were evenly matched, both liking everything. They also had no sexual preferences with one another, so there's no top or bottom in the segment. I still think it's one of the best sex scenes I ever filmed. Just two hot men satisfying themselves and each other.

Now the film was in the can, and I only had to edit the sections, track them to music, and then I'd have a movie. In the meantime, I still had to put together the Byrd show for the fall.

I needed some footage of *Follies*, so that I went to Hal Prince and asked him for two last row seats in the orchestra so that I could take eight-millimeter movies of the production numbers. Hal explained that he could give me the seats but couldn't grant official permission to film. It was definitely against union rules, but he would close his eyes.

However, Hal did speak to the head usherette and ask that she also look the other way while I was filming. If someone else should catch me, I would be on my own. They didn't, and I shot some wonderful film of all the musical numbers. I was actually doing what my friend Ray Knight had done for years. His advice kept me from getting caught: "Only shoot when the music is loud!"

I also went to Dorothy Collins's dressing room and filmed her being made up by Teddy Azar. All these images would be put together to make up the finale of the show: a freaked-out version of *Follies*.

In early November we opened the Byrd show to raves and packed houses. The last few nights we had to turn people away. The Friday night performance was one of the best. Since everything was done by hand, the show was slightly different every night. There were so many variables that it was hard to make things happen at the same time every night. It also made it fun to execute. This performance had gone without hitch. Which reminds me, the entire show started off with an intentional mistake. The opening image was a clip of the Columbia Pictures logo. On the sound track we put the sound of the arm of a record player, scratching across the record, as if backstage someone had hit the record player by accident.

Every night we heard a groan and general uneasiness from the audience. Not an unpleasant groan but a sympathetic one. The film blacked out and started over again. The same thing occurred again. The third time it happened, when the audience realized they had been tricked, they laughed and applauded. We were off and running. They also relaxed and knew this show was going to be a challenging experience. They were going to have to work to get full enjoyment from the experience, and they had to participate by making some sense of what they chose to look at.

After this performance Peter and I were putting all the projectors back in their starting positions when Roger pulled back the drape and announced that someone wanted to say hello.

Still sitting on my little stool, I turned to see Michael Bennett, Hal Prince, and Stephen Sondheim. Hal was raving and couldn't believe the entire show was all done manually. He kept going on and on. He was always curious about new things and how they worked. He still is; that's why he's still directing. Michael stayed uncommonly quiet—he could talk to me later. Then Stephen, smiling put out his hand, took hold of my arm, and held it until he caught my eye. "It was really wonderful, Wakefield!" he said. "I didn't know you had it in you."

"I know," I responded, holding back tears of pride. Stephen's two home movies had inspired me, so nothing meant more to me than his praise. I'd finally made an impression on him. During *Waltz* I always felt he thought I had little or no talent. Now I had created something that excited him and captured his mind for a moment. It was a great feeling and has remained with me as one of my most rewarding experiences.

Suddenly I began to get job offers. Alexis Smith had come to the show and sat on the floor with Hugh Forden. When the film ended she said she'd like to discuss a project. She had acquired the rights to a romantic novel, *Forever*, about a couple who meet and fall in love in the "foreworld," before their lives begin. They're born on different continents, and when they meet for the first time, they're both married to other people but feel a strong attraction.

Alexis and I had dinner one night and went back to her apartment for a nightcap. She was excited and said that after seeing the Byrd show, she felt I could handle the mystical elements of the novel and come up with an appropriate concept for the part that takes place in the foreworld. She gave me a copy of the novel, and as I left we agreed to meet again after I had read the book and developed some ideas.

We talked on the phone several times, but we never had that second meeting. In less than five weeks the first ad for *Boys in the Sand* would appear in *The New York Times*. After that I didn't hear one word from her again about the project.

Hal Prince was so impressed with how great the *Follies* footage looked that he asked me if I would do the same for his other shows. He had five shows running and wanted to bring Zero Mostel back for one performance of *Fiddler* so that we could get it down on film as well. I gave him a quote of $5,000 for filming, developing, and editing each show. He was shocked at how low the bid was.

The only problem was the union. Even though he only wanted to do them for preservation, as a gift for the Library of Performing Arts at Lincoln Center, and not for commercial purposes, the union refused. Today, after agreements were made with the unions, all shows are videotaped for historical purposes.

Kevin Carlisle and Michael Hill also had a project that needed the type of visuals I had created for the Byrd show: a rock version of the Old Testament.

Conrad Matthei, one of the producers of *George M!*, came to see the show and called me after we had closed. He wanted me to do the Byrd show at the opening night party for *The Great White Hope*, a Broadway play he was producing, starring James Earl Jones. I hated that I couldn't do it. Everything had been dismantled and returned to their owners. I had borrowed movie projectors, slide projectors, slides, film, tape players, everything. I told him I couldn't possibly reconstruct it in the few days we had before his play opened. I don't think he knew how disappointed I was not to be able to do it.

While all this was going on, Peter and I were editing my little porno movie and trying to put a sound track to the picture. I also had trouble getting the film processed. I would meet a technician from Guffante Film labs at a coffee shop around the corner, give him the film in a brown grocery bag, and he would return the processed film the same way. It was so covert, you'd think we were trading in top-secret material. At that time, though, we could have gone to jail for what we were doing.

I cut the original footage, not knowing anything about work prints, which are copies of the original footage used solely for editing. Work prints ensure that the original footage is never projected and runs no risk of being scratched. I didn't do anything right. I cut the film in a makeshift editing room in my apartment. At the very end we found ourselves with a fifteen-second overlap in the music and didn't know how to fix it. My friend Bobby Alvarez was editing *Woodstock* at the time and kindly agreed to help.

He liked what he saw and suggested we see Marvin Soloway at Cinelab, which developed film footage for network news programs. This was before wide use of videotape, so all footage was rushed to processing and printing to make the five-o'clock news. Marvin also encouraged young independent filmmakers by guiding them through the rough spots. He still does.

When Marvin asked how he could help, I handed him two big reels of film and a sound track. When he found out I had cut the original footage, he looked at me and said, "You've got some balls cutting the original footage."

"Balls had noting to do with it," I said. "Just stupidity. I've got this film here, and I don't know what to do with it."

"Filmmakers usually know it all. What a relief to meet someone who doesn't—and admits it!"

With that remark he took me under his wing, and with his guidance *Boys in the Sand* was finished.

Now that we had a film, we had to try to get it shown. The man in charge of the Park Miller, the theater where all this started, was in California. Marvin called and he agreed to see the film. In a few days I was in his outer office on Hollywood Boulevard, waiting to meet the porno king of the West Coast. The office door opened and out walked a tall, light-haired, heavyset man with a pleasant smile. "Hello, I'm Shan Sayles. You're Wakefield?" he asked, extending his hand.

"Yes. Nice to meet you."

"I understand you've made a boy-boy picture you want me to look at. I like the title, so that's a good start. There's not much more to talk about until I view the picture. Come back tomorrow at ten and we'll see if we can do some business."

I was a little surprised because I had no idea he wanted to keep the film overnight. I wasn't prepared, so I just said, "I'm not sure I should let it out of my hands. I really don't know you, and I've heard such wild stories about getting ripped off." He laughed and promised he'd take good care and not let the print out of his possession. He wanted to take it home that evening and watch it at his leisure.

I couldn't muster up the courage to say that some of the stories were about him, so I agreed. Still, I left his office with a great feeling of "What have I done?" hanging over me like a dark cloud.

I spent the evening with Frank DeSal, who was now living in Los Angeles, and the next morning I was at Shan's office at ten sharp. We greeted each other, and as he sat across the desk from me he said, "Well, I think your picture is one of the best boy-boy films I've ever seen. How much did it cost you?"

"About $4,000." I was so excited about his response that I didn't even think that the cost would affect his offer. So much for my business sense.

"Well, I'll give you $8,000 for the film outright," he said.

"You mean $8,000 and you own the film?"

"That's right. You get return on your investment and 100% profit. Not bad for a first film."

"Well, if it's the best gay film you've ever seen, it should be worth more than $8,000," I snapped back with a smile.

"Oh, it's worth more, but that's all I'm willing to pay for it."

"Then I think I should talk it over with Marvin. Thanks for your time. I'm glad you liked the film." I told him I'd get back to him, then left.

When I got back to the hotel room, I called Marvin with the news. He was encouraged but said we should go to option B.

Andy Warhol had shown his films at the 55th Street Playhouse, located right across the street from Marvin's apartment. The two-hundred-seat theater, run by Frank Lee, had resorted to showing Chinese films when nothing else was available. Frank operated from a small theater in San Francisco, so that was my next stop.

When I arrived a frail Chinese man escorted me to a dark and dank back storage room. Through another door I saw that a 16-millimeter projector had been set up in what looked like the kitchen of a closed restaurant. After I had threaded the film, another Chinese man, unfriendly and anxious, introduced himself as Frank Lee.

I switched on the projector. After a few minutes he turned and said that the film had class and that he'd be willing to discuss a four-wall deal, which meant we would run the theater ourselves and pay him a fee and a percentage. He suggested that Marvin call to discuss terms.

Marvin struck a deal, and we had a theater. We also had only four weeks to get our ad campaign moving and run some previews and private screenings. Quickly we acquired Bob Ganshaw, a public relations man, as our press agent. We were proud of our work and wanted to promote it like a regular movie. Marvin and I made it clear that everything had to be first-class. I asked Bob to invite all the first-string critics to the press screenings. Let them choose not to come. He did just that. Most of them came, though most chose not to write about it. The ones that did made history.

Boys in the Sand became the first hardcore film reviewed by *Variety*. The ads in the *Times* had everybody talking, and the gay press, what there was, stood behind us. Bill Como, editor of *After Dark* magazine, supported us fiercely, not only taking our ads but also running feature stories about Cal as Casey Donovan. I had known Bill since my old Ballet Russe days. He had picked me up on Central Park West one night and taken me home, and we'd been friends ever since.

We did everything we could to make it work. That, along with good luck and good timing, made the film a resounding success.

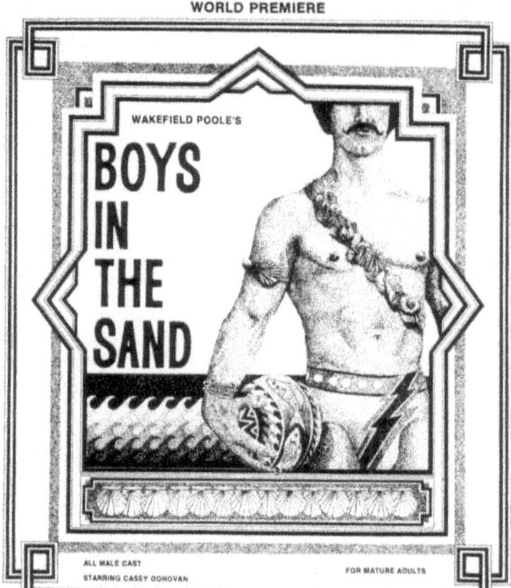

Original ad for *Boys in the Sand* (1971) designed by Ed Parente.

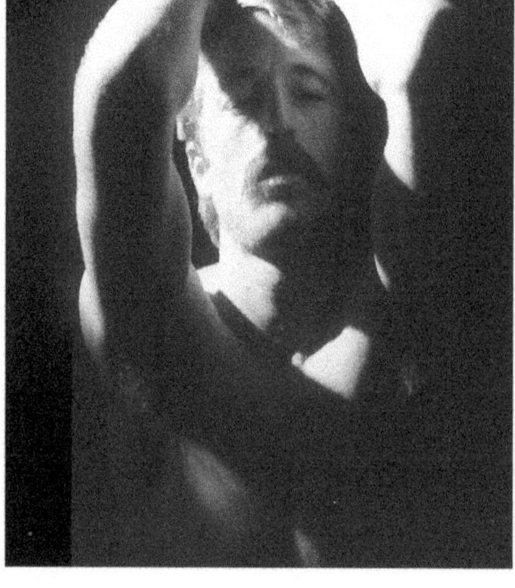
Paul Jasmin

Bill Harrison,
star of *Bijou* (1972).

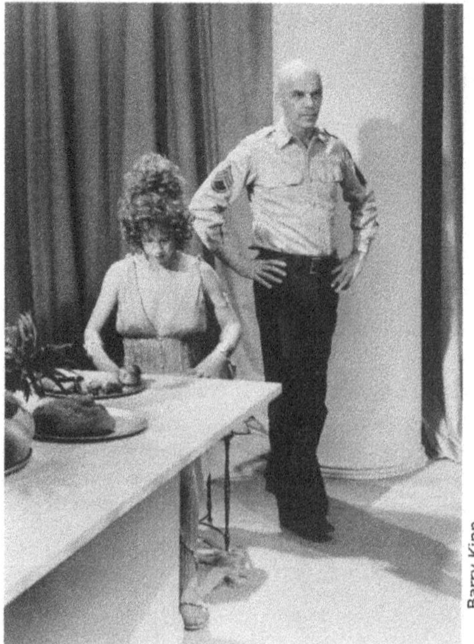
Barry Kinn

On the set of *Wakefield Poole's Bible*: producer Marvin Shulman and star Georgina Spelvin (as Bathsheba).

Chapter Nine

Bijou

New York City, 1971

In the week following the opening, things really got hopping. Everyone was talking about our movie. Holiday parties helped spread word of mouth, and even the negative remarks seemed to pique interest in the film. Hobe's review in *Variety* contained one of our most-used quotes: "The casting seems as if it were done by Dial-a-Hustler." And also from *Variety*: "There are no more closets!"

We changed the quotes in our ads in the papers daily. We actually had readers turning to our ads to see what we were going to say next. This was one of the first instances that gay ideas and propaganda were published daily in *The New York Times*. The more outrageous we got, the better it seemed to be for us. These two-inch-by-three-inch ads acted as our soapbox for the entire run.

I was pretty well-known in the theater world, so a remark like "Did you hear Wakefield Poole made a dirty movie?" just made people more interested in seeing the film. Most people didn't go to see it because it was good but because they were curious. We got the audience we'd wanted: first-time porno goers as well as hardcore aficionados. Paul Soland, a gypsy dancer friend, said he had run into Gwen Verdon and asked if she had heard about Wakefield's "dirty movie." She had and asked him to tell me "Good show!" and to keep on doing them. Even Gwen had read about it in *Variety*.

Two weeks after we opened, *Variety* published an article about our success titled "Amateurs Bring in Bonanza" written by Addison Verrill. *Newsweek* printed a small piece about our success, and along with our "gay" reviews, we definitely had "legs." We made about $20,000 the second week, after our $26,000 opening week.

Paramount called. Howard Koch, the president of the company and one on the most powerful men in the film industry, wanted to screen the picture. I wanted to know why. I never received an answer but provided the print anyway. After all, it was Paramount Pictures. I wasn't proud of the technical aspects of the movie. I had learned so much while making it that I was dissatisfied with the finished product. As expected, Paramount returned the print with no enclosure, not even a thank-you.

I guess after reading about our financial success, Koch wanted to see if I had talent worth exploiting. The film is crude by Hollywood standards, so, unsurprisingly, he must have found the film and my talent unworthy. I admit I didn't know what I was doing when I made *Boys*, but I learned fast. My next movie would be a lot better technically, that's for sure. Later I heard a rumor from Cherry Vanilla, a rock singer and sometime assistant to David Bowie, that Paramount got the film to screen for Mick Jagger and the Rolling Stones. Who knows?

With the publicity I was getting, I decided I should make some explanation to my family. I had never, since the time I was arrested years before, spoken to my family about my sex life. I never hid or explained any of my actions to them, but this was a public event, written about in *Variety* and *The New York Times*. Wakefield Poole was a gay pornographer, and they might have to deal with some negative reaction. I certainly didn't want to embarrass my dad, especially since he had become one of the top ten Chrysler salesmen in the United States. So I phoned my father. My stepmother put him on the line.

"How's it going, Bub?"

"Things are pretty good," I said. "Marvin and I made a movie last summer, Dad. It opened here a few weeks ago. It's making a lot of money, so we're getting a lot of press."

I thought a lot of questions would follow, but Dad only expressed his joy over my success, saying, "Son, that's great! You've worked hard for it."

I continued, "If you want to read about it, go to the out-of-town magazine stand and buy this week's *Variety*. There's an article about us."

It was a chicken way out, but I felt it would be easier for him to deal with it first on his own. He'd have some time to gather his thoughts and not do or say something in haste that could never be taken back. The few guys I knew who'd come out to their families had problems dealing with their parents' hot emotions—as well as their own—accompanied by guilt, fear, and insecurities.

We finished our talk, and I knew that as soon as we got off the phone, he would be heading to Adams Street. He loved any excuse to drive. Now I only had to wonder how he would relate to me after reading about *Boys in the Sand*.

After that night he always made a remark about how well the movie did, or something about the success, but he never mentioned a word about the content. He was, to my astonishment, actually proud of it.

Bob Colacello, from Andy Warhol's *Interview* magazine, wanted to do an article and photo spread on me. I did the interview, which was Bob's first assignment, and Peter took nude pictures of me sitting in a horn chair with my newly acquired Warhol portraits of Marilyn, leaning against the wall. Another had me lying on my side, nude, in front of a TV, with an Oldenberg soft drum set strategically placed. The caption read, "Zenith, Poole, and Oldenberg."

Once the article was published, we were "porno chic." Features appeared regularly in *After Dark*, *Screw*, and other magazines. It just kept growing. Our luck held.

After the second week of our run, Marvin bought himself a new Mercedes. He gave me $10,000 to spend, so I promptly bought a new Beaulieu 16-millimeter camera to shoot my next film. There was no doubt there'd be another film when I was ready.

I got nervous, though, when asked to appear on *The David Suskind Show*. I'd appeared on TV as a performer but never as Wakefield Poole, real person. I was afraid I'd embarrass myself. What if I came off like a big queen?

On the way to the taping, I stopped by Marvin's to pick up some photos that were acceptable to show on TV. When I walked in Michael Bennett was sitting in the office. I was dressed in a Cardin suit with shirt and tie and thought I looked pretty good. Michael, on the other hand, thought I was too dressed up. He took me by the hand—it seems like people are always taking me by the hand—and led me across the hall to his apartment. Going into his dresser, he produced a turtleneck to go with my suit. I removed the shirt and tie, replacing it with his sweater. He was right. I looked better.

The entire show focused on pornography in all its forms. Martin Hodas, who owned all the 25-cent porno machines in New York City, also appeared, along with a man from Philadelphia who printed hardcore magazines and another who owned two hundred porno shops.

I had known David slightly when I was married; we had attended some of the same social functions. When the program started he attacked me. Now here I am with three alleged mobsters and he attacks *me*. At the commercial break David's assistant told him, "You're coming down too hard on Wakefield. Ease up." When the show continued the others defended me.

"He's making porno more acceptable."

"He's got the carriage trade coming to see a boy-boy film."

I loved it. The whole scene was really funny.

At one point David asked me how I could justify what I was doing. Did I have no shame? I responded, "Maybe I've gone beyond shame, but I think that when people make love, they are, or should be, more vulnerable and open than at any other time. I like to capture that moment of vulnerability in all its eroticism and beauty. People are the most beautiful then. It's spiritual."

"That's some rationale, Wakefield," he said. "Do you really believe that?" I can't remember much more, but when the show aired the following weekend, Peter and I were alone in the den. After the first minute I turned to him.

"Thank God! I'm obviously gay, but I'm not a screaming queen! I was so scared I'd embarrass myself." We both laughed at my insecurities.

Promoting the movie took up much of my time. Everyone wanted an interview or pictures or something. I got calls asking to book Casey for private modeling sessions. That was his business, not mine. I had no desire to become a madam, so I promptly turned these over to Cal to handle as he wished. Cal, or rather Casey, had turned into quite a commodity. He would live off his reputation as "every gay's dream," a quote from *The Advocate*, for the rest of his life.

Peter and I continued to live as usual. No big changes in our lives. We didn't move—we already had a spectacular apartment—and we still went out as before. This was still the hippie age, so we didn't spend money on clothes. Torn jeans and T-shirts were more than sufficient, and we still had our Cardin and Bill Blass suits for when we had to dress up.

But we did start to buy more art. We were into lithos, silk screens, etchings, sculptures, as well as African and pre-Colombian pieces. So any "found" cash was put directly into art. We never pondered what to give each other on special occasions and holidays—always a piece of art.

Peter and I also began to have incredible discussions. We were exploding with creative ideas. Success and lack of financial worries made this possible. It was a great time of learning. But all of the potential projects that came out of the success of the Byrd show suddenly vanished. The release of *Boys* had changed people's minds as to my ability to do anything other than pornography. It was strange. I was praised and rewarded for the success of the movie by some, while at the same time I was criticized by people who only weeks before had acknowledged I had talent.

Until now I hadn't realized that when I came out publicly as a homosexual, I was coming out a pornographer. To most people, that was worse than being gay. There's no such thing as an ex-pornographer. Once you've got that title, you keep it for life.

I had no doubt I was going to have to secure my own future, and no doubt that I had no choice in the matter. Marvin supported me. I think he liked the attention, and I know he liked the tremendous cash flow we'd created with the movie. He talked one of his other clients, Edward Villella of the New York City Ballet, into hiring me for a project. My last legitimate job would be creating a dance for him to perform on Ed Sullivan's Beatles special. I was given "Lucy in the Sky With Diamonds" and with the help of John Moffitt, the director, produced a ground-breaking piece. With Eddie and three women from the New York City Ballet, I created a number to show visually what happens during an acid trip, which is what the song is about.

Using an unprecedented amount of cameras and tape machines, we overlaid four to five images simultaneously. Each showed a different view of the same thing, a close-up, a medium shot, a long shot, and a tight close-up, all superimposed over one another. You could actually choose which image to focus on or you could shift realities simply by blinking your eyes and refocusing on another image. It was all done live, except for the twenty seconds of slow motion that we put down on tape. I was thrilled with the end result. Eddie was not.

It was not his usual TV performance—jumping and turning to show his technical ability—but rather a mood piece of the times. Because it was performed to the original Beatles recording, it was actually a music video, but those didn't exist yet. I got two calls after that show. One from Larry Kert who got it all and the other from Ron Field. Both remarked that they'd never seen anything like it, and both agreed that I'd accomplished my goal: It was an acid trip.

We didn't wait too long to open *Boys* in Los Angeles. Marvin contacted Shan Sayles and made a four-wall deal to open at the Paris Theater. We only did two preview screenings there. One, given by Kevin Carlisle and Michael Hill, was attended mostly by New York dancers who had relocated there to do TV. Also, my old buddy Michael Allen, a singer who recorded for London Records, brought Rock Hudson. When he introduced us before the screening, I wanted to say that we had met years earlier in New York, but I hesitated. The memory of that meeting instantly shot through my head as I took his hand and looked into those incredible eyes.

One night, quite a few years before, at the Everard Baths, I'd noticed a man following me around. I'd seen this person before but couldn't place him. Finally he came up to me and said, "I've been watching you all night. I have a friend at home who would like you. Would you come home with me to meet him? You'll enjoy yourself, and I promise you won't ever forget it." Well, I was intrigued and being one who loves adventure, especially when it's sexual, I agreed to go with him. If the guy turned out to be a horror, I could leave.

I changed into my clothes and met him at the front door of the baths. We went to an apartment on the Upper East Side and were met at the door by...oh, my God! It was Rock Hudson. He was in a robe and appeared to be naked underneath. I managed to keep my cool—I think!

We sat on a huge sofa and had a drink. When we were alone he kissed me. Then he began to remove my clothes. He opened his robe, pulled me on top of him, and we had sex right there on the sofa. The only thing I can say is, the guy was right: I've never forgotten it. I never knew who took me there that night, but years later, watching a rerun of *Land of the Giants*, I thought it might have been Kurt Kasznar.

After the screening Rock came over and thanked me but didn't voice any opinion about the movie. I guess he thought that with our balls we might quote him in our ads. Come to think of it, we would have.

The other screening was given by Curtis Taylor, an old friend of Marvin's, and was attended by the hardcore gays in Los Angeles, including Fred Halsted, whom I met for the first time. I found him strange but intriguing. I liked him but didn't find him sensual. This first impression of him never changed over time.

After our New York success Shan Sayles was eager to do business with us and secured other play dates around the country. As paranoid as we were about the porn business, we had to trust someone in-the-know, someone with the information we needed, and we were prepared to pay for it. We weren't greedy and were willing to share the rewards, so we chose Shan.

Our publicity had taken on national proportions thanks to *After Dark*, *The Advocate*, and *Variety*, and it certainly helped our sales. We broke records every place we played, and according to *Variety*, *Boys* even outgrossed *A Clockwork Orange* during our opening week in Los Angeles.

From there the film went to the Nob Hill in San Francisco, the Follies in Washington, the Eros in Portland, the French Quarter in Houston, Le Salon in Washington, the North Station Cinema in Boston, and the Sampson Theater in Philadelphia. That was basically it as far as big gay theaters went. There were a few small theaters in other small towns, and eventually, we played them all.

Suddenly the movie was playing in a theater in Boston, and we had no prior knowledge of it. Someone had ripped off a print, made copies, and was renting it to small theaters all over the country. We had made money in the major cities and were happy about our success. Still, we were not adverse to threatening lawsuits over unauthorized exhibitions.

This was unheard of: homosexuals unafraid of the law, protecting their property instead of being victims. Pride made this possible; pride was everything at this time. Success, money, and the power that comes with it didn't hurt either.

I'd been kicking around another movie idea about a club called *Bijou*, a place of sexual freedom with a mystical, almost religious atmosphere. I wanted to make a film that was totally ambiguous, a film that each person, through his own experience, could make personal. Again it would be nonjudgmental and emphasize a prideful attitude toward sex. I went through several drafts, the first being about a female fashion model who witnesses another woman being hit by a car. Then, after discussions with Marvin and Peter, I decided I should continue in the gay genre and not risk going into the straight field. That settled, I wrote the shooting script in two days. It's truly autobiographical and psychologically rooted rather than physically factual. And it's all about where I was at that time: my beliefs, my insecurities, my ego, my sexuality, everything I was.

It's all done with mirrors!

From the introductory shot of the construction site and rock-laden trucks, we immediately see our hero. He finishes work, leaves the site, and witnesses an accident. A woman is hit by a car. Her purse flies through the air and lands at his feet. He picks it up, hides it in his coat, and leaves. At home he opens the purse and finds ordinary things: keys, a rosary, a snapshot of a sailor, some money, lipstick, an address book, and a ticket to a place called the Bijou. It's good for one night only, that evening at seven.

He picks up the tube of lipstick, opens it, smells it, tastes it, and gets excited thinking of the Playboy models who adorn the walls of his room. But images of the girl being hit by the car interrupt his masturbation, so he gets dressed and leaves for the Bijou.

Up a dank staircase to a loft on Prince Street, our hero enters a world of fantasy. In darkness, lit by star bursts of color and with fog swirling at his feet, he enters an empty sanctum. A sign lights up advising him to Remove Shoes. He complies. At another turn, a second sign commands Remove Clothes. He obliges. Lights direct his path into a room of mirrors. He meets himself at every turn and likes it. He's taken through a series of rooms—one with huge sea urchins, two stories tall, another with a huge Chamberlain foam sculpture.

He then comes across a form lying flat on the floor. The entire room is black except for the body lying ass up before him. He has become so excited that he mounts the almost lifeless form and takes his pleasure without any foreplay. After orgasm, the form rolls over, touches our hero on the chest, kisses him lightly on the lips, and leaves. There's no set, and everything is black. There are no walls, only a black void changed only by the addition of light. Everything becomes truly abstract in this context.

A multimedia, split-image film within a film begins. Our hero is introduced to all the men who will presently service him. They all undress seductively, and simultaneously, and all five images have orgasms. The show ends, and the mood changes. One by one, the men enter the room, and a ritualistic orgy ensues. Suddenly the orgy ends and our hero is alone. He retraces his steps, going back through the rooms. Once outside, he lights a cigarette. As he exhales the smoke, he smiles, and the film goes to a freeze-frame as the credits roll.

This freeze section is the only special effect done in the lab. All the other effects are in-camera, including the multimedia section. This saved us about $15,000 in lab costs, but the film still looked well-produced.

Bijou was an ambitious undertaking, and we had to find the right cast. Most of the people I called, when faced with an offer to be in a movie, admitted it was only a fantasy and that they couldn't bring themselves to do "it" on film. They all had curiosity but not courage. And it takes courage.

Knowing this, I decided to shoot two hundred feet of film for everyone I wanted to use. Each screen test had the same look. I filmed them against a black background to make the shots consistent. I sat each one in a leather-covered horn chair and told him to seduce the camera, to undress for it, to entice the person of his dreams to join him in pleasure. Each would end the test by masturbating to climax. All these tests would be shown in the film, overlapping each other, a sort of multimedia orgy. Since this was the first time in front of a camera for most of them, it was good practice and helped tremendously when we shot the movie.

A lot goes through your head when the camera is running and you're trying to keep an erection. I know, because Mike Ende, one of the men in the film, never came to orgasm, so I had to stand in for him. During filming, when the orgasm happened, I framed each person only from the chest to the knees, so it was easy for me to stand in for him without being recognized.

Peter got behind the camera. It took me more than an hour to get an erection and reach orgasm. That was with my lover behind the camera and no one else in the room. I had always respected my actors, but now that I had gone through what they had, I admired their ability to overcome their insecurities and all the obstacles involved. It's not an easy thing to do, but once you've done it, a sort of freedom comes with it. Get rid of fear and what's left? Nothing. Just a little space to fill with something pleasant.

Marvin returned from a West Coast vacation, and we were having dinner when he announced that he had found the perfect star for our new movie. He told us that one night in San Francisco, Harlan Crandall, who was the fur buyer at Magnin's, had sent a birthday present to Marvin's hotel. It was a scene right out of *Boys in the Band*, when Harold brings Cowboy, a hustler, to Michael's birthday party as a gift. People really started to do this after the play and movie became successful.

"When he walked in I was knocked out by how much he looked like Robert Redford," Marvin said. "I know the reviews said Cal looked like Redford, but this guy *really* does. He was almost six feet tall, and I swear his cock was a foot long. I'm so embarrassed. I don't believe I'm telling you this. Anyway, during the fucking, the headboard was banging against the wall so hard, I thought we might break through. Without missing a beat, he put a pillow between the bed and the wall to stop the noise. Now that's a gentleman!"

Peter and I were laughing uncontrollably when Marvin produced a snapshot of this guy, Bill Harrison. The picture was so bad, had I not trusted Marvin's taste, I might have passed on him.

When we got back to Marvin's, he got Bill on the phone. We talked for a minute or two about nothing, really. I immediately liked him and the way he sounded.

"Would you like to make this movie with us?" I asked.

"Sure, I guess so. Why not?"

"Good. That's done. I'll put Marvin back on, and we'll see you as soon as we get our shooting schedule together. You can discuss all the details with him." I handed the phone to Marvin and that was that. We had the star of our next movie.

I cast the movie mostly with New York men, but we hired one other guy from the West Coast named Bill Cable, who resembled a muscular Warren Beatty (which two reviewers happened to pick up on when the film opened). He was straight and gorgeous—exactly what I needed to counter the openly gay men.

He agreed to do the film, one day's work, only after I promised no one would lay a hand on him. He would just wander through the orgy scene and react to whatever he witnessed. Marvin thought I must be crazy. Imagine putting a naked straight man into a roomful of six hot men having sex with each other and telling him he was safe.

Bill arrived in New York, and just three months after opening *Boys*, we began shooting our second film.

The first day, we planned to shoot outside Lincoln Center. I had envisioned all sorts of shots using the Henry Moore sculpture in the reflecting pool, and the surrounding areas of the Metropolitan Opera House. We had city permits, and even had a traffic cop assigned to us for the actual shooting on the street in front of the Empire Hotel. We thought we had everything covered.

During the first setup a security guard rode up on a motor scooter and informed us that we could not film on Lincoln Center property without a permit. When we produced our papers he smugly informed us that we had to have permits issued by the center and that city of New York permits were no good on their property. I thanked him, we took a break, and while Marvin went to the center office to make arrangements, I spent the time rethinking my shots, just in case.

In less than an hour Marvin returned. "We can't shoot here, Wake, I'm sorry. They want an incredible amount of money, and there are a lot of other things involved, like special insurance. And they want to read the script. Let's just rethink the opening and do it tomorrow."

"No, we can go on, right now. We have city permits, and the cops are here, so let's just move the camera positions off Lincoln Center property and onto the city sidewalks. I'll use the zoom lens and we'll be fine. Peter and I adjusted a few camera setups, just in case."

We did it and even made up the lost time. All the day's work was finished on schedule, and by sundown we had all the exteriors for the opening of the movie.

The next morning we went to dress the set for the apartment scene. I promised not to tell—and for decades I've kept that promise—but Joe Allen let us use an empty apartment over his restaurant on 46th Street. It had been vacant for years and was just unkempt enough to work for me. It was so perfect that it took us no time to clean and dress the set.

Paul Jasmin (our art director and still photographer), Bill Eddy (the second cameraman), Marvin, Joe Nelson, Peter, and I were on the set that day. We were shooting the shower scene, the first time any of us would see Bill Harrison naked—that is, except Marvin. Well, when he took his dick out that first time, everyone on the set gasped out loud—just as the audience would later.

I worked hard to gain Bill's trust, and he was wonderful. He grasped things immediately and gave me exactly what I asked for. This would be important later when we filmed the procession through Bijou. He had to see and touch things that weren't going to be there, so he had to follow directions exactly. It was very much like filming against a blue screen. Again, it went off like clockwork. Another day, and we were ready to shoot the first sex scene.

In the film he comes across a naked body lying facedown. Without any foreplay, he kneels down on the bed and penetrates the almost motionless form from behind. I had shown Bill all the screen tests of the men in the film and let him choose his favorite. His pick was Bob Stubbs. Bob had a naturally well-developed body, a striking face, and long brown hair to his shoulder blades. I was glad he picked Bob. With his long hair, lying on his stomach, he could easily be mistaken for a woman by our hero as well as the audience.

I didn't want them to meet before the scene, so I kept them apart. In the scene I wanted no reaction from Bob Stubbs, nothing at all. I just wanted him to lie there, get fucked, and not move a muscle. Right before we were ready to shoot, I whispered to Bob that he was about to have an experience he'd never forget. That's all I told him, other than not to move. Not a hair! He hadn't even seen a picture of Bill, so again, he had to trust me. I also didn't tell him the size of the instrument that was about to invade his body. My luck held, and the scene went great. Bob later told me that it was the most erotic sex he had ever experienced. Just the few rules I imposed on the scene—not meeting him before, not knowing what he looked like, not being able to react at all, being totally passive—let him experience sex differently that night. At the end of the shoot, Bob remarked, "Wow, you really blew my mind tonight."

The Bijou interiors were shot entirely in my living room. We covered all the walls and floors with black felt and built a platform in the center, which we covered with black velvet.

In the orgy scene I wanted to portray as many types of lust as I could. I hired Bruce Shenton, a friend who was totally into bodybuilders. He never watched porno movies but instead real bodybuilding posing films. Even as I announced to the cast that no one was to touch Bill Cable, I knew Bruce would not be able to control himself. He'd break the rule!

I set up little situations like this without letting the actors in on them. After questioning them at the interviews and filming them, I knew how each would react in a given situation. I knew that Bruce would have to touch Cable, and I knew that when he did, Cable would reject him. The rejection would tell the observer a lot about both characters, and viewers would relate. Who hasn't desired someone unattainable and been rejected, and who hasn't been on the other end as well? I only had to stay aware during the orgy and catch these spontaneous moments on film.

After witnessing the multimedia show our hero closes his eyes and falls into a light, contented sleep. One by one the cast enters the set. Beforehand, each was given a certain body part to caress, kiss, or do to it whatever they chose.

Peter enters first, and I'd asked him to start by caressing Bill's inner thigh and to work his way to deep-throating him. After a few minutes Larry Lapedis enters, and I'd asked him to work on Bill's nipples and stomach and to slowly work his way down to meet and watch Peter as he's blowing Bill.

When Peter becomes aware of Larry being only inches away, he offers Bill's cock to him, and they share him as their lips meet around his cock. Mike Ende caresses Bill's neck and gently kisses his face, as Bob Stubbs massages and kisses his arms and hands. Bob had been unable to see Bill while he was getting fucked in the earlier scene. Now he seems not to be able to take his eyes or his hands off Bill's dick. He gives a look of disbelief that something that large not only penetrated him but also gave him so much pleasure.

I purposefully left no space for Bruce Shenton to fit in. I wanted him not to know where to go so that he would have to just observe the others for a while.

I kept them apart so that no one knew what Cable looked like. I knew that when Cable finally entered the set, Bruce would see him immediately and spend the rest of his time just watching him. I knew this would happen and it did. This is one of the most exciting moments in the film, and it is not even physically sexual. It is an example of pure lust enhanced by Bruce's insecurity in the face of all this masculine beauty. His lust finally wins out over his fear of rejection. A "just to touch him once" look shows all over his face.

When he finally does touch him, he does so fearfully, from behind. He kneels and runs his hand up the back of Cable's thigh to his ass. Cable walks away a few feet before turning to face Bruce, and using the whip I gave him as a prop, holds it over his head in an erotic pose—but it's a threat to Bruce not to touch him again. This ran the chance of being laughable, but because of its reality base and truth on Bruce's part, it became a voyeuristic glimpse at the face of lust and desire.

Cable was a tease at heart and knew exactly what he was doing. He enjoyed making himself desirable to everyone—men and women. His moment of truth comes later. Bill Harrison is lying on his back getting blown by one of the men. Cable sits at his head and expresses his envy by slowly wrapping the whip around Bill's neck. It's a hostile act, but Peter softens it, lowering himself between them to kiss and lick Bill's neck, whip and all.

Most of the little episodic moments I set up happened. The ones that didn't pan out turned into moments on their own and were usually just as good. This whole scene I called section B was the actual sex portion, and it was up to each person to participate as they desired. They way it was choreographed, it had a ritualistic, almost religious quality—exactly what I wanted. My sex with Peter was like that, and sex on psychedelics becomes spiritual every time.

When this section ended, each person was asked to masturbate to orgasm, and in the same order as they had entered the scene, they were to make an homage to Bill Harrison and exit.

Again, the choice of how they manifested this homage was theirs, and those choices were revealing as to what the person was actually feeling at that moment. Some chose to pause and just look down. Others knelt and kissed him on the body or touched his leg. Mike Ende summoned all his courage, sat down, and kissed him gently on the lips before reluctantly leaving. After they all exit, Bill, like most men after sex, falls into a peaceful sleep, and when he awakens he leaves, never to be the same. The only direction I had to give in the entire scene was to call out section A, then B, then C, and except for blowing a fuse, which is pretty normal in these kinds of shoots, everything went well.

I had put Bill Eddy, the second cameraman, behind a drop so that he was never seen. Paul Jasmin, who was taking stills, had another perch to get his shots, and I roamed freely about in the shadows.

Shooting was a totally pleasant experience for us all, and when I called it a wrap, everyone was surprised. The actors wanted to keep going, which is unusual for a shoot like this, but I knew I had what I wanted. I finished the filming but still had lots of work to do on the multimedia section. I couldn't wait to start editing. That's where you really make a movie.

Summer was approaching again, so Michael Maletta, Tom, Peter, and I took a house at the Pines on Fire Island. This time it was a large dramatic house overlooking the bay. It was a happy time, one of the best in my life so far. I was a minor celebrity among the fast-growing out-of-the-closet New York set and was financially comfortable for the first time in years.

All I had to do that summer was edit *Bijou* and get it ready for a late fall opening. We had finished our twenty-six week run of *Boys*, and Jack Deveau had taken over the theater for his first movie, *Left-Handed*. Jack and his lover, Bobby Alvarez, who had helped me with the final edit on *Boys*, had decided that if I could make a film, they could too. They were right, and *Left-Handed* became the first of many pornos that their company, Hand in Hand Productions, would produce. Jack booked Jay Brian's *Seven in a Barn* into the theater until his film was ready. So the 55th Street Playhouse was now known as a mecca for classy gay porn, and Frank Lee, who still had the lease on the theater, was getting rich.

Frank was a greedy man who wouldn't spend a penny to make building improvements. Jack mostly had trouble getting him to keep the air conditioner in good repair, which was essential in the unbearable New York summer heat.

Jack and Marvin had been friends since their early days in Montreal, and the competition between them had always been fierce. When *Boys* first opened, Marvin and Jack would talk every day about the business. In fact, Marvin talked to Jack and Shan Sayles more about the grosses and business matters than he did with me. That was fine because it left me more time to experiment, study film, and learn what the fuck I was doing.

When I was in the city, I'd edit in the early morning. It took a while for me to be able to look at hardcore sex over my morning coffee, but soon I became so detached that it became only a technical task. It still amazes me to this day how unsexy the material becomes when viewed as just a problem to be solved. I found the same thing true when shooting sex scenes. I've never to this day been aroused while filming. When I look through the camera lens, my ego fades and I almost disappear—so much so that I never directed the actors while shooting. I never said, "Move your arm. I can't see what you're doing." I just moved my position. I always used a shoulder harness for that reason. Mobility was key.

After a few good hours at the editing table, I'd pop by Marvin's office to catch up on any details that needed to be discussed, take in an afternoon movie, and then go home for dinner with Peter.

Peter had used the last name Fisk on *Boys*, not because he was ashamed but because Schneckenburger was much too clunky for marquees. Now he wanted to change his name legally to Fisk. I guess he'd become comfortable with his new role as a porno star. I told Marvin, and for his birthday that August, we legally changed his name to Peter Fisk.

Peter was also into tattoos. He had a small one on his left forearm done by Rick Herold in Los Angeles and had been toying with the idea of getting both his lower arms tattooed with pre-Columbian masks. I contacted my old friend, Lou Thomas, who owned Colt Studios, for the name of the best tattoo artist in town. The best, he said, was a guy from Chicago named Cliff Raven, who just happened to be in New York for a few days. We met, and the next week Peter set out for Chicago to spend three days getting tattooed from the elbows down.

The night before he was to go, we were lying in bed smoking a joint. He'd been quiet that evening, and I had no idea what could be bothering him. "Are you OK?" I asked. "You seem worried about something."

"I've been thinking all day. What if they turn you off? What if they look tacky and you don't find me attractive anymore?"

"You mean the tattoos?" I couldn't believe my ears.

"Yeah," he answered, still sounding troubled and insecure. "It could happen!" This wasn't like Peter. He was always so confident.

"Well," I said. "If that turns out to be the case, when we want to fuck, you can wear long white gloves."

I was trying to make light of the situation, but I realized he was deadly serious. "Look, Peter, I know you really want them. The designs look beautiful on paper, and if it turns out that I find them distasteful, we'll find a way, but that's not going to happen."

I put the joint in the ashtray and turned to face him. "I've never been happier. I love you more than I ever thought possible, and I can't imagine the rest of my life without you in it somewhere." He turned his face to me, and I kissed him. We made love that night like never before. There was such tenderness and a total lack of ego on both our parts. It was passionate yet so smooth. And it had a bittersweet quality. Funny, but I remember I was completely taken by the feeling—the kind of lovemaking I'd imagined one has before lovers part for a long time, all tenderness, only lightly dusted with lust. Like a soldier making love to his girl before going overseas. Quiet, passionate, and unrushed. It was memorable sex that night, even though we had been together for more than two years.

Peter returned from Chicago four days later with his arms bandaged from the elbows down. (Actually, he was wrapped in Pampers.) He had chosen three masks for each arm. They were incredibly beautiful, like no tattoos I'd ever seen. They changed Peter Schneckenburger into

Peter Fisk, porno star. He was now even more identifiable. He was now "the man with the tattooed arms."

Our summer on Fire Island continued with guests every week. Marvin came out for a week with his Labrador, Irving, one of the greatest dogs I've ever known. A few months later, when we formed a new company to sell eight-millimeter copies of our movies, we would name our company after him: Irving Inc.

Ed Parente came for a visit, even though he was spending the summer in the country with his sister, Marianne, and her husband, Raymond. Bill Harrison and his lover, John, also visited, spending most of their time watching young straight boys dig for clams in the bay. We had a large telescope on the deck, and they would take turns blowing each other while watching these boys. Whatever keeps you together!

That's what it was all about in the '70s. With everything in the open you minimized the chance of hurting your relationship. All the couples I knew at this time were not monogamous. It was a time of sexual freedom, and sex, though necessary to a relationship, was not limited to your lover. Sure, there were a lot of spats and quarrels. When insecurities crept in, jealousy followed closely behind; then sometimes chaos. Especially with all the drugs everyone was doing, no one was safe, and often the results were breakups. There were exceptions, I'm sure, but everyone I knew at this time was totally hedonistic.

I hated the social scene at the Pines. Peter and I loved to dance, but we preferred to go to the Ice Palace in Cherry Grove rather than to the White Party or whatever color party was being thrown. But since Michael was social, our entire house was usually invited to all the parties. Peter and I declined more often than not. Or if we went, we would leave after our acid or mescaline had kicked in. When we tripped, we liked to stay free. We didn't mind being around crowds but didn't want to socialize. We wanted to boogie, period. When we did go to a party, we usually had a good time, but we preferred public places where you didn't need an engraved invitation. We both objected to the snobbery in the Pines. Even though we liked the lifestyle there, we much preferred to be "trash in Cherry Grove."

One night after we had danced ourselves into a frenzy, as usual, we stopped by the Meat Rack on our way back to the Pines. We sometimes split up as we did at the baths, to chase our own fantasies until dawn. Tonight was one of those nights. I met someone there in the dark, among the bushes. It was a moonless night, so dark I couldn't even see the person at the tip of my nose. Still, we had incredible sex, and when we finished we walked out of the brambles and down to the water.

We soon realized we had known each other in Jacksonville. As a teenager I had danced with Harry Goodwin on the *Virginia Atter* television show, and the director was a young, handsome man named Don Erickson. He was masculine and had a sexy scar down one side of his face. I didn't even know he was gay.

Don and I were very compatible, and for the next few years we had sex together many times. It was always like coming home. We had no romantic interest—we both had lovers—but we enjoyed great sex together and had good times discussing film and theater. Don ranks among the best lovers in my life. Unfortunately, like so many other friends, we would lose touch. I don't even know if he's still alive. Why does that happen so often to me? Or does it happen to everyone?

The summer flew by. When I finished editing *Bijou*, Michael suggested we throw a big party and screen the movie. I'd just gotten an answer print from the lab, and it looked beautiful. So we held a party on a Saturday night in late August for about sixty people. The entire front of the house facing the bay was glass, so those who could not get into the main room sat on the deck and looked through the glass wall. People were not quite sure if the party would turn into an orgy, so there was a lot of tension in the air as well as big expectations.

We had joints all over the place and lots of sangria but no hard drugs or psychedelics. Some had chosen to take them before arriving, but, for a change, we didn't supply them.

During the screening there was little activity. When we had to change the reels on the projector, no one moved or spoke. There was a strange feeling in the air, so I hurried with the reels as fast as I could and started the second reel in less than a minute. The audience remained attentive and almost reverent.

When it was over there was silence in the room. They didn't clap, get up, chatter, or make small talk. A few thanked me and left, but most stayed and conversed quietly, in small groups, about the movie. There was no big exodus; they left gradually, a few at the time.

I was pleased but concerned that the reaction had been so subdued. I wanted it to move people. I wanted them to see themselves in all of the characters. I found out later that even though everyone liked it, most were disturbed by some of the images. Some got one thing out of a scene and others got another view entirely. But I got my desired result. I wanted it to be ambiguous. I wanted each person to believe it meant what he felt it meant. This became evident when we opened the film.

Each review summarized the film differently. Some saw the main character as a straight man. Others saw him as gay, some as a bisexual or a closet queer, while others saw him as a symbol of all men. But the reviews were all excellent, and several critics even called it a masterpiece. It went on to win Best Picture of 1972 from *Screw* magazine exactly one week after *Boys in the Sand* had the dubious honor of being awarded Worst Movie of the Year by the same publication. The only catch was that we had to share the best picture honor with *Deep Throat* because even though Al Goldstein admitted that *Bijou* was the superior film, he couldn't "honor faggotry over heterosexuality." This should give you an example of what the times were like. Even porno king Goldstein was publicly homophobic.

Bijou received more and more press, even getting mention in all the gossip columns. When asked by *Women's Wear Daily* what the favorite thing he did on his visit to New York was, Yves Saint Laurent said, "Seeing *Bijou. Extraodinaire!*"

Every week something nice happened like that. Marvin called one Sunday morning to tell me that in an interview in *The New York Times*, Andy Warhol, when asked why he stopped making movies like *My Hustler* and *Lonesome Cowboys*, answered, "After Wakefield Poole's movies, mine are unnecessary and a little naïve, don't you think?" All this from a man who didn't say much, period. All this publicity helped the box office, and we got a twenty-four-week run out of the movie.

Near the end of the run, I was contacted by the head of the psychology department at Columbia University. Let's call him Dr. Richards, as I don't remember his name. He explained to me that since the film opened, an unusual number of patients had spoken to their shrinks about *Bijou*. Some were disturbed, and some were haunted by the imagery. Subsequently, the film had been a major topic in psychologists' sessions with their homosexual patients and also among the doctors themselves. Dr. Richards asked if I would bring the film to his house on Easter Sunday to show to some of his friends and colleagues.

When I arrived I was greeted at the door by a woman in her seventies, who showed me into the living room, where there was a mixture of people: four psychiatrists, three male and one female. Also in the room were Dr. Richards, his wife, his thirteen-year-old son, fifteen-year-old daughter, and his mother, who had answered the door.

After a nice brunch Dr. Richards explained to his guests what they were about to see. He asked that everyone be prepared to say something at the end of the screening, explaining that he didn't want a review of the film but an indication of their feelings while watching it.

I started the projector. It was so quiet during the screening, you could hear people breathing or sometimes, as when Bill Harrison revealed his dick, not breathing. At the end of the film, they applauded politely. The two children thanked me and explained that they were going to meet friends in the park and started to leave. Dr. Richards asked for their comments.

The girl was a little embarrassed as she had never seen an erect penis before, much less one in the act of sex, but she was careful to point out that she was never grossed out. Her brother, on the other hand, found the film unsettling, particularly regarding the loneliness he perceived in the actors.

The other comments were much the same as others I had gotten in the last few months. The last one to speak was Dr. Richards's mother. "I want to thank Mr. Poole for enlarging my experience and improving my bridge game!" We all were puzzled. "In Philadelphia," she explained, "I play bridge with two gay men. Now that I know what they do in bed together, I can stop thinking about it and concentrate on my game."

We all had a good laugh. I packed up the film and projector and went home to Peter.

Barry Kinn

Gloria Grant as Delilah prepares for revenge on Samson in *Wakefield Poole's Bible* (1973).

Barry Kinn

Wakefield Poole (at camera) and Peter Fisk filming *Wakefield Poole's Bible*.

Chapter Ten

The Bible

New York City, 1972

I don't remember why we were willing to leave our fantastic seven-room apartment on 72nd Street. I think Peter and Marvin decided we needed a change, and before I knew it we were living on Second Street and Bowery. It was a great loft. We put in a new kitchen, bought a huge air conditioner and a washer and dryer, and finally I had an area solely for editing. Best of all, we now had all our art in one room. We had quite a collection of Warhols, Lichtensteins, Stellas, Dines, Oldenbergs, Rosenquists, and as many other pop artists as we could afford, all mixed in with African and pre-Colombian pieces. The room was impressive, a wonderful atmosphere in which to work and create.

I was working on an idea for my third movie, a straight film using some Bible stories from the Old Testament. I had gotten such a positive response from women's organizations about *Bijou* that I knew I could make a film that women as well as men could respond to. Women's lib organizations were beginning to show strength, and some of the more progressive ones had screened *Bijou* at special events and seminars. Basically, they wanted to show that all pornography was not degrading, that it was possible to make a film where tenderness and love were the norm, even if the actors' lifestyles weren't. They wanted to find some way to demand the same on women's behalf in straight films.

We also gave the film to the Council of Designers to show at their annual conference in Aspen. Every year, top designers and media people got together to discuss where fashion was heading and what was going to be hot for the coming year.

Brendan Gill, a critic at *The New Yorker*, gave a lecture, "The Life-Enhancing Qualities of the Blue Movie," using *Bijou* and *The Devil in Miss Jones* as his basis. I received a nice thank-you note, saying it was so successful, they showed the film again late at night for all who wanted a second viewing.

This acceptance from the "straight" world, and women in particular, was amazing. On the other hand, the government was getting aggressive as far as raiding and busting sex films—backlash after the brouhaha over the *Deep Throat* obscenity case.

I was a fervent Bible student as a child and loved all the stories. I went to Sunday school and church every week, and there are preachers on both sides of my family. Baptists and Episcopalians on my mother's side, and Lutherans on my father's. To this day I can still recite the books of the Bible in order. So I decided to tell three stories from the Old Testament from a woman's point of view. In the Bible most of the stories cast women negatively: Eve tempts Adam, Bathsheba seduces David, Delilah betrays Samson. I decided to tell these stories from the woman's perspective.

Eve eats the apple after having sex for the first time with Adam simply because, like so many people, sex made her hungry. Bathsheba seduces David, whom she catches spying on her, only after her husband ignores her and pays more attention to their maid. Delilah decides to do elaborate harm to Samson only after he kills one of her servants in a brawl in the marketplace.

I wanted to make this film with no dialogue but storied and staged to an entire musical composition: an adult *Fantasia*. Hans Boon, a good friend, worked for London Records at the time. His boss, Terry McEwen, was a fan of mine and arranged for me to use London recordings for the film's score. For a contribution to the Musicians Union pension fund, we were given permission to use what we wanted. This made the whole project possible.

I chose music to support each story, starting with Vivaldi for the creation, Albinoni for the Adam and Eve section, Faust ballet music for the comical David and Bathsheba section, and "The Scythian Suite" by

Prokofiev to underscore Delilah and Samson. I choreographed the film to music as I would a ballet.

Surrounding the three stories, I staged the creation leading into Adam's ascent from the dust, earth, and rocks, and concluded with a short scene of the annunciation with Gabriel and the Virgin Mary, played by ballet dancers Dennis Wayne and Bonnie Mathis.

Money was still pouring in as we had started to sell our movies on eight millimeter for home use. This was before videotape, and feature-length films weren't yet available for home use. We were the first to do features on eight millimeter, and the response was spectacular. We ran full-page ads in *After Dark* and *The Advocate* as well as smaller gay magazines and in *Screw*. We made more money here than we ever did with theatrical releases. People wanted to own the movies. Enclosed in each set was also a list of suggested music to be played along with the film.

We received many requests from famous people for 16-millimeter sound prints for their private collections. Bruce Williamson, film critic for *Playboy* magazine, obtained copies of *Bijou* and *Boys* for Hugh Hefner and Sammy Davis, Jr., and while he was appearing on Broadway, Sir John Gielgud came to Marvin's office to pick up eight-millimeter versions to take back to England. Even though we didn't—or rather, couldn't—send them to Europe, people arranged to have friends pick them up and carry them through customs. I found out a few years later that an eight-millimeter copy of *Boys* had actually played in a small theater in Berlin for more than two years. They had purchased the print for $99, showed it all that time, and we didn't make a penny off it. It did, though, help to establish an international reputation for the movie.

I met John Schlesinger! One afternoon when I stopped by Marvin's, there he was sitting in the office. He was staying in Michael Bennett's apartment across the hall and had dropped by for a drink. I was thrilled talking about film with him. He had just seen *Bijou* and was astonished that it was only my second film and I'd done so much of the work in camera. I was proud that someone I respected was giving something back to me. I was always starstruck and knowing some of them wanted to own something of mine was mind-blowing.

I loved hearing stories about their reaction to my movies. Harry Kraut, Leonard Bernstein's manager, told me one of my favorites. When my friend Tim Wernet introduced us, Harry said that one day Lennie had gotten a call from Jerry Robbins suggesting that he see *Boys in the Sand*. He said Jerry told Lennie, laughingly, "The music is good, and it even has a story!" I loved that.

Craig Zadan was writing his first book, *Sondheim and Company*, and he wanted an interview to discuss *Do I Hear a Waltz?* I didn't really want to stir up all those negative memories, but I accepted. It was my chance to be honest, even with myself, about the entire episode. I was. Later when the book was published, I received a signed copy with a note from Craig expressing his and Stephen's gratitude for my candor.

It must have been my time because I was prominent in another book that year. Kenneth Turan and Stephen Zito wrote *Sinema*, a book about porno films and the people who make them. I had a chapter, Cal had a chapter, and we were both in the chapter on gay films. They certainly were good to us.

About this time, my sister Pat decided to come out of the closet. She had three children and a wonderful husband who was a great father, whom she loved. But now she had a girlfriend, Joan, who was her neighbor. She had written letters to everyone she knew, including all our relatives, expressing her newly acknowledged sexuality and her desire to live her life honestly as a lesbian and a mother. That was brave, especially in the early '70s. As it turned out, her son, Billy, also came out. Now don't tell me we weren't all born gay. It has to run in the genes. This was obvious to me. I also had several cousins, all on my father's side, who were gay, and who, eventually, all came out of the closet. Even our next generation has a few gay individuals. I wasn't shocked at all to discover so many of my relatives were gay or lesbian. I remembered looking at our family tree from my father's side. The number of men and women who never married was staggering, but only one, a great-uncle, had always been referred to as "strange." There were so many limbs on the tree that just stopped. Funny thing about that family tree: It disappeared after my mother's death.

I began casting my Old Testament movie. I was a big fan of Charles Ludlam and his Ridiculous Theatrical Company from the beginning, so I wanted Charles and Lola Pashalinski to play David and Bathsheba.

It was to be a comedy segment, and I thought they would be great. We had several meetings, but in the end Charles wanted to control the segment, the design, the set, costumes, everything. It wasn't a clash of egos, just his way of protecting himself. It's what he did. Instead I decided to use an old friend, a Carol Haney dancer, Chelle Graham, better known as Georgina Spelvin of *The Devil in Miss Jones*.

Peter and I invited Georgina to dinner one night and gave her the script—or rather, a treatment—for her section. She excused herself and went into the bathroom, the only place in the loft with a door and some privacy, to read. When she returned she kissed me. "I'd love to do this," she said. "It's funny, and I don't even have to get 'double dicked'!" She was speaking of the famous scene in *Devil* when she takes it from both the front and behind. A difficult feat, indeed.

I asked John Horn, a neighbor from 72nd Street, to play David. John was a good actor, straight, handsome, and from what I understood, just in case we decided to shoot hardcore, he was really hung. After my divorce I had spent many hours smoking grass and discussing the state of the world with him. He was recently divorced too. I found him attractive, but I never made a pass. Although neither of us acknowledged it, when we were together the sexual tension was unbelievable. I knew he would be terrific.

He agreed to play the role, especially after he had heard that Georgina was going to play Bathsheba. He didn't want to risk hurting his career, so he became Nicholas Flammel, a name used in repertory companies when an actor of stature had to perform a minor role and didn't want to be listed in the program.

The name Georgina Spelvin was the female counterpart to that custom. Now I had them both in one segment. Robert Benes would play Uriah, and Nancy Wachter would play the handmaiden. Nancy was the hat-check girl at 21.

Paul Jasmin approached me several times to consider Candy Darling to play the Virgin Mary. She loved my movies and had heard from him what I was doing with this new film. It was a small part at the end of the movie, but she wanted it. To this day I'm sorry I didn't use her. Within a year Candy would die from cancer. I opted for Bonnie Mathais, a soloist with the American Ballet Theater, for the role, and

Dennis Wayne, who had his own dance company, to play the angel, because the scene was a sort of desert ballet.

For the role of Eve I selected a young redhead named Caprice Cosselle, and for Adam, Bo White got the part. Caprice had made several porno films, but she had a shyness and naïveté that were amazingly photogenic. A friend of Michael Maletta's, Braum van Zetten, was hired to play Samson. He was a masseur, a bodybuilder, and gorgeous, like Bill Cable in *Bijou*. For Delilah I selected Gloria Grant, a beautiful African-American waitress from Steak and Brew. We used to eat there often. I watched her move gracefully through the tables, so one day I just asked her. She said she'd talk to her old man (so much for women's lib), and he gave permission for her do the role.

Now we just had to find a location for Eden. Bill Boyd suggested the Virgin Islands because he had been a border guard there. Bill was amazing. He could do anything—build things, repair things, hang wallpaper. You name it, and he'd try it. And he was dependable. We went on a location scout.

We stayed at a small resort, Marina Cay, owned by an ex-football player and his wife. It was a sixteen-acre island not far from Virgin Gorda, the location of the world-famous Little Dick's Resort. I remember I laughed when Bill mentioned Virgin Gorda and Little Dick's in the same breath.

"How can it be wrong to shoot there with those two names?" I asked. The baths at Virgin Gorda were so primal looking, with enormous rocks emerging from the ocean. It was a perfect Eden.

This was the first section we decided to shoot. Peter, Bill, Bo, Caprice, Barry Kinn, a still photographer, and I set off for the Islands. While we were staying at Marina Cay, Hume Cronyn and Jessica Tandy anchored their boat in the channel and stayed at the resort awaiting the arrival of their son, who was also a filmmaker. Marina Cay was a very down-home place. Everyone had his own cottage, but we ate all our meals together in the center area of the main building. Hume and Jessica were so pleasant to us even after I told them we were shooting an X-rated version of the Bible. They asked many questions about pornography and even pitched the idea of my giving their son a job on the movie. Jessica was exceptionally nice to Caprice and spent a lot of time talking with her on those balmy evenings after dinner. There was no formal entertainment at the resort: no radios, no TV, no nothing. Only good food, beautiful scenery, and conversation.

I finally decided the movie was going to be R-rated. The mood of the country was still very much against hardcore films. *Deep Throat* was still in deep trouble, and the mere notion that I was going to do an X-rated version of the Bible was considered insane by some of my friends.

While we were away in the Virgin Islands, Marvin found a large garage on Mulberry Street in Little Italy for our studio. We spent our days scrubbing the cement floors to remove decades of excess oil, and we painted the entire place stark white. After two weeks we were ready to shoot our Samson and Delilah scenes. Peter and I had designed the sets using natural 2-by-4 planks. We'd seen an art exhibit of stacked wooden planks at the OK Harris Gallery. Depending on how you laid them, you could create many different structures, and no nailing was required. We decided to use the 2-by-4s since we could use the lumber to construct the set for David and Bathsheba when we were finished with the segment.

We hired Stanley Simmons as costume designer. Frankie Welch, one of Richard Avedon's favorite makeup men, came on board to do hair and makeup. Gene Kelton, who'd lit *Bijou*, was asked to repeat his good job on this project. The whole enterprise was staffed with friends. What better way to work? Joe Nelson, who was choreographing the Bathsheba scene, remarked, "This is going to be the most expensive home movie ever made."

I decided Delilah would have two midget servants, one male, one female, along with a number of muscular men to do her bidding. I wanted to show Samson as a bully, a guiltless brute. When he catches Delilah's servant trying to steal the knife strapped to his side, he picks him up by the throat and strangles him—the motivation for Delilah's revenge.

When I interviewed for the midgets, I learned a few good lessons. They like to be called little people, not midgets or dwarfs, and usually they're the most "together" people you'll ever find. They have to put up with so much discrimination from the start of their lives that by the time they're adults, they're either really fucked-up or very real people. Willie and Kathy were in the latter category. Fantastic people.

On the first day we shot the bazaar scene. For the set we used white upholstery rope with white sheer rayon fabric mounted on crossed 2-by-4s to create walls. We covered the floor entirely with kitty litter to resemble sand, so everything was either white or ecru. Color would appear only in the costumes. For the extras, Stanley created beautiful purdah costumes from assorted pastel Italian fortuni. Delilah wore a skintight white dress with a scarlet floor-length cape. It was a nice palette and looked striking on film.

We arranged for Marvin Soloway to make dailies for us to view, and we were impressed with the first rushes. Gloria looked gorgeous, as did Braum. After we viewed the rushes we prepared to do the day's schedule.

But about midday, I was frustrated. Gloria was falling all over herself and couldn't kneel down without stumbling. After several bad takes and three hours of disaster, I broke for lunch. I went over and sat in the corner by myself with a cup of coffee and about ten cigarettes. Finally, it dawned on me. When I filmed I didn't shoot at the normal rate of twenty-four frames a second, the speed necessary when synching dialogue with picture.

Since there was no dialogue, I upped the count to thirty frames a second. This takes the edge off any harsh movement. It's not really slow motion, but it makes all movement attractive.

After seeing themselves on film the first time, Gloria and Braum kept trying to accomplish that look without the aid of the camera. They thought they really moved that way. I explained to them that it wasn't possible to move that way naturally, that they should just do the movement and the action and let the camera take care of the rest. They both said, "Yes, that's exactly what we were doing, trying to make it pretty." Once they understood the difference we sailed through the rest of the day.

Peter and I argued a lot about artistic choices. We argued our points until we both came to a mutual decision without anyone winning, losing, or keeping score. We finished the segment after six days of shooting, and the raw footage was spectacular.

For the next ten days we went about building the set for Bathsheba's section and buying the props we needed. Bill did an exceptional job, right down to the fountain, which was big enough for Bathsheba, a huge goldfish, and the water lilies.

I had decided not to edit any of the film until the shooting was complete. We still had to go to Arizona to film the last section. It was going to be very simple. The Virgin Mary would fetch water from an oasis in the desert and start her journey home. She sees an angel, becomes frightened, drops her urn of water, and runs across the dunes, chased by the angel Gabriel. His wings were suggested by sixteen-foot plastic poles extended from his own arms. When she accidentally falls and covers her face in terror, he touches her with the rods. She turns to face him, and a shimmering light covers her as she lies back in ecstasy. We dissolve to a neon sign that reads: BETHLEHEM INN, NO VACANCY. The credits roll, end of movie.

Despite the heat, our shoot in Yuma, Ariz., went well. We had to film early in the morning to avoid the hot sand. By noon we were done for the day, and after two days we were finished. Bonnie rejoined the American Ballet Theater on tour, and Dennis went to Los Angeles.

Peter, Joe, and I drove from Yuma to Disneyland in Anaheim, Calif., while Marvin flew back to New York with the exposed footage. We had finished all the major photography, so we decided to take a little vacation before editing. We spent two days at Disneyland on acid. It's surreal anyway, but the acid enhances everything: the rides, the visuals, and the food.

But on the way there, Peter and I had an argument like no other. He complained that we hadn't done sufficient filming on the last section and that we were going to come up short once the editing began. He didn't let up. What could we do about it now? It was done. I knew I had what I wanted, but Peter wasn't convinced. I was so distressed when we arrived in Laguna that I went to bed at six P.M. without dinner, and Peter bunked with Joe.

We'd had our first unresolved dispute. Unresolved disputes lead to more trouble, but I thought that once he viewed the footage, he'd realize there was enough and that would be the end of it. I managed to push all this to the back of my mind and enjoy the rest of the vacation. This was a big mistake!

After two days we piled into the car and took off for the Los Angeles airport. Joe and I boarded the plane for New York, and Peter took a flight to San Francisco. He was going to drop off a print of *Bijou* for exhibition at the Nob Hill Theater. We never sent the prints through the mail; instead, we hand-delivered them to circumnavigate the obscenity laws. Carrying them was much safer than using a delivery service or the U.S. mail.

When Peter returned the following week, we began editing. By late January we had our rough cut finished.

Randy Fields and his girlfriend, Jane, both friends and neighbors of Marvin's, were extras in the Samson and Delilah section. Randy also worked for Joseph E. Levine in his New York office. After seeing the rushes he encouraged us by saying that if the film turned out to be as good as the rushes, he should be able to get us a distribution deal with Embassy Films.

This encouraged us that we had made the right decision to make an R-rated movie. We knew we had to prepare the audience to accept something else from Georgina and from me. A deal with a major company such as Embassy would accomplish that. This casual remark by Randy would influence all the decisions we would make in the future concerning the film.

We decided to blow up the film to a 35-millimeter negative. All the prints would be 35 millimeter, the format we would need to play in regular theaters. Also, the film was a tribute to silent movies. Wide screen was the rage in the early '70s, but I wanted the movie screened in the original format of early movies.

We asked David Byrd to do the poster for the film. I knew if anyone could handle the problem of letting people know what they were going to see, it would be him. David came up with the perfect concept: He drew the Virgin Mary, looking like Kate Smith in a '30s dress, holding a baby in swaddling clothes in her arms. They both wear sunglasses, and she seems to be truckin' (a famous jitterbug step). The only reference to their identity is the halos over their heads. There was no doubt, seeing this poster, that this film would be humorous and out of the ordinary. We decided to call it *Wakefield Poole's Bible*.

Marvin asked that I do a screening for Michael Bennett and Bob Avian before locking in the final cut. I agreed, since we were both eager to hear their reactions. When it was over neither had much to say. Michael did suggest that I show it to Larry Cohen, a friend of his and a film critic and screenwriter. He said Larry would have a better idea of what we had. I was disappointed that Michael didn't have more to say.

When he had asked my opinion in the past, I hadn't hesitated to give it honestly. I expected the same from him and from Bob. That's what friends are suppose to do: tell the truth. Anyway, I set up the screening for Larry. When it was done he looked at me and said, "Wakefield, you should direct operas! The imagery you've created is so operatic, the color, the photography!" He went on, but I had stopped listening. He was no longer talking about my film or what he had seen. He was talking about another career entirely. I knew then that he didn't like it much and was trying to find something to say before fleeing. I felt abandoned by my friends. No one had said anything constructive, and not one of them said, "Wow, Wake, did you fuck up!" or "You should have made it hardcore" or even "You should stick with gay movies." Nothing.

From that day on Marvin began to pull in the purse strings. I knew my friends must have said things to him that they didn't say to me. But we plunged ahead.

We got tremendous play in the straight magazines as our still photos were spectacular. *Penthouse*, *Viva*, *Bachelor*, and *After Dark* all did layouts of at least five pages. All this occurred after one press screening in our loft. Everyone in attendance was a writer or critic for sexually explicit magazines, except for Tennessee Williams, who came with Billy Barnes and Paul Jasmin. The magazine people truly liked the film, and their articles reflected their pleasure. One critic stated that "a copy of the film should replace the Gideon Bible in hotel rooms across the nation." We still didn't have a distributor, but we were getting press.

In the middle of all this, Peter began a campaign to move to the West Coast. He discussed it with Marvin, and even while trying to get the film into distribution, we were considering leaving New York. Marvin spoke to Shan Sayles about the possibility of setting up offices there. We were gathering information so that when we opened this movie, we could come to some decision about whether to stay.

We finished the film without any expert advice as to content or how to market it. Randy offered us the screening room at Embassy Pictures to view the 35-millimeter print for the first time. We wanted to see what the finished film looked like in a real theater environment. While we were still in the first reel, "Adam and Eve," who should open the door to the screening room but Mr. Joseph E. Levine. He looked at the screen for exactly five seconds, no more, and said to Randy, "Is this ours?"

"No," Randy answered as he started to explain who we were.

"Good!" he responded, cutting Randy off mid-sentence as he pushed open the door and left. Randy didn't know what to say; he was so embarrassed. I was stunned, and Peter was angry. I asked Randy to stop the film, as I had no interest in seeing the rest. I wanted honesty but only after someone had seen the movie. How could anyone voice an opinion after five seconds? Waiting for the projectionist to rewind and pack up the print was murder. We just sat there in that bright-red projection room in total silence. I remember thinking, *What an ugly shade of red and so much of it.*

Mrs. Levine had decorated the offices, so this was my way of rationalizing that Mr. Joseph E. Levine and his wife had no taste. I had counted on making a deal with Avco Embassy and knew Randy would never get Levine to look at the film now. We picked up our print and left. I was really depressed.

We started pushing the picture to independent theaters in New York, including Cinema Five, the Plaza, Ruggoff Films, and art houses on Third Avenue. No one was willing to take the film, even on a four-wall deal. We had this movie that cost us more than $100,000, and no one wanted it. That is, no one except Jack DeVeau, who ran the Lincoln Art Theater on 57th Street as a gay house, having taken over the lease from none other than Joseph E. Levine. In fact, the theater had been decorated by Mrs. Levine, and now it was showing hardcore gay films, so we went with it. Actually, we had no choice. Most gay theaters only had 16-millimeter projectors but Lincoln Art had both.

We held our press screenings, and the advance reviews were excellent. That heartened us a little. We submitted the film to the MPAA for a rating, which cost us three hundred fifty dollars. There's no hardcore sex in the film, lots of nudity, and some frontal shots of Adam but not an erection in the lot. When I got the call from the board members, they said that even though they enjoyed the film and appreciated what I was trying to do, they had no choice other than to award us an X rating.

Now I knew we were in trouble. We were opening in a hardcore house, and the movie was made by me and starred Georgina Spelvin. The film was called *The Bible*, and now we had an X rating. People would be disappointed because they would all expect hardcore. It was now up to David's poster to let them in on what they were about to see. Our first ad appeared in the Sunday *New York Times*, and at the bottom was the MPAA seal with an X rating. It also read OPENS WEDNESDAY.

The following Monday we got a call from our advertising agency saying the *Times* would no longer run our ad. They'd received hundreds of calls protesting it, saying it was sinful to depict the Virgin in such a way.

"Take out the halos," they suggested. We did. Then the next day, "Take off the shades." We did. Then finally, "Do a new ad! This one is unacceptable." Two days later, we got a call from Jack Valenti, president of the MPAA.

"We do not recognize an X rating, and therefore, you must remove our logo from your ads." He insisted, even over my protest that we had paid a fee and received an X rating from his organization. He suggested that we could remove the implied fellatio in the Samson and Delilah scene, cut the frontal nude shots of Bo White, cut a shot of David on top of Bathsheba (though both are fully dressed), and submit the film for a new rating. Of course, another three hundred fifty dollars should accompany the request. It was just too much. This was on the opening day of the movie.

If you ever have any desire to make a religious film other than the DeMille type, don't. Every filmmaker who tries to do something different asks for trouble. *Greaser's Palace* and *The Last Temptation of Christ* come to mind. People are not broad-minded, and they have no sense of humor where religion is concerned. It's a shame. Humor is a necessary element to life, even though it's not so evident in the good book.

We pulled the film during its second week. It was making expenses, but we had no advertising campaign and people didn't know what to expect. Reviews were favorable, but most never appeared in print. Some of my friends didn't even know we'd opened. Once the protest started over the poster, most papers wouldn't print anything about the movie. The only coverage we got in the dailies appeared in the Letters to the Editor section of the *Times*, and a few items of outrage over the poster showed up too.

Now I had my first failure to deal with, and an expensive one at that. Most of the profits from the first two movies were used to finance this film. Even so, we proceeded with our plans to move to the West Coast. I was still pushing for Los Angeles. Shan Sayles was there if we needed something, and he was willing to get involved with production.

Peter, on the other hand, wanted us in San Francisco. He'd been there recently, on another trip when he took a print of *The Bible* to Carmel to show to Shan. Shan loved the movie and wanted to open it in his gay houses in San Francisco and Los Angeles, but I didn't think gay audiences would accept a softcore movie, much less a straight one.

He did a sneak preview, and the cards were mixed. Most wanted hardcore and wanted to know why I'd chosen to do a straight movie. Marvin and I decided to give up. We gave the distribution to Joe Green, who booked mostly drive-ins and small theaters in the South and Southwest. We never made our money back. It was a total financial disaster.

I don't remember how or when we finally decided, but we were moving to San Francisco. Since I really didn't care where we lived, I gave in to Peter's wish. Our plan was to go out, find a place to live, and within the year Marvin would follow.

We threw a little party at our loft before we left. We were only taking our records, books, and art, so we gave away everything else. We said good-bye to all our friends, swearing to keep in touch, as friends always do. Marvin and Joe drove us to the airport. I don't remember the good-byes at all.

In a flash, Peter and I were on a plane, going to a new city, a new life, and starting a new adventure. As soon as we were in the air, I leaned over to Peter and whispered, "I'm a little scared. I just realized I don't have any keys. I don't have a key to anything. I don't belong anywhere."

Peter managed to squeeze my hand. He was not much of a flier, so he was concentrating on keeping his breakfast down. I put my head back on the pillow and closed my eyes. We had each other, and that, I thought, would be enough.

Chapter Eleven

Paul

San Francisco, 1974

After just two days we found an apartment and bought a Volkswagen van, thanks to stopping by Castro Camera to say hello to Harvey Milk. He and Scott, his lover, had been friends of Peter's in New York. One of his customers had just told him about a place for rent up the street. It was the bottom right corner of a huge Victorian building—a two-bedroom apartment with a living room-parlor and a huge kitchen. There was also a small room that could be used for editing. We signed a lease that afternoon. I didn't know it, but Castro Street was the Mecca of the gay community in San Francisco. It was like living on Christopher Street in Greenwich Village—it was the gay ghetto.

The first thing we did was buy ferns to hang in our sunroom at the back of the house. It was right off the kitchen and was where we'd end up spending most of our time. We hung dozens of crystals from the ceiling, and in the afternoon until the sun went down, they reflected their prisms all around. It was just a room, mostly windows, with banquette seating around a large table. We hadn't brought any furniture with us, only our art and a few special things, so the built-in table became the center of our world. All our art went into a closet.

We didn't drink, so we met people at cafés, the Laundromat, and, of course, the baths. People recognized Peter instantly, but as soon as I introduced myself as Wakefield, they would say, "Wakefield Poole? You've got to be kidding!" Or, "I don't believe you." I don't know what their expectations were, but I wasn't it. Many times, I'd have to show my driver's license to prove it.

Peter and I were minor celebrities—actually, big fishes in a little pond, the pond being gay people, and even then, only gay people who were into pornography. We were known among our pornographic peers, so to speak, or so I thought. Then, for the first time, I realized that almost every gay man in America, who'd had the opportunity, had seen *Boys in the Sand*. It had become a classic, and I had become a champion of gay rights and sexual freedom. I heard many times, over the years, how much it changed people's lives. How it made them less afraid the first time they went out with a man. How it made them feel less guilty about their sexual desires. And in some cases, how it made them proud.

In New York I'd known most of my friends before I made movies, so there wasn't a big change when the movie came out. I wasn't just Wakefield Poole, the pornographer. I was a little more complex. I came with a lot more baggage.

In San Francisco everyone we met related to us as gay, successful, sex-loving, hedonistic pornographers. It's something I never got used to, living up to the reputation of Dirty Poole. I didn't fit the mold, really.

Life was pretty good for us. We slept late, ate well, smoked good pot, and went to the baths a lot. As in New York, each bathhouse catered to a certain clientele. The Club Baths clientele primarily consisted of young college or go-go boy types as well as the older men they attract. The Rich Street Baths attracted the young, hippie, pot-smoking variety. The Sutro got mostly bisexual men since it was coed. Another, at the Embarcadero, I favored because of the transient clientele. Lastly, there was the Barracks, where the customers did heavy drugs and heavy things. I liked the Barracks in small doses, but Peter favored it. Consequently, we saw less and less of each other.

At the Gay Day parade, where I was shooting a short documentary, I realized how much Peter and I were growing apart. At Peter's suggestion we parked the van and met Harvey on the corner. He was selling film from a pushcart and said his location would provide a nice vantage point. We decided he was right.

When we came back later to shoot, Scott, Harvey's lover, was behind the cart selling film to a young red-haired man. Harvey came over to help us through the crowd. I was attaching the camera to the shoulder harness when I looked up to see Peter talking to the redhead. Harvey took the camera case and, putting it in his cart to keep for me, introduced me to Rusty.

I peeked around the camera and offered him my hand.

"Rusty works at the Barracks, Wake," Peter said.

"Really, how do you get any work done?" I laughed.

"If it's OK, Rusty's going to hang out with us for a while," Peter said.

"Great, he can help run interference." I turned to Rusty. "Just keep me from walking into people!" We laughed, and as if on cue, the parade began.

It was a terrific day, a wonderful parade, and different from any I'd ever seen. We ended up, thousands of us, dancing in front of city hall until the sun went down. Rusty lived only a few blocks away, so we stopped by his apartment to feed his birds. I thought they'd be in a cage. Surprise. Three baby finches and their mother were nesting in Rusty's chandelier. He'd throw seed onto the carpet and the mother bird would come down, pick it out of the rug, and then take it back to the nest. Rusty, like us, had very little furniture.

After dinner Peter and Rusty decided to make a night of it. It was a festive time, and they wanted to party. They asked me along, but I was too tired to spend the night walking the halls of the baths. I declined, so they dropped me home and took off for the Barracks.

I had noticed that Rusty and Peter were having a good time together. When you have a camera hanging on you, and your eye is stuck looking through a lens, you're pretty much left on your own. So they talked with each other. A month later I found a nightstick under the seat of my van with Rusty's name carved into it. You might say that a blow from a nightstick woke me up. They were having an affair and had been even before our move out here.

One afternoon when Peter came home, I was sitting in the sunroom smoking a joint. I hadn't seen him for two days. He was crashing. He poured himself a cup of coffee and joined me.

"Peter, I'm not very happy. I don't see you much, and when I do you're usually crashing. Other than having an occasional meal, we don't do anything together."

He didn't speak. He just looked down at his cup. I wanted him to tell me he loved me, but in my heart I knew he couldn't.

I was already history. Peter was still here because he couldn't just walk out with nothing. He had invested too much, and he hadn't found a way to resolve his problem. He couldn't just ask for his share. That was too straightforward. I had to do it for him.

"Peter, I know you don't want to be here anymore. You want to be with Rusty."

Tears formed in the corners of his eyes as I fought to hold my emotions in check.

"It's OK," I said calmly. "I know you're worried about...things...all the art we have together and what you're going to have to show for the last six years. Well, before any of our hurt turns to hate, let's split everything right down the middle."

Tears flowed from his eyes as he took me in his arms. Then, as he started to tell me how sorry he was, he began to sob—I think more out of relief than sadness.

After holding each other for a while, we pulled ourselves together, then listed everything we had in one column or the other. When we were finished I gave him a list and said, "I once told you I couldn't imagine the rest of my life without you in it. I still feel that way. Now go. We'll move your things later."

He hugged me. Then he got up and walked out of the house. Suddenly I realized I'd just played out the last scene of my favorite opera, *Der Rosenkavalier*. At the end, the Marschallin gives her lover away to a younger rival and bows out gracefully. That's just what I'd done, so I got stoned, put on my favorite recording of the opera, and indulged—no, wallowed—in self-pity for the rest of the night. It's not every day Richard Strauss serves as background music for a real-life drama.

A few days later Marvin called. Our cash flow was dangerously low, and he wanted us to do another movie as soon as possible, but it had to be made on a shoestring. Money from the mail-order business wasn't coming in fast enough, and *The Bible* had been a financial disaster.

After much discussion it was decided that I should make a film exclusively for mail order, which would cut down the budget since we wouldn't have the expense of scoring the picture or the hassle of distributing. Just make the movie, send a brochure to our mailing list (which had become extensive), and wait for the money to come in. That was the plan.

When I spoke with Peter about starting pre-production, he told me he didn't want anything more to do with making movies. I had lost more than a lover when we decided to part. Peter did make one concession. He would star in one segment of the new film.

"I owe you that much," he said. He would, however, have nothing to do with the production. That would have to be my department, and this would be his last appearance on film.

I started to think about what kind of movie I wanted to make. It would have to be simple and made as cheaply as possible. I was going to have to make it on the same budget I had for *Boys*: $4,000.

In the middle of all this, Hans Boon arrived from New York to attend the opening of the San Francisco Opera. We had invited him to stay with us, and it wasn't until he arrived that he learned Peter and I were no longer together. We had plans to attend the opening together, to hear Pilar Lorengar sing the role of Desdemona in *Otello*. We'd heard her on many occasions in New York and were both fans and friends. Hans got an extra ticket so that Rusty could join us. Rusty had never been to the theater or an opera. He was speechless. At the curtain, we all rushed to the footlights to cheer Pilar. Hans was dressed to the nines, while Peter, Rusty, and I wore jeans and leather jackets. When we went backstage to see Pilar, Rusty was flabbergasted. His naïveté was obvious and at the same time endearing.

When we got home Hans and I spoke briefly about the breakup. I was glad he didn't press me for details. I didn't have any. One moment we were together, the next we weren't.

After Hans returned to New York, I began to feel lonely. I saw Peter and Rusty once or twice a week. Here I was in a new city, with no lover, no friends, and no creative support. I should have packed my bags and gone back to New York, but I was too proud. I had to turn this whole experience around.

I began to spend a lot of time with my neighbors on Castro, especially Bruce Fergason, an aspiring filmmaker who lived upstairs. He'd come down with a little cocaine and we'd get high, then spend the rest of the night talking about film. Up until now I hadn't done a lot of coke because it made me too hyper. Now it was just what the doctor ordered. So I began to do more. In a few weeks I asked Bruce to introduce me to his supplier, George. In general, addicts and dealers use only first names, so now I was entering a new "first name only" phase. A new period of my life was beginning: I was on my way to becoming an addict.

I had always based my movies on my life experiences, so I decided to do a film about what I'd just experienced: moving. Three segments would again make up the basis of the film. "House for Rent," "Room for Rent," and "Apartment for Rent." It would focus on not only physically moving into a place but also moving in new directions sexually.

Cal was doing a play in Los Angeles, so I called about the new movie. He once said that I need only to call and ask and he'd do anything for me. He was true to his word, even helping me acquire the house I wanted to use for his segment, a beautiful home in Beverly Hills, with a swimming pool, tennis court, greenhouse, and gardens.

Lou Thomas of Colt Studios helped me land one of his models, Val Martin, to star with Cal. He was definitely into S/M and quite visibly a top. Naturally, he turned Cal on.

It was a simple idea. Cal arrives to check out a house for sale. He wanders around, imagining Val and himself in every situation: playing tennis, swimming in the pool, and ending with sex on the lawn. The segment went well with one exception. Val was into fisting, which was becoming more and more popular, but Cal wasn't about to let that happen on film. Not yet, anyway. There's an indication and an effort on their part to make that happen, which I put into the film, but it was never accomplished. Cal's struggle to let it happen or should I say, to not let it happen, is the main action of the segment. His desire and resistance to Val's urges gave me the tension I needed. It became a competition between Cal and Casey.

A few months after the film was released, Chanel, one of the top fragrance houses in the world, copied action right out of this segment, shot for shot, in a commercial. Cal at one point imagines Val at the opposite end of the pool. Cal dives into the pool, and swims under water to the edge of the pool where Val is sitting in a deck chair. Then he rises out of the water holding on to the edge of the pool. It was a strong sexual image, and it worked. Chanel still uses that image after more than thirty years.

Burt Edwards, one of the hot new models on the porn scene at the time, was a sexual animal and new to life as a porno star. He was Canadian, not too experienced, and still had some naïveté. I paired him with an aspiring actor, Curt Gerard, whom I'd met through Paul Jasmin. Paul was always helpful to me, and he knew people on the cutting edge willing to take chances. I shot them in a motel on Sunset Boulevard. Budgetwise, I was doing all right. I didn't have to pay for the house, and I only had to pay for the motel room for three days. The third section didn't cost me anything since I shot it in my apartment.

I had planned for Peter's section to have a lot of heavy imagery. A young man would come to rent an apartment. Finding no one there and the door ajar, he goes in. Entering the living room, he finds a straightback chair and sits for a moment. Double doors dividing the room then open to reveal a full-size drawing of Peter, naked, arms crossed, showing his tattoos. The young man rises, walks to the drawing, touches it, and as if by magic, Peter becomes real. The sex scene follows. At the end, the man is once again in his chair and the doors are closed. Did he imagine what transpired or did it really happen? This was the little drama I had planned, and Peter added his own drama to the action. This section remains one of my favorites.

Peter introduced me to Terry Weekly, whom he had picked to star with him. He wasn't plain, but he didn't show himself to his best advantage. His self-esteem was also obviously low. I was struck by his innocence, as he reminded me a lot of myself.

When we spoke I ended by telling him my standard truth about participating in porno films: "Your life will never be the same. You're hot, and you'll see that on film. You'll never again be able to use your appearance as an excuse for not getting who you want."

We shot the segment, and I was prepared for everything and anything. Peter didn't disappoint me. Although he didn't plan to, he acted out of love, in homage to our six years together. He was, at that moment, everything I'd loved about him.

This segment turned out to be, in my estimation, one of the best examples of S/M relationships on film. Terry totally submits to Peter's desires. His face shows total trust, even when Peter shaves his head and they get into heavy fisting. But the outstanding thing about the segment is the love that shows through all these usually sordid activities. Visual proof that love is trust, that love can be of the moment, that all love is not eternal. In all its abrasiveness, this segment is quite beautiful.

I edited the section, and invited Terry and Peter over to see the results. After they watched it Terry hugged Peter, and with tears running down his cheeks, he said. "My God, I *am* hot! I really am!" He was overwhelmed, and Peter too was pleased.

I'd never gotten into fisting, finding it nonsexual and too mental. Hell, it was all mental. On the one hand, it's physically uncomfortable, and on the other, the arm is not a sensitive appendage. It receives no pleasure and can't have an orgasm. Still, Peter was able to show me his fascination with this new form of sexual expression, and I was able to catch his enthusiasm on film.

Moving turned out so well that after viewing the finished product, we put on a music track and opened it in theaters. We didn't promote this movie as we had the others; we just opened with a moderate advertising budget and let it play. Our mail orders were doing great, and this was all gravy.

Ed Parente came to visit and stayed for a few months, so I wasn't as lonely. But I still missed New York. If it hadn't been for my pride, I would have returned after we'd broken up, but it never was a choice. I had San Francisco, some celebrity status, money coming in, and Peter was close by. That was enough for now. And, oh, yes, now I had cocaine.

I happened to look in the paper one day and saw that *Boys* and *Bijou* were playing at a local porno theater. It wasn't the Nob Hill Theater, where our movies generally played, but a cheap little theater in the Tenderloin. I got on the phone to see if Marvin had booked the theater. He hadn't, and we decided to proceed legally, to get back our ripped-off prints and to stop the exhibition. Elliot Lefcowitz, our lawyer in New York, recommended that I contact a colleague, Mel Honowitz.

Mel immediately got a sheriff to serve the theater with papers demanding our prints and their receipts, and that they refrain from showing the picture. We got our prints back immediately as well as a few hundred dollars. Mel said we might sue for damages later because the ripped-off prints were so poor in quality that they damaged our reputation. It was nice to fight back and not be the victim of thieves and rip-off artists. It takes balls to steal someone's film and exhibit it—and they not only exhibited it but also advertised it.

Well, it takes bigger balls to sue someone for doing it. We're talking legalities about a business that wasn't really legal. It was scary, but we won, and I was grateful for this small victory. Lawyers on both sides planned to meet in a few weeks to discuss a further settlement.

Ed had been seeing Michael Monroe, a waiter who worked on Amtrak trains to Chicago and back. He was six foot two, stocky, butch looking, and nice, but he kept trying to fix me up with a friend of his, saying the guy was perfect for me. I resisted; I wasn't ready. Finally, he told me he had invited him to my place for dinner the next evening. I always hated blind dates, disliking the idea that someone else's taste is brought into the formula. How could anyone know what I wanted from a relationship when even I didn't know? Still, I agreed to cook dinner and meet the guy.

The night arrived. I chose a dish that would keep me busy in the kitchen so that I wouldn't have to worry about much until after the meal. I could just get up and go to the stove anytime I felt uncomfortable. This was my plan.

Ed had decorated the sunporch with flowers and about a hundred votive candles. Those, along with the crystals and the ferns, made the place quite beautiful yet informal. Ed was lighting the last candle when the doorbell rang. I heard Michael answer the door, some muttering, and some light laughter, followed by footsteps coming down the hall.

Michael entered, followed by a strangely attractive young man dressed in torn jeans, a plaid shirt, leather jacket, and a Cub Scout cap. He was about five foot seven, with black hair and a Fu Manchu mustache. The cap, along with the mustache, accentuated his man-child appearance—his most endearing quality. He didn't evoke an immediate sexual response from me, but he did intrigue me. His name was Paul Hatlestad, and his handshake was as warm as his smile.

They all took seats around the table. Michael poured the wine and

Ed lit a joint, taking a few puffs and filling the porch with that pungent scent of freshly lit grass. That smell, mixed with the aroma of roasted chicken coming from the oven, began to work its magic on our appetites.

It wasn't long before I started to enjoy myself. And it also wasn't long before I regretted planning such a complicated main course that kept me getting up so frequently to baste. It amazes me that we all indulge ourselves in such hopeless activities. Worrying should be the eighth deadly sin.

Paul was charming, intelligent, sometimes shy but always interesting. When I asked him what he did for a living he said, "I'm a creative design consultant for Minnetonka."

"Now that you've told me what you do for a living," I said, "what do you do for a living?" They all laughed. I was curious to hear about what he did, but I guess they didn't think I was serious. He never answered my question.

The dinner went off without a hitch. Around midnight Michael and Ed left for the Barracks for another evening of debauchery. When we were alone Paul asked to see one of my films. I started with *Andy*, then showed him the Gay Day parade film I had just finished, which was being shown in the theaters along with *Moving*. Even though these films were nonsexual in content, it wasn't long before Paul and I were in bed.

It was a unique experience for me, like making love to myself. We were so comfortable: no fumbling, no hesitation, just warmth and pleasure. It was as if we'd done these things many times before. I knew this was special, but I didn't know yet that I'd found my soulmate. We spent two days in bed until Paul left to spend Thanksgiving in Monterey, Calif.

That Wednesday had been set for our meeting with the porno theater owners. Three men arrived at Mel's office: two guys who looked like hoods, and their lawyer, who looked like a lawyer. The meeting was going really well when one of the men asked if I knew George Tresler, a theater owner in Chicago. I said I didn't. He looked straight at me and said, "He was killed last month. His car blew up." He didn't change his expression. He didn't blink. He just kept staring into my eyes, trying to read my reaction.

"I thought you might know him. A shame, really."

After a few awkward moments Mel abruptly ended the meeting. They got up, shook our hands, and left the office. Mel closed the door after them. "I'm not sure, but I think they just threatened your life."

"You're kidding. Is that what that was about?" I asked. "It was so out of left field."

"That's why I think it was a threat. You've got your prints back, and you've got three hundred from the box office. That's not bad. I think we should just sit tight, watch our backs, and decide later what, if anything, we want to do."

I left the office shaken but aware of everything around me. When your life is threatened you become very much in the present, aware of what's happening. I noted to myself on the drive home that when I'm comfortable, I become selectively observant. Safety numbs my senses. I never thought about these things. Was this the beginning of cocaine-induced paranoia or was I seeing a new reality? I didn't know. I was scared and alone.

Ed was spending the night at Michael's, and I was spending it cooking the next day's Thanksgiving dinner. At about ten o'clock the front doorbell rang. I'd done a few lines of coke, smoked a joint, and the stereo was going full blast. I wasn't sure I'd heard anything, so I didn't respond immediately.

The bell rang again, followed by rather loud knocks. When I came out of the kitchen and looked down the hall, I saw a figure peering through the glass. The porch light was behind him, so I couldn't see any of his features. I proceeded down the hall, reached for the knob, and opened the door. "Mr. Poole? Wakefield Poole?" a voice asked.

I still couldn't see a face, but I nodded, thinking all the while that I had to do something about that damn light.

"I've got something for you," he said as he brought something from behind his back. My mind flashed to the threat earlier in the day, and I took a step back. Then I saw the small package. I took it carefully, and he backed away. When he turned to go down the stairs I saw that the entire back of his jeans was in shreds, exposing a very cute little ass. I relaxed as I thought, *This guy doesn't look like any hit man I'd ever seen.* Of course, I'd only seen them in movies, but they always looked the same. I closed the door and returned to the den.

Covered in beautiful earth-colored paper, the box was tied with a gold cord. When I opened it, under the thinnest sheets of tissue paper in the world lay a bed of tiny dried rosebuds. There, in this fragrant mass of red and pink, was a Chinese figurine, carved from ivory. She was nude, her arms lifted, with her hands touching her shoulders. The bun on her head was removable and attached was a small spoon. I knew these types of figurines were originally made as ear wax removers but were frequently used to snort cocaine. On the lid of the box was a lovely thank-you poem from Paul. It was the most beautifully presented gift I had ever received; it totally attacked the senses.

I had a good laugh at my paranoia. Then I used Paul's gift to take a toot. I used it just that once, returned it to the box, rewrapped it, and placed it in a drawer for safekeeping. I returned to my chores.

I loved doing drugs while doing ordinary things. Cooking is wonderful when you're stoned, not to mention eating. I could never understand doing drugs and just vegetating. I guess that's what kept me away from heroin.

The next day, Thanksgiving dinner went wonderfully. Then about six o'clock that night, the phone rang. It was Paul, calling from Monterey. He wanted to come back to be with me. Was it OK?

He came back that night, and we spent the next few days together. As it turned out, we would be together for the next ten years. We had no choice. We were meant to be together. Paul was the brother, friend, and lover I'd always wanted.

It was in this atmosphere that Marvin came to visit for two days on his way to Los Angeles. He was my house guest, but except for meals I didn't spend much time with him. I was in the first throes of a love affair and had no time for distractions. I assumed and took for granted that Marvin would understand and not be hurt.

I was wrong, since from that time forward our relationship changed. Maybe Marvin felt he was no longer important to me and that there was no place for him in my life. Maybe he saw this as an opportunity to distance himself from the porno field, or maybe the idea of leaving New York now seemed foolish to him. I don't know the reason, maybe it was all those reasons...but things began to change.

I had a new lover and was starting a new life. I'd just released a new movie, and money was coming in again. Now I could relax for a while. After a few months I gave up the apartment. Ed moved in with Michael, and I moved into Paul's beautiful little house on Divisadero. He had wonderful taste, and it was reflected everywhere. Antiques and collectibles were mixed with contemporary objects—all done with the same sensibility as the gift I received. Altogether, it was a perfect and creative atmosphere.

Charles Sinclair

Paul Hattelstad (on phone) in Hot Flash of America store, San Francisco, circa 1977.

Charles Sinclair

Interior of Hot Flash of America store, San Francisco, circa 1977.

Chapter Twelve

Hot Flash of America and Take One

San Francisco, 1975

Rusty and Peter had taken a storefront on Market Street and moved in, setting up a little shop and living in the back. They called the shop Hot Flash, only opening it when they felt like it. They filled it with collectibles they found at flea markets in Alameda and Marin counties. Those things, along with Peter's art, made for an interesting browse.

We spent a lot of time with them, and once Paul saw what they were doing, he was intrigued. A real entrepreneur, he saw some value in the store. A few years back, Paul had opened the first mainstream head shop in America in Minneapolis. The shop, called Now and Then, immediately took off, selling items from fine soaps to psychedelic posters. Paul was also the primary promoter of a new product, soap balls and soap on a rope, which his friend Bob Taylor had created. In just a short time Bob had sold enough soap to start Minnetonka Inc., which sold personal care products. Not long after, Paul had sold his store, retired to San Francisco, then started to worked as an advisor to Bob, long distance. When he was needed for a project, he'd just hop a plane. I finally understood the meaning of "creative design consultant."

One night Peter cooked Chinese food for all of us at their place. While we smoked a joint between courses, Paul asked if Rusty and Peter would be interested in expanding Hot Flash. They kicked the idea around a bit, and then moved on to other things.

On the way home Paul said that together we could all make the store a big success. We could help Rusty and Peter get the store they were dreaming about, and we could chase their dream.

Paul and I began to pull things together to make it happen. We scouted locations, since their present store was too small. Paul located a pre-quake building that had been a hardware store for thirty-five years. The owner was near retirement and ready to sell. On Market Street, right off Castro on the fringe of the gay ghetto, it was a perfect location to establish the store as a gay-run business. We would also use my reputation to secure press coverage and publicity for the store. As it turned out, it worked very well for us.

We entertained two friends one night, and by the end of the evening, Don Van Derby and Don Lyles, a doctor and a college professor, had agreed to buy the building, make the renovations, and give us a lease we could afford. Paul and I agreed to do all the necessary work when possible. When we needed a plumber, we would call one, but we'd do all the painting, flooring, drywalling, etc.

Now that we had a space, the concept had grown. The shop would be an art gallery, an antique shop, a hair salon for men and women, and a general store all in one. Besides the four of us, Paul had brought in three other people as partners. Darryl Useman, one of the finest hairdressers in San Francisco, would run the salon. Clark Kostner, a stockbroker and finance man, would handle finances, and Timothy Callas, a good friend of Paul's who'd delivered the figurine to me that night, would help in the day-to-day operations. Now we had to get investors.

Raising money turned out to be the hard part. I sent a prospectus to Marvin, asking him to send $5,000 for my investment in the partnership. To my surprise, Marvin told me there were no funds left, even for my share. Marvin had put all available income into a new project, the workshop of a new musical of Michael's called *A Chorus Line*. He was sorry.

Yes, I remembered that right before we'd left New York, Michael was having a session with some dancers. They were going to get together to talk about their lives. It had turned out well, and now they were doing a workshop. I didn't know until years later that the reason Marvin asked me to make *Moving* was to increase his cash flow and that the money from the movies allowed him to help Michael produce the musical.

Despite my failure to bring in any investors, we did raise $35,000. Still, we were about $25,000 shy of what we needed. But we plowed on. Friends came in to help. We worked harder. We wanted this store to be fabulous. We were exploiting it as a totally gay-owned enterprise and wanted to make sure it represented a truly complex view of the homosexual experience. We still did our drugs. We still had our sex. We certainly had our share of artistic differences, but we were all dedicated to this one task to open our store, where our motto would be "Everything you want but nothing you need!"

Timothy brought in more friends to help. We planned to open in October, and we needed them. They all worked for nothing, with the hope that later we could put them on salary. Beverly Blair and Mary Ann Thompson became the backbone of the shop, and, as they'd hoped, we kept them on staff.

For our grand opening we decided to give Ed Parente a one-man show to exhibit his sculptures, the plastic boxes that housed plaster-cast body parts: faces, hands, and fingers, along with natural objects: dried flowers, butterflies, dragon flies, tiny skeletons, and skulls. They were eye-catching, complex, and beautiful.

Things were moving along. About four days before the opening, I was making calls on the balcony (now our office). Rusty was organizing the back room. Peter was working on the collectibles display, and Paul was in the attic wiring our security system. At one point I heard a thud, followed by a flopping sound. I called up to Paul. No answer. I ran to the ladder leading to the attic and shouted up. I heard Peter say, "Leave him alone or he'll never get that job done. He's OK."

As I reached the top of the ladder, the flopping sound grew louder, and as I turned to face the front of the building, I saw Paul's legs from behind a partition, both kicking about six inches in the air and landing on the floor making that terrible sound. He still didn't answer my call, and before I even reached the partition, I screamed for Peter to call an ambulance.

As I rounded the wall I saw Paul lying on his back. His arms were by his sides, his legs still kicking and his head looking straight at me. He was actually hanging by a gold chain around his neck. The chain had gotten caught on an exposed electrical wire. As soon as I saw that, I yelled to cut the power switch. I knew I couldn't touch him. It felt forever waiting for the power to be shut off.

I picked up a push broom to knock the gold chain from the wire. Just as I reached for the wire, Rusty threw the master switch and that awful sound of Paul's feet hitting the floor abruptly stopped. I took him in my arms and tried to talk to him. He was unconscious but, remarkably, still breathing. I kept talking to him as I heard sirens.

Suddenly, there were two firemen in full regalia standing next to me. They made no effort to do anything, instead discussing how to get him down from the attic. The only exit was down a six-foot ladder through a hole in the floor. I heard them talking about taking out the windows and lowering him down the truck ladder. I couldn't believe how matter-of-fact they were.

After a few minutes they left to talk the situation over with the fire chief. I became agitated. They hadn't even touched him. So I stood up, threw Paul over my shoulder, and carried him down the ladder, all the time thinking about the scene in *Carousel* when Digger puts Carrie over his shoulder and says, "This is how firemen carry folks." Talk about weird.

I got Paul down and laid him on the floor just as the ambulance arrived. They checked him out, wrapped him up, and took him to San Francisco General. I stayed with him until I knew he was out of danger and resting in the burn unit. He was in critical condition.

Thank God for that gold chain. It had been the cause of the accident, but it had also saved his life. He was on the wire for a long time, but the electricity kept going around in circles rather than through his body. The chain had burned into his neck and was only a millimeter away from his jugular vein. Another few more seconds on the wire and his throat would have been cut.

Well, miracles do happen, and we not only opened a few days later, but also, with the doctor's approval, Paul attended, accompanied by a nurse named Ellen, another friend of Tim's. After the opening Paul went back to the hospital for another three weeks.

On the day of our opening, the barricades for the new BART train system, under construction for more than two years, were taken down on Market Street. This amazing piece of luck fit into our plans perfectly. We'd left the outside of the building untouched during the four months of our construction. The entire façade was built off site and put up the night before we opened. Then we draped the entire building like a Christo with white nylon. It would stay there until we revealed the store at eight that night At the stroke of the hour, a harpist, placed in the window, began to play. Our guests waited behind a roped-off area on the sidewalk as we unveiled Hot Flash of America.

The opening was a huge success, and we received unbelievable press. "A walk into Hot Flash can brighten even the bluest spirit. They raise the concept of gift shops almost to an art form. Novelty items priced for a dollar to art in the thousands, you can be assured of finding something to please your heart and your budget," wrote *The Advocate*.

"I saw things in Hot Flash that amazed my aesthetic sense, and for all of us with any percentage of child left in our perspective, Hot Flash is ours," raved *City Magazine*.

We were thrilled with our press and overwhelmed with the personal responses. We were having the time of our lives yet still not making a living for ourselves. Paul and I had income from other sources, so we gave up our $28.50 a week so that Mary Ann and Beverly could attempt to pay their bills. When the rest of us needed extra money, we'd sell something we owned.

We had consignment items, quality items that helped give the store its basic elegance: antique French marble candy counters beneath Lalique mirrors, next to San Francisco street lamps, beside a wicker chair, covered with Mao silk pillows, alongside a rubber chicken. And that was just one corner of the store. Great and entertaining, but we needed small things to sell. Affordable things, because everyone who came in wanted to take something away, no matter how small.

We started to sell T-shirts and gym shorts with the Hot Flash logo, which became so popular that we couldn't keep them in stock. We became an art gallery that survived by selling more shirts than art or antiques. I remember Marvin calling from New York one day to say he'd just seen one of our T-shirts on a customer in Lamston's. He was impressed!

Hot Flash also became a showcase for gay craftspeople and their wares: coffee mugs made resembling a pair of cutoff Levi's, porcelain soap dishes shaped like a woman's upturned hand, erotic cloisonne jewelry, beautifully crafted sterling silver drug paraphernalia, coke spoons, joint holders.

We changed Hot Flash every six weeks, closing on Saturday night and reopening Monday night with an invitation-only reception for a designated local artist. We'd totally re-merchandise the store, a tremendous undertaking, to support the style of the artist. During these marathon weekends we did a lot of drugs to get us through. Drugs were new enough to us to aid to our creative juices and keep us awake and alert for the two days.

Our openings became so successful that after the few months people were paying twenty-five dollars to attend. So many people tried to crash these parties that we hired an off-duty policeman, Bob Cato, another friend of Tim's, to man the door. Several years later, Bob would gain attention by driving the car that caused the accidental death of Janet Gaynor and injury to Mary Martin.

Marvin called to say that Michael's show, which opened at the Public Theater, was moving to Broadway. It was a smash hit. He went on to say that the porno business no longer interested him. The distance between us, he said, had made it difficult to maintain our partnership. Marvin wanted out, as Michael would be taking up more of his time. But he would, however, send me the inventory we had in stock and the necessary things I'd need to continue the mail-order business. All the money invested in *The Bible* was paid back. That was good news, but when *Boys* opened I owed Marvin $70,000. In three years I had reduced that figure to $2,000. Marvin said he'd write that off as a tax loss and we'd be even. I'd have no money, no security but would own the rights to all of my films.

We sold enough eight-millimeter films to cover our loss on *The Bible* (more than $100,000) and to generate enough cash flow to finance Michael's first workshop of *A Chorus Line*, as well as wipe out my debt. We sold a lot of films to show that much profit. They were post peak, but as he told me, it would be a way to make some extra money for myself—and I would need it. After four years of hard work and making good money, I was back to zero.

Marvin was dumping me as a partner and a client. He'd been my business manager, and for fifteen years he had paid the bills. I lived on an allowance, and I had no bank account of my own. I was stunned. I understood that with the success of *A Chorus Line*, he didn't need the movies anymore. They might even become an embarrassment. After all, Michael had just won the Pulitzer Prize for *A Chorus Line*.

What I didn't understand was that after I received everything, I was also dumped as a friend. It wasn't official. He became what I call a "passive friend," one who never calls or writes but when you contact him, is civil, preoccupied, and uninterested. This was the second blow to my soul since moving to San Francisco. I'd made money making porno movies, but I'd never thought of myself as a pornographer. I was the only one who didn't.

I still wanted to make movies, but I no longer had Marvin, and along with that, I no longer had financial backing. The lab that did our eight-millimeter prints refused to mail them across state lines, so I had to find someone in California to do it. This was difficult because I had no credit at the new lab and everything was COD.

Mary Ann came to work for me, and we ran Irving Inc. from my house. Marvin was right: There was still a little life left in the films. We didn't have any money to advertise, but the orders kept dribbling in from our mailing list. We made enough at least to pay for the cocaine. I never used drugs secretly. I always shared with whomever was around, and we were all using more. The store was doing well, and the gay publications were wonderful to us. We were a publicly advertised gay-owned-and-operated business. In the four years I was active with the store, *The Advocate* alone did five interviews with me, as well as feature stories that resulted in national exposure for all the gay artists we showed at Hot Flash. We received total support from the gay community, yet we had to really work to pay the bills. When you open a business underfinanced, it's hard to get ahead. You always have to restock the store. Cash flow is everything.

One day Michael Bennett called from New York to ask for my help. *A Chorus Line* was opening at the Curran in San Francisco in May, and he was looking for a place for the opening-night party. Michael wanted me to take Bernie Gersten—who was coming out to scout a party location—around town, and I agreed to help.

When the day arrived I picked Bernie up in my van and drove him to a few places. The last and the best was the City, a disco owned by a friend, Tom Sanford. Tom went out of his way to give Bernie everything he needed to make it work. It was a done deal.

Barbara Rossi, Marvin's secretary, was also a photographer and Michael had given her permission to shoot during the rehearsals of *A Chorus Line*. She came up with some remarkable shots, and I asked her to do a one-woman exhibit of her photos. She was thrilled, so we booked her, and the framed prints started to arrive. Later, I brought her out for the opening.

Hot Flash also did a tie-in with the musical's T-shirts, and later we'd become the official California supplier of *A Chorus Line* T-shirts. Making this opportunity available was Michael's way of saying thanks for helping him get his show produced.

When the company arrived at the Curran Theater, each member received a Hot Flash T-shirt, gym shorts, a cap, other gifts, and an invitation to a party at Hot Flash after the first preview. We sent the trolley to pick them up. The cast was blown away by the store, but Michael and his companion, Donna, weren't there. They had requested a special showing a few nights later.

When they walked into the store, I could tell they were both impressed. "Well, this is what I'm doing now that I've left show business," I said.

To which Michael responded, "From the looks of this place, you haven't left it yet." We laughed and spent the next hour drinking wine and catching up. We spoke little about the show because I hadn't seen it yet; I planned on seeing it in a few days and could hardly wait.

When the big night finally arrived, I invited our whole staff. They were picked up in a limo, a first for some of them, taken to the show, and then to the party.

Paul and I sat in Michael's house seats. Tenth row center! About ten minutes into the show, I realized that the entire cast was playing to me, or so it seemed, and not much later my cheeks were bathed in tears. I'd never had an experience like this before. By the end of the show, I was a wreck. I knew so many of the cast; some had auditioned for me, some had even worked for me.

Even though Carol, now Kelly Bishop, was not in the show, the role of Sheila touched me as I had shared in the experience of her not being able to audition well. It was the same with the other characters; I saw myself in so many of their stories. I think that's the key to the success of this show. I'll never forget that night as long as I live.

After the show, I was standing in the lobby of the City waiting for my whole group, when Michael walked in with Bob Avian. He came right over to me, and as I put my arms around him, I spoke in his ear. "Michael, it was perfect, right down to the bows, leaving me wanting just one more...so I could scream my head off...and then, not giving it to me!"

He tightened his embrace and asked if I remembered what I'd said to him the opening night of *Follies*. Of course I didn't, but evidently he did. "You said I almost did a perfect show, that there were places where I settled for the ordinary. Rehearsing this show when I was pressured, I heard you in my ear: 'Almost a perfect show, almost a perfect...almost...' When it happened I just stopped rehearsal. Thanks for that."

Michael hugged me once more and lightened up by saying, "I tell everyone now that Bill Harrison and Casey Donovan kept me for a year while I was working on this show. It's really true, and it always gets a laugh. Now let's go party."

Just as he turned to go in, Marvin Hamlisch rushed over. "Michael, the waiters have on nothing but jockstraps. What kind of place is this?" He was clearly upset.

As they walked away I heard Michael say, "Marvin, relax. You're so fucking uptight. I guess if they were topless waitresses, it would be OK, huh?"

It was a fantastic night—one of the best, the peak for Hot Flash. But everything from here on went downhill.

I saw Michael twice more while he was in town. He and Donna spent a evening at our house. We had dinner and watched the silent film *Intolerance* while listening to Scott Joplin. Michael told us he and Donna were engaged to be married. I got up, went to the bedroom, reached into a drawer, and brought out the gift from Paul that Timothy had brought me that November night. It was still just as I had received it. I gave it to Donna and told them the story as she unwrapped the package.

She caught her breath as she opened the top, smelled the pot-pourri, and saw the tiny ivory figurine. She was pleased but said she couldn't possibly keep such a lovely thing, especially since Paul had given it to me.

"Please," I said. "You can pass it on to someone else. One day when it's right, you'll know. Then just give it away." Paul agreed, so she accepted it graciously. That spring, Michael and Donna married in Paris. They sent me an invitation, which I still have. Considering what was to come, it's a miracle that it's still in my possession.

At Hot Flash we worked hard and played hard. It's amazing that we all got along so well. Of course, there were disagreements, but we always managed to reach a mutual decision without too many bruised egos. I'd made some new friends, and a few moved out from New York. Michael Maletta and his new lover, Steve Barnett, made the move to San Francisco, eventually helping out at our openings.

Michael was so impressed with our parties that he formed an organization called Creative Power that planned large parties and sold tickets. It became successful, and organized partying became a thing of the '70s. And it's still going on all over the country. No one minded paying money to attend a party where you were safe to do whatever drugs you wanted. The music was as good as could be had, disco was just peaking, and there was nothing to worry about except having a good time.

Since the accident, Paul had changed. Nothing really major, only his outlook. He lost his fear of dying, so he became more aggressive about pursuing a good time. He said that when he was "on the wire," he could only give into it. He just relaxed and let the current flow through him; he accepted death. He had experienced it, even though he didn't die. Consequently, he no longer practiced caution of any kind.

We both had to consider new ways to increase our income. We were making no money off the store. Paul started to sell drugs—just grass, MDA, and amyl nitrite—and I started to expand our eight-millimeter business. I contacted Toby Ross, a local filmmaker, and made a deal to distribute his film *Reflections of Youth*. The Gage Brothers' first film, *Kansas City Trucking Company*, had been a great success, so we also made a deal to distribute that.

Paul and I learned that each time we did a new release, we could expect the same response. People on our mailing list liked our product and didn't mind paying $99 for a complete movie. But it took capital to release a new film. The mailing alone, including the printing of the brochure, ran into the thousands, and the number of films I could handle was limited. When we generated enough money to do another release, we did.

Cliff Newman was managing the Nob Hill Theater and booked my films when he had a date he couldn't fill. They still did good business, and the extra money always came at the right time. Cliff didn't know until later how many times he'd saved me from disaster.

To learn more about the retail business, Paul arranged for me to sell baskets at the Los Angeles Gift Show, even though I was already a good salesman. On the last day I looked up from my order sheet and standing in front me was my ex-lover Dick Colacino, who told me he was still living in Las Vegas. We arranged to meet later that evening.

I arrived at his hotel around ten o'clock to find he was already in bed. Immediately, I realized I still wanted to jump his bones. He looked great, a little heavier, but his sexuality was still potent. He was traveling with a woman who was in the next room, so I decided not to make a move. Instead, I settled myself on the floor next to his bed. We talked for an hour or so before I had to leave. I often wonder if I had made a pass how he would have reacted. It wasn't too late, so I went to see Joe Layton, who also lived in Los Angeles. Evelyn had died of cancer recently, and I wanted to see him. When I arrived Joe was drunk and in bad shape. He asked me to come back into his professional family and promised we'd have great times again.

I explained that I had my own family now and that we were all depending on each other for our survival. I had no choice, I was already committed. I've had just a few moments in my life where I've reflected on what might be if....This was one of them. Just before sunrise, I put Joe to bed, kissed him good-bye, and left.

One day an attractive guy came into Hot Flash and introduced himself as Nick. Over the next few weeks we spoke more and more about film. He introduced his roommate, Edd, a quiet, pleasant older-looking man. Soon after, we went off to the Café Flore for a chat.

Edd, it turned out, was also a filmmaker. His company, Cinematherapy, made short films dealing with all sorts of medical problems. He owned most of his own equipment, and his editing facilities were top-notch. Together, we owned everything it would take to make a new film. We agreed to think seriously about forming a partnership. It was a way to make another film cheaply and well.

I wanted to do a documentary about San Francisco gay men and their sexuality, something real but still with some fantasy to it. A lot of people had been stopping by the store to tell me they wanted to be in my movies. Now I would have to start asking if they were serious,

The previous year, Sam Christensen and Tim Kincaid had come into the store. They wanted to produce a movie, and I thought they were asking for my help. What they really were looking for was money. I said I was sorry and that if I had money, I would make one myself. I gave them what advice I could: "Just make it. Use credit cards. Borrow from friends and relatives. Just make it!" They did. They became known as Sam and Joe, the Gage Brothers, using pseudonyms since they both worked in other areas of the industry.

When Edd and I met again, we decided to start auditioning, even though we hadn't formulated our ideas. I thought the actors themselves would help bring it all together. We videotaped anyone who expressed an interest in being in our movie, formed a questionnaire, and asked each person to respond on camera. They were general questions: What was your first sexual experience? What is your favorite sexual expression? What do you enjoy most? What is your most secret sexual fantasy?

We experimented on Nick. Edd and I had agreed that he would be in the film. After all, he had initiated the whole thing and was hot and willing. When asked about his fantasy, he told a story about his 1956 Buick convertible, which he had restored. It was breathtaking, with that wonderful '50s purple. He had restored the seat covers using white duck cloth, then airbrushed it to create a leather look, right down to the painted buttons on the seats. His license plate read KATE, the name he had given her. Nick loved Kate and said sometimes he wished he could fuck her.

This is what I meant—the cast would make this all come together. I felt encouraged. We interviewed and filmed perhaps twenty-five guys before we felt we had enough. Edd invited me, Nick, Joey (our production manager), and Charlie (our soundman) to Hawaii for a week. We brought all the videotaped interviews to complete the casting and start a screenplay. We returned with our casting complete but still without a concept. Edd and I decided we would each work separately on an idea.

When the time arrived Edd presented his concept first. It wasn't bad, just ordinary. It probably would have made a hot movie but not for me.

"It's pretty good, but I've already made that movie," I said.

He looked a little hurt by my words, so I added, "If you want to do this movie, you direct it, put your name on it, and I'll support you. I just don't want to do a film that's not different from my last one." I started to explain what I meant. I wanted to do a "docufantasy," envisioning it as very Robert Altman with a *Nashville*-type feel and editing. The film would document the whole process of making the movie, right up to the premiere, which would also be in the film. *Take One* would be the title.

It was simple, yet complex in its approach. I wanted to make every cast member's sexual fantasy real. Two of the selected cast members were brothers, Rudy and Dutch Garcia. During their interviews I realized that they both desired each other. When I confronted them they not only admitted it but also agreed to make love together for the first time on film for me.

This section started with Dutch telling a story (actually a scene from the video audition) about their youth. Dutch would leave the house to go into town. Rudy would call a friend and tell him that Dutch was hitchhiking on the highway. His friend would go pick him up, put the move on him, and then relate the experience to Rudy. Dutch never knew about this until Rudy came out with the story during their interview. Dutch laughed and said he wondered why he always got a blowjob from every guy who picked him up. This section turned out to be one of my favorites.

At one point, when they start to have sex, the music softens and under the lyrics of a song written especially for this segment, you hear young kids in a playground, running, and laughing. It is a very tender moment.

With Nick we let him have his wish. He actually fucks his car. We did an "autoerotic" section where Nick actually inserts himself into the exhaust rings on the side of the car. He runs his tongue around the rings, slides naked over the hood, and eventually has an orgasm on the steering wheel.

Glenn, a bartender, had leather fantasies, so we did a multimedia scene using all his fetishes. And Philip and Bill were lovers who only wanted to see themselves fuck on film. That was an easy one.

Richard Locke's fantasy was to fuck his lover on the roof of their cabin in the desert. We did that too, in a scene that evokes the desert of Georgia O'Keefe in pastels and pinks.

Sal Guange was a strange local dancer. He was untrained but danced naked with abandon. We opened the film with him performing on the stage of the Nob Hill Theater. The screen dissolves from his interview into a scene in which we're actually shooting his segment. I tried to really fuck up the sense of time in the film. Sometimes I brought cast members together in the same frame without their knowledge that others are there.

In one scene I'm at the bar of La Caracole, talking to Glen, the bartender, about his being in the movie. Over Glen's shoulder, through a huge window, we see Phillip and Bill sitting at a table across the street at the Café Flore. Richard is at the corner pay phone talking to his lover, while he's giving Philip and Bill the once over. At the same time Nick cruises him while driving his car down Market Street. Six cast members in the frame at once.

The film's last section deals with the cast members watching their movie in the Nob Hill Theater. As they view it from different places in the theater, each fantasizes about having sex with another member of the cast, a sort of separated orgy. When the screening ends they all exit the theater while I'm in the lobby, still filming the movie. As the last one leaves I look directly at the camera and say, "I'm out of film," just as the orange-colored film end runs through the camera.

And then there are other production scenes where everyone gets in the picture: Paul works on the set, Mary Ann talks to the lawyer about contracts, and Cliff Newman even changes the marquee to display the title of the movie. We worked hard, and finally all the major photography was completed. All that was left was the editing.

We had raised money to make the movie from outside sources, but when I discovered that Edd was presenting bills for camera rental and other equipment, I realized we were going to have a huge budget and needed more capital. If he was going to charge the company, then I would have to as well. It was by the books, but to keep my budgets low, I'd never charged my company for using my own equipment. Regardless, I agreed to the method and was certainly glad to have some money coming in for a change. I could present bills for my camera, lights, office space, even for the use of my van.

I approached Don Collins, a friend in Los Angeles, to invest in the picture. He agreed to come in for the remaining money we'd need, and Edd also agreed to invest. Both Edd and Don knew the kind of money my movies had made, and they formed expectations based on my previous profits. I didn't realize it, but with these two investments, I no longer had controlling interest in the film. But money was never my motivation to make a movie. The only film I'd ever made strictly for money was *Moving*. Now I had investors for the first time who expected huge returns. They were looking for a blockbuster.

We finished editing, and the day of the mix arrived. The mix is the first time you get to see the film with all its elements together. You see it complete, except for any special effects done in printing. It gives you the first real sense of the film and what you have. It was exciting, and Edd, who had doubts until the mix, was amazed at how it fit together. He loved it.

I was doing a lot of cocaine then. Unfortunately, when I did drugs, I always did them in public. I never went to the bathroom and snorted secretly. I always put them out to share. Edd did occasional toots, but he wasn't a user. I'm sure he wondered many times whether I was really in control.

We premiered *Take One* at the Nob Hill and received the best reviews I ever got.

"Poole is the Neiman Marcus of the porn film world!" wrote George Robert in the *Bay Area Reporter*. "Poole is back BIG!" said Jon Roberts from *In Heat*. "Go see this film. You'll never be the same, and after seeing it, you wouldn't want to be!" Michael Schmitz wrote in *Calendar*. We didn't receive one negative review.

Cliff, the manager of the Nob Hill Theater, had made a good deal with us, and we received fifty percent of the box office. No one ever gets that kind of deal in the porno business, but Cliff knew how much love and care had gone into the filming. Actually, the film was a love letter to the Nob Hill Theater. It was the finest gay theater in the world, and I wanted people all over the country to see and know that somewhere gays were treated like first-class citizens.

On a black Monday in June 1977, Anita Bryant caused a major upheaval with her "Save Our Children" campaign in Florida. An ordinance passed by the Metropolitan Dade County Commission mandating that qualified homosexuals not be discriminated against in the hiring of teachers was overturned by her vigorous attacks on homosexuals and her slanted biblical interpretations.

Nothing was organized, but on that evening hundreds of people flocked to the Castro and to Harvey Milk. Plans were made for an organizational meeting the next day to find some way to fight this action. I remember sitting on the ground in the courtyard with Harvey on one side of me and Paul on the other. People were offering their thoughts, expressing their anger and fears. At one point Harvey leaned over and whispered to me, "We have to watch out, you and I. We're in for some hard times, and a lot of hate is going to come out of nowhere. We're both 'out there' and are easy targets. So be careful and watch your back."

That's all he said, and to be quite honest, I thought he was being a little dramatic. After all, I wasn't political and never had been, officially. The possibility of losing a newly found freedom scared us, but the fact that so many people had rallied together made it bearable and turned many of us into activists overnight.

The next day, a group of us met to discuss how we could unite to fight Bryant's attack. I offered to pay for a full-page ad in *The Advocate* to inform people about it and to urge them to participate however they could. Paul and I had spent the night drawing up the ad to present to the group. At the bottom, in small letters, we had placed one line: Donated by Irving Inc.

Everyone was pleased with the ad, but Edd objected to the line at the bottom. He felt it associated the group with pornography, which might cause a backlash. I was stunned. My partner on *Take One*, which was still playing at the Nob Hill Theater, was embarrassed by his association with "dirty movies."

After much discussion I withdrew the offer, and my time as an organized gay activist came to an end. In my efforts to fight discrimination, I ran into a wall of it. I'd been told I was a second-class citizen because I was a pornographer, not because I was gay. I was devastated.

Paul and I went back to quietly supporting Harvey with financial aid. When Harvey lost his lease Paul took an option on a building across from Hot Flash so that Harvey could move Castro Camera to Market Street.

At this point we were strapped for cash. Everyone in our group owed each other, and we were financially log jammed. I owed money for drugs, I owed money to Mary Ann, she owed Timothy, he owed Peter, and so on.

I decided that we had to change our situation or disaster would surely come. Someone wanted to buy my set of Warhol *Marilyn*s. After much agonizing I sold them to him for $7,500. I had paid only $2,500, so I at least made a profit. I, in turn, bought the Warhol *Electric Chair*s back from Peter for $2,000, giving him cash to catch up on his debts. I paid my drug bills and caught up on some film lab payments for Irving Inc. This was the first time I'd sell my art to support my drug habit.

It did take the pressure off our little family for a while, but was it worth it? Later, the *Marilyn*s were valued at $750,000. Their sale would result in one of the few regrets of my life, not only because of their monetary value but also because they were truly my favorite possession.

Poster for *Take One* (1977), a mix of sex and documentary that was Wakefield Poole's last feature shot on film.

Richard White

Wakefield Poole, Casey Donovan, and Frank O'Dowd (left to right) shooting *Boys in the Sand II* in the Fire Island Pines, 1984.

Chapter Thirteen

Bottoming Out

New York City, 1977

At the request of Shan Sales, I went to Los Angeles to catch the act of a hot new model entering the porno scene. His professional name was Roger, and Shan had decided he was going to be the biggest male porno star yet. Roger had starred in a movie with Jack Wrangler titled *Heavy Equipment*, the first 3-D all-male porno film. Roger's stage show accompanied the film around the country.

I took a seat in the audience. His act consisted of go-go dancing and stripping. It was an ordinary act, but the raw material was exciting. By raw material, I mean Roger, whom I found strikingly handsome. He had a "you can have me" quality, and at the same time projected a macho image of "you can look but don't dare touch." This quality made Roger desirable to almost everyone, but everything he did in his act worked against him.

His music selection was bad, and his clothes were too cute. But the main problem was that after disco dancing for twenty minutes, when he finally took off his clothes, his dick was the size of a cocktail frank. This was the problem with all live acts. Public masturbation is against the law. You could do it on film but not onstage. I decided I could fix all of these problems.

After the act was over I was still in my seat watching the film when Roger slipped into the row behind me, tapped me on the shoulder, and introduced himself. I shook his hand, rose from my seat, and we walked into the lobby. There I met his manager, Jim Bacon. Roger took my criticisms well.

After a few minutes I agreed to restage the act for its opening at the Nob Hill. His show would run with my new film *Take One*. Cliff and I could make this happen.

Roger came to my studio in San Francisco, and we shot footage of him masturbating, something he did really well. I shot him against a black void so that all you could see was him. He enjoyed playing with himself and easily kept his erection for hours. We started the film with his back to me. After fondling himself and rubbing his body with oil, he turned to face the camera. He then began to slowly masturbate, continuing until he reached his orgasm. Roger was a joy.

The act started with slides: a multimedia extravaganza showing him in fantasy situations and dress, playing ball, swimming, jogging, and working out. In the middle of this Roger appeared wearing one of the outfits from the slides and performed his disco number with slides flashing all around him. As he removed his clothes down to a posing strap, the music slowed and the lights changed. The slides around him took on a more sexual tone as he began to do a bodybuilder pose down. He slipped off his posing strap and began to oil his body.

At this point, on the opposite side of the stage, the movie began to play. Now there were two Rogers, one on each side of the stage. There was no background onstage at all, and Roger's film image appeared life-size. He mirrored everything we had done on film live. When the image on film turned to face the audience, Roger turned his back to them. The lights lowered slightly so that the audience could watch him work his way to orgasm on film, while at the same time, even though his back was to them, see it live. After his orgasm, the process was reversed. The image on film turned his back to the audience as the live Roger turned to face them with a raging hard-on. You could actually hear a gasp from the audience as he turned around. Then they screamed and yelled like they were at a rock concert.

The act was very theatrical, worked well, and was legal. It also added three extra weeks to the run for *Take One* at the Nob Hill before showing *Heavy Equipment*. I created this act for no pay, but we agreed that Irving Inc. would release a short solo film, *Roger*, and that the act would run with *Take One* in its final weeks. I also gave Roger rights to all the footage shot for his act.

I decided to return to New York to run the 55th Street Playhouse, so Mary Ann and I went east to secure a deal with Frank Lee to lease the theater again. I planned to rerun all my movies, build up the patronage while improving the ambiance of the place, and in the fall open *Take One* there. It was a good plan, but I didn't realize the theater situation had deteriorated so tremendously. For the last few years, Frank had made tons of money off gay audiences and had put none of the profits into the theater. It was in worse condition than when we'd taken it over for the *Boys* premiere six years before.

This time I needed to paint the walls of the lobby and bathrooms. The movie screen was so filthy I had to wash it by hand, which took three days. Everything we did made the place better, but the air conditioner still went out every other day. When the air-conditioning was out, we lost about two out of three customers. Those we didn't lose left the theater dripping wet. I began a four-month plea to Frank for a new air conditioner. It was a losing situation, and I should have pulled up stakes and gone home, but I had too much riding on this.

I was staying with my friend Joe Nelson, who also worked at the box office along with Jay and Charles. They were old employees of Jack Deveau's and eager to help out. I told them both that I knew they would steal from me but to try not to be greedy. It was easy to slip a bill into your pocket and not issue a ticket. Because of this, I spent about ten hours at the theater every day, seven days a week. If I took a day off, proceeds showed a definite drop.

I was still doing a lot of cocaine, but it enabled me to keep the long hours and to stay positive. I wasn't doing anything else but working, so I wasn't spending money on other things. I was also sending money to Paul to keep Irving Inc. running.

Ever since I'd arrived in New York, I entertained the idea of getting back into theater. Running the playhouse was depressing, so I began to daydream again. Michael Bennett and Bob Avian's new show, *Ballroom*, would be a perfect opportunity. They needed older dancers, and I certainly filled that requirement. I asked them for a job. After two weeks I realized that old age and years of abusing my body had taken its toll, so I dropped out. My attempt to come back failed miserably. So I did more coke.

I received no invitations from my old friends, which is common when you abuse drugs. Even Joe Nelson eventually turned away. One night I returned after closing the theater to find Marvin, Joe, and Mark Glascow having a nightcap. I laid out some coke, and things got nasty. Mark said I should stop doing so much coke and that I should pay Joe rent or move out.

When Marvin and Joe said nothing, I had to assume they'd discussed this and agreed with Mark. My two oldest friends just sat there, silently looking at me. So I got up, packed my bag, and moved into a hotel on 55th Street. This was really a clumsy attempt at intervention!

This incident shows why people do cocaine privately. I never was a sneaky drug user. I took drugs to enjoy them and wanted those with me to have the same experience. Otherwise, do your drugs alone and jerk off when you need to. When people know you're a user, it colors every decision they make concerning you. But I put the hurt in my back pocket and went on with my life. I was of no use to my old friends, so I'd have to develop new ones.

One of these new friends was Frank O'Dowd. He, his lover Steven, and Gene Stavis produced *Emerald City*, the first gay TV show, which had a huge following. The format consisted of anything of interest to a gay audience, ranging from an interview with producer Alan Carr to a discussion of photography with Kenn Duncan. Frank did an hour show featuring my films as well as interviews with Cal and me.

Later, I conducted some interviews for them: one with Michael Stewart, author of *Hello, Dolly!* and *George M!* and another with Joe Gage. I enjoyed interviewing and was good at it. Frank became a close and dear friend.

I made other friends too: friends who were into film and promoting anything gay: writers, painters, musicians, even gay restaurant owners... a whole new culture. And here I was, Wakefield Poole, gay filmmaker.

Soon after, I booked a feature film, *The Right Number*, into the playhouse. On the night reviews came out, I went down to 42nd Street to get the first copies but was early. While I was waiting, the owner asked me to watch his stand while he ran down to the subway bathroom.

Before I could answer, he was out of the stand and running into the subway.

I stepped into the stand and stood behind the counter. Immediately, Bill Como appeared, friend and editor of *After Dark*. He recognized me. I saw it on his face. He just stood there, his mind grabbing for something to say. "God, Wakefield, are you working here?" he finally asked with a look of shock. Just as I was ready to answer, the owner returned and thanked me. Bill, realizing the situation, plopped down his quarter for the paper and walked away laughing, as he said to give him a call.

I had to return to San Francisco to edit *Roger*. While I was there Michael Maletta asked that I arrange a party for him on gay pride day. He was producing a party for the evening before the parade and wanted something for the afternoon after the parade. I agreed and *Abracadabra* came into being.

I asked five San Francisco filmmakers to participate. The six of us would stand at different spots along the parade route, and each would have 1,000 feet of film to shoot as he liked. I had the film picked up by motorcycle at each locale and rushed to be processed. The party started immediately after the parade.

We had scaffolding built in the orchestra pit to hold six projectors and the cameramen. It rose up on elevators, as the screens, which were hanging over the dance floor, descended—an immense undertaking. Less than an hour after the parade, the audience was watching the entire event from six different points of view, simultaneously projected by the filmmakers themselves. This was all raw footage, and we were all seeing it for the first time together. It was amazing.

I returned to New York and spent the rest of the summer trying to make a living off runs of *Boys*, *Bijou*, and *Moving*. I couldn't afford to pay rentals for other films. The theater just wasn't taking in enough money, and my main purpose became to hold on until the cold weather returned; then I could open *Take One* in New York.

Artie Bresson had made a documentary called *Gay USA* but was having trouble booking the film. We made a deal: For the first time, the word *gay* was displayed on a theater marquee. *All-male* had appeared but never *gay*.

The rock documentary *The Last Waltz* by Martin Scorsese was playing at the Ziegfeld right around the corner. One night when the show broke, the audience poured out the doors and moved past our theater. Sitting in the box office, I witnessed mob violence for the first time in my life.

This hate started from just a few kids shouting "cocksucker," "fag," and "asshole," and grew and grew until someone threw a garbage can at me, breaking the glass doors. Simply because of some words on a marquee. This wasn't even pornography; it was a documentary, so I can only guess that it was more threatening. All I could do was repair the doors as Harvey's warning rang again in my ear: "We have to be careful, you and I."

I got through the summer since I deducted the cost of the air-conditioning repairs from the rent. They required cash, so Frank Lee suggested it. I didn't think to get it in writing, so later I was served a summons. Frank was suing me for $26,000 in unpaid rental fees, the cost of the air-conditioning repairs for the summer. I hired a lawyer.

Take One opened in New York, again to the best reviews ever. We should have done really well, but it took everything I could do to get a seven-week run out of it. Even though it was cooler inside, people still didn't come. Too many times they had to ask for their money back because of the unbearable heat. Too many times they had their pockets picked. It was a degrading experience again.

The golden days of porno chic were gone.

I prepared for the court hearing and had all my records in order. Two days before the trial, Paul became ill and had another bout with death. This time, his liver. He wasn't taking care of himself, and I wasn't around to see that he did. Of course, I left for San Francisco immediately but not before asking the lawyer to get a postponement.

Jay took charge of the theater, and I took off for home. Four days later, Jay called to say that I had defaulted and that Frank Lee was taking all the receipts. The lawyer hadn't asked for a postponement as I requested. He was too busy getting control of the theater for Danny Mamane, another client, and I'd been sacrificed to achieve this. But I really didn't care about the theater. *Take One* had finished its run, and I was leaving anyway. I lost my case, Danny got the theater, and Jay went to work for him. Conspiracy or too much cocaine?

Paul recovered from this bout, but his doctor warned him to change his lifestyle. My nose was blown out from too much coke, and I was in such pain that I decided to give it up. Paul's health would make it easier and provided another incentive for us both to get clean.

Irving Inc. was distributing *Take One* theatrically in the United States, and the bookings were coming in. But the gay-porn business had already peaked. Rental fees were slashed, top fees cut in half.

Don and Edd had had such high expectations that they were bitterly disappointed with the receipts. But I remained positive. I knew we'd recoup, as well as show a nice profit with the film's eight-millimeter release. Also, I saw a revolution starting in the home video market, which was just around the corner, and I intended to be in on the ground floor.

Don and Edd couldn't wait that long. They accused me of cheating on the New York grosses and squandering their profits on drugs. We never went to court, though, since they had no case. I had kept such good records because of the trouble with Frank and proved without a doubt that the figures for the New York run were actual. Still, using their combined interests, they took the film and its distribution rights away from me. From that day on, to my knowledge, the movie has never been seen again. I called Edd years later, offering a video deal for the film. He told me that he'd cut out the section in which Nick makes love to his '56 Buick and had sold it to his own company, Cinematherapy, to illustrate masturbation. So the film was now incomplete. He added that he wasn't interested in a deal for the film because he couldn't trust me. So the film sits on a shelf somewhere, and no one has ever made any money on it.

Why did they want control of the movie if they never intended to do anything with it? Did they hate me so much they had to get even for some unknown, horrible act I did? They even did a new edit. Why? I still don't understand.

On my lawyer's advice, to avoid paying Frank $26,000 from the judgment of the New York trial, I went into bankruptcy. It was an unpleasant experience, made even more so by Don Collins's public exhibition of his feelings. In the hall outside the courtroom, he screamed his disgust for my morals and his belief of my dishonesty. It was the most embarrassing and humiliating moment of my life. When he was finished I turned away and left the building.

I was still struggling to make Irving Inc. successful. The Gages had made so much money with us on *Kansas City Trucking Company* that they were eager to make a deal for their latest film, *El Paso Wrecking Company*. It was arranged. I would go to Los Angeles and edit the film with Joe.

On the morning of my departure, I stopped by Castro Camera to see Paul, who was making some minor repairs to the building. After a short visit he and Harvey walked me to the car. Harvey loved to tell bad jokes. I got in the driver's seat as he asked me, "What's purple and has 1,200 legs?" I shrugged, and as I closed the door, he said, "The residents of Jonestown!"

"Harvey, that's so bad you should be shot." I laughed, put the car in reverse, and backed into the Market Street traffic. I waved good-bye and drove off to Los Angeles. It was the last thing I'd say to him. Two days later he died from gunshot wounds.

I was devastated and left for home the minute I heard about the murder. I was so upset that I couldn't participate in any of the vigils or demonstrations. I went into seclusion. I hate to admit it, but I was so drugged out that I didn't go with Paul on the boat to spread Harvey's ashes into the bay. I was not only grieving for Harvey but also feared for my safety. After all, Harvey had warned me that this could happen.

Paul told me about the ceremony when he returned. They were all drinking champagne, snorting coke, and toasting Harvey. It wasn't a sad time but a celebration of his life, his dedication to his ideals, and mostly to his sense of humor. Paul said that the highlight was the throwing of the ashes. No one tested the wind, he said, so "Harvey" ended up flying back in all their mouths when the wind took a sudden shift. They laughed and spat out his ashes all the way back to the dock.

Harvey's death spurred a change in my life. I became paranoid, venturing out only occasionally to the baths or to visit Cliff at the Nob Hill.

But I did have a friend, Dan Taylor, an artist who often came into Hot Flash, whom I saw frequently. We had hit it off, and for a few years we were fuck buddies. Sex with him was comfortable. We played no permanent roles with each other, and he wasn't a threat to Paul.

Freebase also entered my life. I had really damaged my nose, so Len, a dealer friend, taught Paul and me to smoke pure cocaine in a water pipe. It gave me the most incredible rush I'd ever had. After the first hit you spend all your time trying to get the same rush again and again.

Paul had gotten into dealing heavy drugs. The more coke we used, the more he had to sell to help cut the cost of our own use. We didn't see much of our friends, having replaced them with drug dealers. I knew them all by their first names only: Slag, Nancy, Len, Kattie, Russell—last names didn't matter.

I forbade only one thing in my house: shooting up, of any kind. If you overdose on pills, the body will try to expel the poison, make you throw up. When you shoot up there's no safety valve. Too much drug into the bloodstream and you're dead. I have never mainlined.

This was a terrible period, and I can only say that, thankfully, I don't remember all of it. My whole life was suddenly about getting and doing drugs. I rarely worked, and Irving Inc. showed my neglect. Paul and I had thrown caution to the wind for various reasons, but here we were together in all this craziness.

Parties just happened. One night turned into two days, which turned into three. I passed out one night during one of these parties. When I woke up after crashing for about eighteen hours, the party was still going on. I didn't know one person there. My guests had invited other guests, who'd invited other guests until none of the original were left. The party was in its third day. I asked them all to leave.

There were still moments of sanity, but they became scarcer. I withdrew even more and seldom left my house. At one point Paul moved out and got his own place to conduct business since it would help curb my use. Naturally, before long, there wasn't enough money to pay the bills. First the lab bills went unpaid, then the rent, then the royalties to my other filmmakers. After the lab refused to extend my credit and to make any more prints, business stopped, dying a slow death.

I made one last stab at pulling it together. I had an idea for a new film called *Mirrors*. Rey Richardson and his lover, Larry, agreed to put up the money to film the segment. Cal came up from Los Angeles and Lewis deVries agreed to do it. Everyone worked for scale, so film stock was the only other expense. With the exception of some mylar mirrors that didn't work, everything went as planned. Maybe there was some magic left.

In the middle of the shoot, Divine called, asking me to play pimp for him. I told him I didn't do that, but he vamped me, "You must have one of your movie stars just sitting around who'd love to date a nice girl. I'm so tired of jerkin' off!"

I put him on hold and asked Cal if he wanted a date with Divine. He said sure, and I put him on the phone.

"Divi," I said into the receiver, "Let me introduce you to Casey Donovan." He screamed as I handed Cal the phone. They laughed and made plans for Cal to call when he got back to Los Angeles. He kept his promise. They really enjoyed being seen together.

Shortly after, I received an eviction notice. I was two months behind on rent and had twenty-four hours to pay up or leave. Frantically, I set about getting rid of my things. I took all my art to Zahn Artman's house, where he agreed to keep it for me. Art is not immediately negotiable, or I would have lost it all by snorting it up my nose or smoking it.

I always had a way of generating money when I needed it. That is, until the first time it didn't happen. I'd asked Theo, a dealer friend, to get me some coke, come over, and play "baseball" (freebase). At the end of the evening, when I couldn't pay for the coke ($500), he said his female supplier wouldn't be very happy. He couldn't wait until the next day, so I took my Warhol *Mao* off the wall and gave it to him.

"Ask her to take this as collateral until I can pay. It's worth five times that amount."

He took the piece and left.

I managed to salvage the most important things by moving them in the dark of night to different places. My film negatives were all in storage in New York, so they weren't at risk. But so many things were left that I can never replace. This was the biggest mistake of my life, leaving so much behind as I fled from the sheriff.

When things really looked bleak, out of the blue I got a call from Joe Layton. He was doing a new show with Michael Stewart, and they both wanted us all to work together again. I'd be assisting Joe, and a lot of film work would be involved. Michael had written a sequel to *Bye Bye Birdie* titled *Bring Back Birdie*, starring Chita Rivera and Donald O'Connor. I couldn't believe my ears. Joe asked to see two of my films, *Bijou* and *The Bible*, so I drove to Los Angeles where I met his lover, John, and showed them the movies. When we were finished Joe agreed that I should handle the film work and offered me the job. I was saved, or so I thought.

On the way back to San Francisco, I was driving down the highway in a borrowed truck, thinking how my luck was starting to change. I'd be able to get myself straight and have everything I deserved. Just at that moment, I blew a rod on the truck. It should have been an omen, but I wasn't seeing things realistically. I still had hope. A chance. A new dream.

Oh, I forgot one important thing: I was still a drug addict.

Chapter Fourteen

A New Start: Broadway-Bound...Again

New York City, 1980

I flew to New York and started work on *Birdie*. I thought this job and, mostly, Joe would help me put everything back together. With his help and my hard work, I could do it.

The second day, I discovered Joe was as much an alcoholic as I was an addict, and he had the same thoughts as I: "With Wake's help I can have a hit show again and...."

We were both wrong. The entire experience was disastrous. I can't remember one pleasant thing other than getting to know Chita, who'll do anything for you. I'll not go into details about this show other than to say it was terrible and it reflected the experience. Michael Stewart left the country, unable to deal with Joe's drinking or my drug habit. I still regret letting him down.

I worked hard all day and did drugs in the evening. That was a real accomplishment, not doing drugs until evening. This lasted through the rehearsal period and into previews.

Then one day I came into the theater. Tony Manzie, the stage manager, asked if I'd seen the Post. He walked me to the bulletin board. I don't understand why anyone would post it, but there for all to see was a clipping from page six of *The New York Post*:

> Joe Layton is well-acquainted with family entertainment. He's executive producer of the upcoming film version of *Annie* and

> director of shows like *Barnum* and *Bring Back Birdie*, opening March 5. But Layton's right hand man on many of his projects is Wakefield Poole, whose forte is aimed at another type of audience. Listed in the *Birdie* credits as a director of "art" films, Wakefield is known for his work in porno films. One of his many classics: *Boys in the Sand.*

This cast was basically made up of young people, and their reactions to the article upset me. Most, being minors, brought their mothers to every rehearsal and performance. Their reaction was the obvious: I was watched carefully when I approached their children or even touched them on the shoulder. I could see their backs stiffen and feel their eyes on me.

This was not drug paranoia—it was reality. No one instigated conversations with me, speaking to me only when they had to ask for direction. Even Tony Manzie blamed me, saying, "With all our troubles, we certainly didn't need this."

Again, while I still thought of myself as a filmmaker to the rest of the world, I was a pornographer. Well, I ran to the pipe. I was just waiting for some reason, I guess. For the next few weeks I was in the worst shape ever. I was totally unwanted. My presence made everyone uncomfortable. Joe tried to console me, but he was in a state of denial about everything. Even Frank DeSal, who we hired to dance with Chita, distanced himself from me. Frank O'Dowd was the only one who tried to support me. He was my assistant on the video work and did his best to keep things going. Nothing mattered at this point. All I wanted was for the show to open.

I begged Paul to come to New York, but he was much too ill, now living in a motel on Market Street. That's the way it is. You spend your time doing drugs and trying to get more. If you can't pay the rent, you go somewhere else. That's why so many addicts become homeless. It's gradual, the bottoming-out process. You begin to make compromises, always favoring the path to more drugs. Little by little, you make sacrifices. Objects of value disappear, sold or left in some abandoned apartment or with a friend who takes advantage of your situation.

Zahn Artman was the exception to this. Zahn worked for Bill Graham, so he was no stranger to drug abuse. He was a true friend and kept my art safe until I could take responsibility for it. The only work of art I traded for drugs was the Warhol *Mao*, which somehow ended up in the possession of Grace Slick. She was being interviewed on some rock show, and I saw it in the background of the shot. I had given it to Theo, in lieu of $500, to pay his dealer for some coke. I can only surmise that she was his supplier or that he had sold it to her for the cash. Regardless, it found a good home.

In these final steps of bottoming out, you're aware of what's happening, but you can do little about it. This was my state at the end of previews for *Birdie*.

The show opened to awful reviews and closed after two weeks. I left for home immediately and was told to call Rhoda, Joe's secretary, in a few days, about staging *Barnum* in London. Joe was working on the film version of *Annie* and couldn't do it. When I finally reached her by phone, weeks later, she explained that she had left messages at the motel office and that when I didn't return the calls, Buddy Schwab had taken the job. I knew she was lying; I knew it was over. The bottom was here.

For the next few months Paul and I lived in the motel room in San Francisco with our two cats, which were gifts from the Grateful Dead, who raised Abyssinians. It was just the four of us, the pipe, and a fixed idea that we were doomed and waiting for the end.

Paul's health deteriorated rapidly. I knew we had to do something, but what? At one really low point I borrowed $10 from Michael Maletta so that we could eat. I paid him back a few days later. We were fronted some coke to help us out. We sold what we needed to pay the motel bill and to pay back Michael. The rest went up in smoke.

When I returned Michael's money, I was in much better shape than when I'd borrowed it. But I noticed he looked thin. He told me he'd had diarrhea for months, and added that he was concerned about Paul. Michael made me promise that I wouldn't let Paul go without food and that I would come to him before that happened. He was still cutting hair out of his apartment and had a pretty good cash flow. Michael never judged anyone, including us. But he made it quite plain that he wouldn't support our habit. Michael had, we later found out, what they were calling "gay cancer." In less than a year he would be among the first to die from what we now know as AIDS.

One night as we were crashing, I took a good look at us. We had run up a large motel bill. Marlo, Paul's brother, came to our aid one last time and paid our motel bill through the end of the month. At least now we wouldn't have to sneak out. If we still had any hope, this was the time. Paul and I made plans to save ourselves. We had quit before, but this time we really started to fight our demons.

I called our friend, Robin Tuchaine, and asked if he still wanted to buy my Lichtenstein *Brushstroke*. I made him a good offer of $500 and he jumped. This gave us money to exist while we were making our life changes.

We decided that I would go back to New York and try to get work. My movies were being sold on videotape by TMX, and in New York I could make sure I wasn't getting ripped off too badly. I would go to the office and just sit until he wrote me a check.

Paul would go to Nevada City to live with Charles and David, friends who owned the American Victorian Museum. They loved Paul, had room for him, and would see to his needs. They would take care of him, and when I got it together, he would come to me.

I had destroyed all my friendships in New York, but I needed help. I called Jay Conway, who was still managing the 55th Street Playhouse, and asked to stay with him until I could find a place and a job. I didn't know him that well, or even like him that much, but I was desperate.

To his credit and my surprise, Jay agreed. I was surprised because I no longer had anything to offer. The side effect of bottoming out is that you're no longer of any use to anyone. Uselessness is the bottom, the most horrible feeling in the world. Everyone wants something, and when you realize you have nothing left to give, nothing with which to barter, it's devastating. I'm sure, in many cases, this feeling of uselessness—not helplessness—leads to suicide. For me, though, that wasn't an option.

Paul went to Nevada City, and I took off for New York with everything I had left in a Vuitton trunk and twenty-five dollars in my pocket.

I didn't understand Jay's hospitality. I was definitely an inconvenience, as he only had a small studio on Gramercy Park. I was grateful, but what did he want out of it? In less than a week I'd have my answer.

Jay worked until midnight and then hit Julius's Bar before coming home. One night I was sound asleep on the bottom half of his hide-away bed when I heard his key in the lock, followed by drunken whispers. "No, no, it's OK," I heard Jay say to someone. "He's really nice. It's OK!"

Before I realized what was happening, a head was under the covers, and a warm mouth had found its way to my dick.

"This is Jim," Jay said, slurring the words. "He's a big fan of yours and wants to blow you. I told him you wouldn't mind, you were staying with me, how you used to love to get blown and...." He went on and on, as the head under the sheets bobbed up and down. I was lying there, wanting sleep, trying not to think about drugs, getting a bad blow job, and listening to Jay's drunken ravings about anything that popped into his head. It was a sobering experience.

It was also the last time I would ever have sex. I didn't plan it, but from that moment on I would abstain from sexual encounters other than occasional masturbation. Sex with or without drugs had become impossible. Survival took all my energy, and thoughts of a better time refused to give way to sexual needs. Sex was no longer a desire or an option.

To my surprise I found I did have some "use" left. At least to Jay. He had only to find someone who remembered who I was, say that I was his house guest, and invite them home to blow the geek. To be honest, I didn't really care about his reasons. I had a place to sleep. It was the first big step toward turning my life around, and I'm still grateful to him for that.

I surmised all this from his drunken babble that night. Two days later I moved into a cold-water fifth-floor walk-up on Ninth Avenue, a sublet for $280 a month.

When you're drying out from drugs, especially cold turkey, the last thing on your mind is sex. Actually, even when you're doing drugs, sex isn't as important as the next hit on the pipe. For this reason I hadn't had sex with anyone during the last year in San Francisco. I'd been experimenting with self-gratification, partly because I had become afraid to go out, and partly because I was determined to have multiple orgasms. I'm not talking about many orgasms during one evening—I'd been doing that since I was thirteen—but multiple orgasms during one erection was another story entirely.

I did attain this goal simply by refusing to let any guilt enter my mind after the first orgasm. I just kept my mind on a sensual tract and kept the fantasy active. Most men have this unwanted, unsolicited feeling, lasting only seconds, immediately after orgasm, even when they're with someone they love. I don't know the source of this feeling. It could be religious or simply leftover guilt from our first orgasm. After all, we're taught not to play with ourselves, that masturbation is a sin, and that orgasms are for reproduction only. I've questioned many friends, and most agree to having a similar feeling after orgasm. I think that's also the reason most men, right after orgasm, feel an incredible need to withdraw.

I spent my time not only fighting off my craving for drugs and missing Paul but also trying to find something, anything, to secure my future beyond the next rent payment. I was reasonably confident that every month, if I hounded Danny, he'd come up with enough video sales to write me a check. Since I had no bank account, I had to cash the check at his bank. I was starting all over again.

This wasn't an easy time. My energy level was so low that I spent hours in bed every day. I had no job prospects, so I passed many hours playing games with myself. Well, not really games, but "tasks" to help pass the time. I'd look away from the clock on the table and try to imagine seeing the second hand go around the face of the clock. After what I thought was a minute, I'd look back to see how close I was to being right. I did this for hours. It helped to keep me from getting depressed, from thinking about drugs, and regretting the mistakes I'd made.

I also became a TV addict. I had escaped to TV once before, but this was worse. The TV was always on, keeping me from feeling alone. Reruns of *M*A*S*H*, *Charlie's Angels*, *The Rockford Files*—they all helped save my life. I also began to hum. I don't mean just songs but whole musical scores. I'd hum complete symphonies, concertos, even operas, anything to keep my mind off freebasing. I found that when I relaxed, my mind would go to drugs, so I stopped relaxing.

I'd clean my apartment every day. Clean and hum, clean and hum. To this day, I still hum whenever my mind isn't on something specific. I remember reading somewhere that Greta Garbo distrusted people who hummed. It bothered me that she wouldn't like me.

Steven Barnett, Michael Maletta's ex-lover, returned to New York too. His problem wasn't drugs but trying to come back after dropping out for so many years. He'd been living in Los Angeles with a friend who, for Steven's sake, had asked him to leave. Now he was living just a few blocks away, and it was comforting to know I could talk with him or at least see him for a cup of coffee. There had been periods during the last few months when I went days without speaking to anyone other than the checkout lady at the supermarket.

I tried to get work in the theater, summer stock, anything, without much success. Bob Fishko was one of the few people who gave me a hand. He'd been my manager at one time and got me a job directing and choreographing the show *This Was Burlesque*. I got the show done on time, but it was terrible. There was no budget, and it was nonunion. I made enough money, though, to bring Paul to New York.

When Paul arrived I was shocked to see how frail he had become. I forgot sometimes that he wasn't just fighting his drug habit, he was also fighting for his life. His liver condition had changed his coloring to a light orange-brown, and his eyes were clouded. Still, he was the best sight I'd seen in months. I thought it would be easier having him with me. I was wrong. Nothing makes it easier. It has to be hard—it's part of the process—or it doesn't work. Still, lying in bed, holding him next to me, hope began to work its way back into my heart, and I could see beyond next month's rent.

Out of the blue, I began to get support from Frank Ross, who worked for Danny at TMX Video. Frank produced films for him and talked me into directing a video for Danny. I needed to make some money other than my royalties from the old pictures. I thought this would help. Again, I was wrong. Danny paid me $1,000 for making the movie, no royalties, and he owned the film.

I went to work, with Frank producing. When you're down you're going to be exploited, and I was satisfied getting what I needed for the moment. This was a temporary fix; it certainly wasn't going to make me secure. Everyone thought of me as a pornographer. Now, to survive, I had to become one.

I called Cal and asked him if he'd like to be in the movie. He didn't disappoint me, even when I explained that I couldn't pay him royalties. I remembered so long ago, Cal had told me he would do anything for me, anytime. Well, he was true to his word, and we did get Danny to pay him quite well for his participation.

With this movie, *Hot Shots*, I became a pornographer. I'd never thought of myself as one because I'd always had other reasons for making a movie besides showing men having sex. It was always a learning experience. Something new. But this was different. I had nothing new to say. This film was just like every other movie: a setting, a situation, a hard-on, some sex, and an orgasm, shown from two different angles to make it appear eternal. Enough for some, and for now, enough for me. I did it for money, not much of it, but we could at least eat well.

Paul got stronger every month, and in early December Bob Taylor, his friend from Minnetonka, came to New York. Paul got dressed up and met him for lunch. I remember looking at him right before he left, in his one suit and my overcoat. He looked as handsome as when we'd first met, before all the unwanted drama. God, we both had so much to offer then. The scene was very *La bohème*. Christmas in a cold-water flat.

When Paul returned home he brought the news that he had his old job back. We were so happy until we realized we'd be apart again. I wasn't trained to do anything but theater and porno movies. I couldn't do either in Minneapolis. Within a week I put Paul on a plane. He would live with his brother and Kathy, his pregnant third wife, and their two children. At least I knew he'd get three meals a day and a chance to better his health.

Frank Ross continued to champion my recovery, making other jobs available to me. He got me involved with how-to tapes and directing a food show, an exercise tape, and a fashion show. These helped me regain some self-respect.

I found a new apartment on 43rd Street and Ninth Avenue, only five blocks uptown, but it was like moving to a new city. I bought a bed, a chair, and a TV. All mine and a new start in collecting, as George Carlin would say, stuff. I wanted stuff again. I was getting better. Proof of this came when I received a telegram inviting me to a birthday celebration for Michael Bennett, a Red Party held at 890 Broadway. I was excited that I was going to see my old friends—Marvin, Joe, Bob, Michael—all of whom I hadn't seen socially in years. But it turned out to be one of the worst nights of my life. My expectations were so high that it couldn't have been otherwise.

Everyone greeted me with reserve and, after the initial courtesies, walked away to join someone else, as if I had no past with these people. I was just an acquaintance and one they'd rather not face. Only Marti Stevens showed no reserve. We sat and had a nice talk before Bob Avian rescued her. I don't blame them. Trust is hard to recapture. Friends tend to be leery. Your very presence makes the ones still doing drugs nervous and forces them to witness what could happen to them. The others are just scared of you, period. I still had to regain their respect. Disappointed, I left early.

A few days later Cal appeared at my door with a bouquet of flowers, dropping by to see how I was doing in the new apartment. In the middle of our visit, Billy, my nephew, phoned to say my father had just died. He hadn't been well for a few months, so it didn't come as a total shock. Cal stayed while I packed my bags.

That day I flew to Jacksonville for the funeral. I couldn't afford new clothes, so I wore one of my father's suits. After a few days I returned to New York never to see my stepmother or her family again. Shortly after my father's death, Myrtice sold the house and moved away without a word. My nephew rang her doorbell one day, and a stranger answered the door.

When we knew we could handle it, Paul and I decided to meet in San Francisco, see our friends, pick up my art, and drive across the country. We had a nice visit, though things were a little strained with no drugs. We spent the day with Cliff Newman, had dinner with Zahn Artman, loaded my art into a rented station wagon, and took off for Minneapolis. We also stopped by Nevada City to get our cat from Charles and David. We were pulling together all the remnants of our lives. We were on our way to recovery.

I still thought about drugs every day, but my desire to use them faded as my memories became more clear. I'd remember things and become so embarrassed. *I didn't really do that,* I'd say to myself, knowing I had.

Now that I had my art, when I needed something or just needed money to live on, I'd put a piece of art on auction at Sotheby's or Christi's. First a Ruscha, then a Stella, then a Warhol, then a Christo. One by one. The single pieces went first. I'd bought art because I liked it and also as my social security. Well, I could think of no better time, so the things I loved became our instruments of salvation.

Paul was doing well in his old job, but it took all the energy he could muster to work full-time. Every three weeks or so, I'd fly to Minneapolis and spend hours cooking meals and packaging them in Seal-a-Meal bags. When I left, his freezer would be filled with entire meals and soups. When he ran out I'd make another trip.

We'd been through so much together. We no longer had any secrets. We knew each other. We never fought anymore. We didn't have time for drama. We were loving and supportive.

Bob Taylor, to help us out, again transferred Paul to New York for a time. Minnetonka had acquired Calvin Klein Cosmetics and was in the process of building it into one of the most successful fragrance companies in the world.

We moved into Madison Green on 23rd and Fifth avenues. In less that two years we'd gone from a cold-water flat in Hell's Kitchen to a one-bedroom apartment on the 26th floor of a luxury building. We were proud of that. Paul was doing well in his job, but I was still trying to find work. I was determined not to make another film for Danny. I wanted no more of him.

One day Frank Ross called and told me that he was offered a job at MaleExpress, a company that produced photo layouts for the major all-male magazines. He turned it down but mentioned that I was available. Bill Adkins, the owner, was interested and after only one meeting offered me a job. He planned to produce all-male videos as well as the photo spreads.

I would interview prospective models, set up photo shoots, supervise them, and see that they were done within budget. Between asking these young men to undress in my office and show me how they could get an erection, I'd write scripts and prepare to shoot MaleExpress's first video. The interviews were the most difficult. I'd never asked anyone to drop his pants and had hired most of my actors without ever seeing them naked. It was demeaning to ask someone to drop his pants and get an erection under such circumstances. Before, I'd gotten people to do things because I showed them respect. Now it would have to be different. There was no longer any denial on my part: I was a pornographer. There were no more lofty visions, just a product to be made.

Bill wanted to turn out videos at the rate of two per month, which he would sell outright to video companies for 100% profit. The main thrust would be quantity. My mind went back to the interview with Shan Sales when he'd offered me $8,000 for *Boys in the Sand*. He had doubled the cost of the film to arrive at its value. This was the formula Bill was using now, so things hadn't really changed much. I received a salary, nothing more, yet I was grateful. Paul and I had stopped using drugs cold turkey and lived through the nightmare of being addicts. The shakes, the body aches, the sleepless nights, the bad dreams, the fears, and thoughts of failing were all behind us.

Chapter Fifteen

The End of an Era

New York City, 1984

After doing magazine layouts for a few months, we were finally ready to shoot our first video. I had put together a cast from all the interviews and asked Cal to star in a segment. He was to play a father who has a three-way with his son and another man. I saw to it that Cal was paid what he wanted. I simply said to Bill, "If you want Casey Donovan, that's what you'll have to pay!" He was greedy enough to realize that Cal was worth it, and he paid.

Cal and I were great together. We seemed to give each other what was needed to accomplish our goals. I had never had a friend like him before or since, as our relationship was built on total trust and respect. Also, it's strange to say, but we were still both naïve. We saw the good side of things and refused to acknowledge the bad. That was our strength and allowed us always to see hope, something better just around the corner.

At first Cal and Frank Ross were my only supporters, but Joe Nelson and Bob Avian decided it was time to add their support. When I needed a beautiful house to shoot a segment for *Split Image*, Bob offered his home in Connecticut. Sure, like everyone else, he was curious to watch a porno movie being shot, but it was more than that. He did it for me. I didn't photograph the main house. The pool, pool house, and gardens were enough. It was definitely an inconvenience, and if Bob ever had regrets, he never showed it. In just two days we shot two segments there, one by the pool and one in the woods surrounding his estate. *Split Image* was really three loops (a series of unrelated sex scenes), showing contradictions to mainstream images. The straight-looking businessman returns home to find a "house stud" instead of a housewife. Nothing earth-shattering, just a reason to have sex, then on to the next scene.

I accepted many invitations to Bob's house over the next few years. Those personal visits were important to me. I was back with friends.

After *Split Image* I decided to develop an old idea for a film called *The Hustlers*. I originally intended to make this film with Cal and Robert La Tourneaux, who had played Cowboy in *Boys in the Band*, but I'd never made it. I talked with Bill about doing it as our next video. He agreed, and two days later I had a finished script. This was my first scripted all-talking all-action video.

It's the story of two guys who meet at a sex club called the Glory Hole, leave together, and fall in love. They become hustlers to stay together as lovers. It's hot and funny, and through their experiences, they grow. I was trying to get back to something more than loops, and so far Bill was with me. He wasn't afraid to let me put humor into the videos, so I was beginning to experiment again.

I wrote one that included a transvestite. When it got down to the sex, to make it more palatable, I did the scene with a series of still photographs and a voice-over. I wanted to expose the viewer (and myself) to something offbeat. It turned out to be a nice segment. Maybe with Bill I'd found what I needed: someone to handle the business side as Marvin had done so that I could be free to experiment and perhaps stumble upon something new.

I was leery at first because I found out that MaleExpress also provided escort services. Because of possible legal problems, I wanted no part of that end of the business. Bill honored my wishes. The escort service did help supply actors for the videos, though. If they could get it up for their clients, they'd have an easy time with a peer in front of the camera. Thus, the professional porn star/hustler became part of my environment. I used to get all my actors through friends, but now I had an office, went to work every day, and had become a full-time professional pornographer.

The Hustlers turned out to be fun to make, and I began to enjoy the process again. I'd never been turned on sexually by making films, so my state of celibacy at this time had no effect on what I found hot or put on film. In the two years I'd been clean, I still hadn't had sex. Paul and I both had lost our desire. We were burned out not only from the drugs but also from the sexual addiction. When you're fighting so hard to keep yourself rooted, you don't want to do anything that might alter the consciousness you're striving so hard to obtain. Sex definitely takes you to another reality, and that's enough to fear. When you're a recovering addict you have to forget the positive side of drugs. We had to forget that drugs are fun and that sex becomes even better on them. This is a truth, or they'd never continue to be so popular. Antidrug advocates never acknowledge this.

To give up our addiction cold turkey, Paul and I had to concentrate on the negative side of drugs. We had to recall the loneliness and total feeling of helplessness. We had to constantly recall how bad our bodies felt when we crashed. We had to remember the abuses we inflicted on our friends, each other, and ourselves. Once these memories outnumbered the pleasures, we were on our way. Sex, and the memory of it, was difficult to make negative, so I just deleted it—ironically while trying to make a comeback in the sex industry.

Right after I finished *The Hustlers*, Paul took very ill, and I flew to Minneapolis. After his year with me in New York, he'd gone back there. His doctors ran all sorts of tests to see if he might be eligible for a liver transplant. Bob Taylor, his boss, once again proved his friendship by offering to pay for the transplant. Unfortunately, it wasn't to be. He was denied a transplant and was given a prognosis of a year, maybe two, at the most.

I returned to New York with mixed emotions. I wanted to be with Paul, yet I was finally making a living again.

After the last video, Bill and I decided to enter into a partnership. We'd release our own videos and also run our own mail-order business. To start the company off with a bang, I agreed to do *Boys in the Sand II*. Of course, I immediately called Cal. That accomplished, I set out to find a new star for the sequel. After seeing about twenty of the hottest men making porno at that time, I decided on a newcomer, Pat Allen. He was striking, tall, thin, and pleasant. He was also well-hung and, like Cal, versatile. He lacked only that intangible substance that set "Casey" apart from the others. Still, he was the best around and thrilled to appear in the movie.

I finished the shooting script to the sequel, and we cast the parts. Dave Connors, a "monster-dicked" professional, signed on and brought a young friend, Tony Williams, to perform in his scene. Paul Irish was also signed on, and Victor Houston agreed to do the opening scene with Cal. Cal personally requested that Victor be his partner.

That accomplished, I rented a house on Fire Island for a long weekend at the end of the season. We had to shoot in two weeks or we'd have to wait until next summer. It was past Labor Day and just starting to get cold. I went into Bill's office the night before we were to start shooting. He stood up, gave me a hug, handed me the three quarter-inch tapes for the shoot, and wished me luck.

The next morning, before I was to leave for the island, the phone rang. It was Diane Pearlstein, Bill's lover. I'd met her several times and liked her. She was smart and, most of all, thought *Bijou* was the sexiest movie ever made.

"Wake," she said quietly. "I have some bad news. Bill had a heart attack last night. He died an hour ago."

"My God, Diane. Are you all right?" I said, not even thinking what this would mean to me.

"Yes, I'm OK. Look, you can go ahead and make this video. It's one of the last things Bill said. He wanted you to finish your movie. Just stick to your schedule. Explain to everyone that I'm taking over the business and that I'll honor all of Bill's commitments."

Then it hit me: I was in a bind. Did I really want to make this movie now? I had scheduled the cast, rented a plane for aerial shots, even bought food. Everything was set. Robert Richards from *Stallion* magazine was even planning to cover the first day's shooting.

"I guess you're right. We have to go," I said. Diane asked that I call every evening and report our progress. That's the way the shooting for *Boys in the Sand II* started.

The first scene we shot was the same as the opening of the first movie except that Casey ended up running into the water, being replaced in this adventure by Pat Allen. I didn't want it to appear that I was killing him off, but Cal said not to worry, a fitting end, should he never work again. I had so many mixed emotions. It was hard not to think back to the time when we were here shooting the first movie. At our location site there was another beached boat on shore in exactly the same place as before. It was a little surreal.

All the sections went well. Even the night scenes were great, though Pat and Paul Irish almost froze to death. Pat discovers Paul in his pool one night, and the sex scene takes place both in and out of the water. How they kept their erections during that scene was amazing. Each time I yelled "Cut!" they'd run to the clothes dryer in the shed by the pool to warm up. It's a hot scene, and you'd never guess they were so uncomfortable.

We only stopped to eat and sleep because we were shooting still photos as well, which Bill intended to sell to make back the cost of the movie. They'd enable us to pay the actors more and would promote the video at the same time. This was our plan, and it was a pretty good one. What would happen now was uncertain and a little scary.

It was a chilly, damp day when we returned to the city. Jimmy took the three-quarters-inch masters home with him, promising to have the half-inch VHS transfers by the next afternoon when I would show them to Diane. He finished them on time and sent them to the office. When I arrived that afternoon, Diane, with the tapes in her possession, informed me, "I'm selling the movie outright to Teddy at Los Angeles Video, and I'm closing down the office. By the way, you're fired."

I tried to explain that selling the movie wasn't possible, as some of the actors were on a percentage, but she said that all those agreements ended when Bill died. She was his legal heir, she had the tapes now, and there was nothing I could do about it.

I started to laugh. I mean, I really laughed. She watched in disbelief as I picked up the few personal things I wanted from my office. She couldn't understand why I was laughing. She had ripped me off royally, or so she thought, and I was laughing.

When I was ready to leave, I told her she'd been a little premature in making her plans known. She only had transfer copies that I would have used for editing. The originals were still in my possession. The half-inch copies she had were time coded, meaning that across the bottom of the picture were running numbers used as the basis for exact editing. They were otherwise useless.

I was still laughing as I left. She was standing in the doorway of her office, red in the face from overplaying her hand. This time I wasn't going to be a victim.

Soon after, Pat Allen called up *The New York Post* and informed them that Diane, a local schoolteacher, was running a male escort service. The next day, it made the front page along with her picture and name: BROOKLYN TEACHER'S SECRET LIFE IN ESCORT AGENCY.

Diane thought I'd been the informer, but she was wrong. Pat had exacted his revenge for not receiving his royalties.

In two weeks Paul was back in the hospital, and I was back in Minneapolis. I was jobless again, so I had no urgent reason to return to New York. It was time to be with Paul, so I packed up the apartment, cat and all, and moved to the Midwest.

I planned to devote all my energy to extending Paul's life. He was still able to work, and with my help—making sure he ate properly and took good care of himself—those attacks might come less frequently. I was right, and we had almost a whole year together.

To fill my time, I set up an editing area in the corner of our bedroom and worked on *Boys II*. On the weekends Paul would stay in bed most of the morning to regain his strength for the upcoming workweek.

Once again, irony entered our lives. Paul began to travel back and forth to New York. Calvin Klein Cosmetics, a subsidiary of Minnetonka Inc., was moving into new offices at the Trump Tower. This time Paul was in New York supervising the renovation, while I was in Minneapolis, working on a video project. Bob Taylor had asked me to create the visuals for their upcoming sales meeting in Key West.

Paul and I talked daily on the phone. But one Sunday I couldn't reach him. The next morning, when he didn't show up for work, Betty Paitson, a friend from the company, went over to the Plaza to check on him. They used a master key, found him unconscious, and rushed him to the hospital. I wanted to be with him, but I had to finish my project for the sales meeting, which was just days away. After Betty assured me that there was nothing I could do and that he was in good hands, I agreed to finish my work and see him as soon as possible.

Paul had contracted a blood infection and was given heavy antibiotics. These massive doses of drugs were hard on his liver, and despite severe pain and jaundice he continued to fight. By the time I was to leave for Key West, Paul was just as determined to meet me there. He promised he would make it.

Paul kept his promise. I waited for him in front of the hotel. When he stepped out of the taxi, I hardly recognized him. He had lost about ten pounds, which he could ill afford, and his color was burnt orange. As I hugged him I felt him let go a little. The trip had taken real effort on his part, and I felt his relief that he'd made it. I held him in my arms for a few moments right there in front of the hotel.

I'd never seen Paul this bad, and even though he tried to keep his energy up, it was too much. The last day of the meeting, Bob Taylor presented Paul with a small trophy recognizing his contribution to the company. He could barely walk to the podium as his coworkers urged him on with shouts of praise. It was like a movie moment. Paul was so touched. He was proud again. He had respect again. He had made it back.

I stood in the back of the hall waiting for my next video cue as I watched him. It was special, and for an instant I saw that young man-boy in a Cub Scout cap, the one I'd first seen in my apartment on Castro Street. Paul said a few words then walked to where I was standing. He put his arms around me and whispered in my ear, "Help me out of here. I need to get to the room."

As the lights lowered I punched up the next video cue and got him back to the room. He was unable to participate in the closing event and grew progressively worse. I spent the next morning arranging our trip back to Minneapolis. We had to change planes twice, so I arranged a wheelchair and escort at each stop. On the plane I held him in my arms to keep him warm. We didn't care what anyone thought. Afraid, I held him thinking this could be the last time we'd be together. I arranged for an ambulance to pick him up at the airport and take him straight to the hospital. It was already dark when we arrived, so after putting him in the ambulance, I took off for the apartment to drop off our bags.

When I finally got to the hospital, it was after visiting hours and they wouldn't let me in. To get into see him, I had to be a family member. The nurse told me there was nothing she could do.

"Look," I said softly but with great confidence, "he's my lover and has been for years. I am family. I have no desire to hear your feelings on the subject, and I don't care if you're homophobic. I only care about him. I know he's close to death, and if something happens to him while I'm discussing the rules with you, I'll sue this hospital for every cent I can get. Now tell me, where is he?"

The nurse answered, "Fifth-floor isolation."

Things were going to be done our way. If this was the end, it would be as Paul wanted: no hassles, no lies, no prejudice, and no hypocrisy. This was the way we'd structured it when I moved here. I loved his mother, Eva, and we'd become close. Everyone could see Paul and I loved each other, and they saw our love expressed by the way we treated each another. We'd never had any trouble with his family. It would have to be the same way with his nurses and the doctors who treated him. I was going to be there all the time, and they would have to accept our situation.

Slowly, after observing us over next week, even the most homophobic of the bunch began to show us some respect. During the first three days I left the hospital only to feed the cat. After all we'd been through, she was still with us.

Once Paul had stabilized, I'd go home, sleep for a few hours, and then return to the hospital. Some nights he'd ask me not to leave, so I'd sit in the chair next to him, holding his hand or just resting mine on his thigh. So many people go through this experience, squeezing every bit you can out of the short time you have left, while at the same time hoping it's not the end.

At times, when Paul felt pretty good, he could charm the nurses as no one else could. He had brought perfume and products from work and lavished gifts on those who took care of him.

The hospital staff began to treat us as a couple. By our being honest, most, if not all, of the people who came in contact with us observed a gay relationship for the first time. In doing so, they saw no differences between us and a heterosexual couple.

Every day I'd get to the hospital at about seven A.M., give Paul a bath, then pick up Eva. We'd sit with Paul all day, taking time off for lunch and dinner. Eva was in her eighties and tireless. Those last few weeks in the hospital room were wonderful. Hearing Eva and Paul talk of old memories became treasure for me—treasure that I stored up.

Every afternoon I'd put Paul in a wheelchair and take him for a walk. On a little hill overlooking the hospital stood a small bench and a picnic table. We used this as our private place. This became the most important part of my day; we laughed at old times, spoke of old friends, and planned for the future. Every afternoon I looked forward this time. Then one day, after we had reached the top, Paul asked me to take him back. "I'm so tired. I'm tired of fighting," he confessed.

I knew then that it wouldn't be much longer, and I regretted that I had fussed at him for being negative. I wanted him to continue to fight. I was being selfish. I didn't want to lose him. I tried to boost his energy again, but he took my hand and said, "It's time to stop."

Paul had certain thoughts about his funeral that he made clear to me. It's no longer unusual for people to plan their funerals, but in 1985, it was thought of as bizarre. These were creative, not morbid, conversations, much like the ones we'd had so many times at Hot Flash. He asked that I take care of his mother, and I promised I would. By the time the end drew near, everything pertaining to his death had been arranged. I remember the doctor coming into the room and saying that Paul's kidneys were shutting down and that the end was coming. He had put a tube directly into Paul's chest to fight the blood infection that had continued to drain his strength. Paul was confined to his bed, and I could no longer take him for his bath or even a walk around the floor.

One by one, all the things that made up our existence began to disappear. All I could do was sit by his side, hold his hand, and try to make him comfortable. After a few days of intense pain from the tube in his chest, Paul asked for it to be removed. He wanted to be unrestricted and free at the end. I spoke with his doctors, who agreed but told me that once the tube was removed, Paul would be gone within twenty-four hours. I instructed them to remove it.

When I realized I had started Paul's final death process, I began to tear up for the first time. One of the nurses who had been close to us took me in her arms and hugged me. That did it. I broke down and began to sob. All I could think was that tomorrow, sometime tomorrow, he would be gone.

After a minute or two I pulled myself together and went back into Paul's room. Marlo, Eva, and Kathy were all sitting around talking. I took Paul's hand and told him the nurses were going to remove the tube to make him more comfortable. He knew immediately what that meant. He perked up instantly and began to make small talk with his family. I knew this was taking every bit of energy he could muster. I had to get out.

I explained that I was tired and wanted to go home for a few hours' rest. I did this so that he and his family could have this last evening together. I'd come back early in the morning and have my time with him.

After the tube was removed and I saw the look of relief on Paul's face, I left. As I walked down the hall, I could hear Paul recounting some childhood story about his father taking him hunting and him saying all he wanted to do was pick wildflowers.

I smiled and let the tears run down my face.

The next morning, I arrived at the hospital at about five o'clock. In the last few hours Paul had become so weak that he couldn't form words. His kidneys were no longer working, and his fluid intake had been limited. His throat was dry, and he looked helpless, waiting for the disease to finish him. The bad flow of blood caused a lot of pain in his legs and feet, so massaging helped.

"Would you like me to rub your legs?" I asked. He just opened his eyes, nodded, and managed a small smile. As I rubbed I felt his tension ease. I began to speak and rub him in the rhythm of his breathing. I said all the things that were important for me to say. I told him I'd never forget him, that I'd think of him every day, and that I was so grateful we had met and shared at least part of our lives. I had no apologies to make. We were beyond that.

A nurse came in, looked at the machines, and quietly told me that

I should phone Paul's family. He was going fast. If they wanted to be with him at the end, they should hurry.

When they all arrived I spoke to them in a group. Paul wished that no one hold him back from his journey. He didn't want crying or pleas of "Don't leave" to be the last words he'd hear. This was his last wish. Eva, Marlo, Kathy, and Bob all agreed. One by one, we took turns spending our last few minutes alone with him. I was last. After only a minute the nurse said quietly, "He's going. Get the others fast."

I ran to the waiting room and told them to come. I took Eva by the arm and helped her down the hall. We stood around the bed, and as we heard sound of the monitor change and knew at that moment his life was slipping away, we all shouted our own wishes.

"Fly high, Paul."

"Go to God."

"Go with love, Paul."

We were a rowdy group shouting at him with tears rolling down our faces. Only once did I hear Eva say, "Oh, my baby." When she realized what she was saying, her words trailed off, replaced by gentle sobs as she patted and kissed his hand.

We were all touching him when he left us, and the sound of the machine became a constant tone. He was gone. I kissed him on the forehead and closed his eyes. It was over. His pain, his suffering, and Paul were gone.

Chapter Sixteen

Life After Sex

Minneapolis, 1985

Steven Barnett flew out to be with me after Paul's funeral. He was struggling to repair his life, trying to get back into advertising after dropping out for ten years. I was glad he came, since I needed a friend. When he left I started closing out Paul's accounts and paying off his debts. Paul had made a list of people to whom he still owed money in San Francisco; he wanted them paid. Another list was for thank-you notes to those who sent flowers and gifts to the hospital. He also wanted to leave his nieces and nephews a bond to start an education fund. I also honored his request to take care of Eva.

Eva lived in a retirement complex. I fixed up her apartment and got her everything she needed be comfortable: a new sofa, a microwave, a color TV, and a new winter coat for those bitter days in Minneapolis. We had dinner almost every night. For the next two months, we grew close. It was easy, since we both had loved the same person.

By the time I left Minneapolis, I had finished Paul's list. He was clear of all debts, at least as far as I knew. I received a card from Paul's nurses at the hospital, saying they were so affected by his death that a support group was formed. They also thanked me for our honesty. One nurse, who was there at the end, said she'd never had such an uplifting experience as when she watched us during his final moments. She said every bit of energy from us went into making Paul's journey joyful, and she would never forget it.

Paul and I, when we tried, could make magic. We really put out our best effort here, and it worked. I left Minneapolis with a feeling of accomplishment and success, but I also left with a hole in my heart.

I had no idea what I was going to do with the rest of my life, but I decided to go back to New York, since it was still home to me. Tim Wernett found me a nice apartment in his building. Tim had been manager of the Chelsea Theater Group, and I asked his help in resolving the difficulties with *Boys II*.

Tim found a lawyer, and finally we reached an agreement with Diane and signed a distribution agreement with Los Angeles Video. Diane turned out to be not such a nice woman. The video had been in litigation for more than two years, and I ended up paying her $8,000 for all the rights. By the time everything was settled, all the advance publicity had been wasted. Even Robert Richards's article for *Stallion* and the special issue devoted to *Boys II* had been on the stands for eighteen months.

Although I won the battle, she won the war and ended up making more money than anyone. After the initial payment from Los Angeles Video, which covered costs, I never received another penny. To my knowledge, they're still selling it, under the title *Men in the Sand II*. But I never sued for my royalties. After my life was threatened in San Francisco, I learned to be afraid of suing anyone in the porno business.

While all these negotiations were taking place, Dave Connors came to me with an idea to shoot a movie with six people who would travel around the country on a personal appearance tour along with the movie. The opening night in each city would benefit AIDS research, and the video would be sold in the theater. It was a great idea, so Tim and I financed and produced it. I was making movies again. We received great support from magazines, and Robert Richards once again did an article for *Stallion* magazine. Both he and Jerry Douglas were supportive. The idea I came up with was simple.

I called it *One, Two, Three*. Part 1 starred J.D. Slater, and I had him talk directly to the camera while bringing himself to orgasm. It was full of dirty talk, with him urging viewers to do things to themselves while watching and listening to him. Part 2 featured Dave Connors and Steve

Kaye. Their sex was accompanied by a voiceover reading a sexually explicit story unrelated to their sex scene. Part 3 starred Ryder Hanson, Ron Pearson, and Tom Stone. This time the dialogue was spoken by Ryder, who stood on the sidelines, instructing Ron and Tom on what to do to each other. When he could stand it no longer, Ryder joined the action. I finished the film with a real circle jerk. All six men stood in a circle, and one by one, in order, they brought themselves to orgasm while being urged on by the other members of the circle.

It's a terrific movie, and the guys are all great. But once again fate intruded. By the time the film was finished and bookings were being set up for the tour, Dave Connors took his own life. He was diagnosed with AIDS and three days later took an overdose of sleeping pills to avoid the suffering and waste that was beginning to affect so many. The tour was canceled, and, of course, all involved in the movie had to worry about being infected. Even though Steve Kaye was the only one to have sex with him in the film, some of the others had had sex with him before.

I had made arrangements for Los Angeles Video to distribute this film and then to follow it up with *Boys II*. So now I had two new films released and problems with both. The advance publicity for *Boys II* had been out for more than a year. All the interest it generated had cooled, and Los Angeles Video had no intention of spending any money promoting it. Dave's death had put a negative slant on *One, Two, Three*, so prospects looked slim for both. One thing was sure: Neither would be profitable.

I had almost decided to stop making films when I received the strangest call from Daniel Holt, a porno actor I met once and to whom I'd never said more than twenty words in my life. To this day, I don't understand the reason or motivation behind his call. He told me how disgusted he was with me for letting people in my movies fuck someone infected with the AIDS virus. He ranted, telling me how I would pay some day for my greed and insensitivity.

I finally broke into his tirade and explained that I knew nothing about Dave's illness before or during the shoot and that even Dave didn't know until after the film was in the can. I expressed anger that he would assume my guilt and asked how he could pass judgment on something that he knew nothing about. I hung up, and from that moment, I knew I never wanted to make another film.

Daniel had driven the first nail in the coffin, and Los Angeles Video finished the hammering by never paying me one cent in royalties on either film. I had no strength or desire left to fight for what was contractually due to Tim and me. We had become partners on these two films, and even Tim was afraid to push for our rights. It's so easy for unscrupulous people to take advantage of anyone dealing in X-rated material. You never know how each law enforcement agency will respond to a "gay" complaint, especially a pornographic one, and on the other side, you're never sure that the things you hear about the so-called underworld figures and their methods are fiction. I only know that all responses and inquiries about money owed were never responded to. The last communication from Teddy informed Tim that both films had been sold to another company that he had nothing to do with but that he would look into it. I still have the letter. That's all I have. In the middle of all this, Tim developed AIDS and eventually returned to Ohio. We talked every day until he died.

I needed to find a way to make a living. No more theater! No more movies! What could I do? I was totally unemployable. What did I want to do? What was I good at?

I realized that for my entire life I always cooked for my friends—and I was good at it. I found it relaxing, so I made up my mind that at the ripe old age of fifty, I would embark on a totally new career. I applied for entry into the French Culinary Institute. Dorothy Cann, the head of the institute, didn't think I was serious. Someone had told her I was a pornographer and that I was doing this on a lark. I informed her that it was a matter of life and death to me. I needed to earn a living.

Dorothy accepted me and suggested that I apply for a grant to help pay my tuition. That, and a loan from Marvin Shulman, made it possible. Once again, Marvin was there for me.

Over the next eight months I lived and breathed cooking. I was the oldest in the class out of seven students, and it was the hardest time of my life. I had to memorize countless recipes and techniques. My age and all the drug abuse made memorization difficult. But on graduation day it all came together.

A few weeks before, I'd been offered a job at La Caravelle on 55th Street by chef Michael Romano, now of Union Square Café. I accepted and had been working there for a week or two when I took my final exam. Michael Romano, now my boss, was one of the four judges for my final, which added even more pressure.

We had to prepare two dishes that we drew out of a hat. Forty-five recipes were the basis for all dishes we were to cook. I was so nervous, and, unlike being on the stage, it didn't manifest into positive energy like it does when you perform. Still, I passed the test. Three students I tested with failed.

I continued to work at La Caravelle for several months. Then I took a position with Annemarie Huste, who had been Jackie Kennedy Onassis's chef for many years. Annemarie had a townhouse, and she catered dinners mostly for stockbrokers. She was wonderful, but after several weeks even she had to ask me about my films, wanting assurance that it was in the past. It seems everyone is bothered by being associated with the porno industry. I assured her, laughingly, that I wouldn't suddenly appear on the front page of the paper, or if I did, I wouldn't tell them where I worked. I was no longer involved with the porno business, period.

She believed me, and for the next four years I would learn from and work for Annemarie. When the market went bad in 1989, I went to work for Calvin Klein Cosmetics as manager of their food services. Bob Taylor still owned the company, but shortly after I went to work there, he sold it to Unilever. I've been with them now for more than ten years.

Yes, I've held a salaried job for ten years. Amazing what you can do when you put your mind to it. If I still had all my friends around, it would be a perfect life, but like so many of my generation, my friendships have been devastated by AIDS.

Paul's death was just the prelude to what was to follow. One by one, news of infection and death invaded my life. Michael Maletta was the first, and from there it seemed as though death was using my address book to make his house calls. Over the next few years most of the people I loved, and in whom I had invested time, would leave this world. Mostly with great pain and suffering. Some, like Peter Fisk and

Ed Parente, would take their own lives so as not to burden their loved ones.

I spoke to Ed the night before he died. He called, as he promised he would, to say good-bye. Just six months before, we had managed to have a weekend together at his sister's farm. We had a wonderful time making pies, walking in the woods, and laughing a lot. But now we were having our last talk. It was the strangest conversation I've ever had, talking to someone, knowing that in the morning he would no longer exist. He explained that he couldn't fend for himself anymore and that it was time. We expressed our love and our gratitude to each other for being friends and sharing our lives. It was surreal, but I was grateful to be able to say to him how important he had been to me. Finally, I said "I love you" and hung up the phone. I could still cry then, and I did.

Tim died shortly after Ed, and one by one, most of my friends followed. Even Steven Barnett finally admitted to me that he was HIV-positive. As soon as I heard, I looked for an apartment where we could be together and I could look after him. He lived in a fifth-floor walk-up, and I knew that wouldn't do for long. He, as did many of my friends, had no family in the city.

I found another apartment in my building, which was 2,000-square feet with two floors, two bedrooms, two baths, a beautiful terrace, and a great kitchen. It was a real find, but I had to practically beg him to move in with me. He didn't want to be a bother, he said. I learned with Paul that I was good at taking care of people, and enjoyed it. The instant Steven saw the apartment, he knew it was the right thing to do. We would live together for almost two years.

One day the phone rang. It was Steven, asking if my passport was up to date. He said we'd been invited to the Olympics in Barcelona, Spain, as guests of NBC. I spent a total of twenty-five dollars of my own money while we were there. Everything was paid for, and we lived on an ocean liner docked in the harbor. We had a wonderful time, even seeing the Dream Team win its medal while we sat directly behind Jack Nicholson and his family.

I was amazed at Steven's stamina. He worked full-time up until three weeks before his death. Since he worked in the advertising end of the TV industry, he had kept his illness secret. Although filled with homosexuals, it's one of the most homophobic institutions in the world. He was fearful that if they discovered he was HIV-positive, they would fire him. Imagine being really sick and still going into work. Now imagine not letting anyone know what you feel like. It's amazing. He was amazing. They were all amazing, my friends. God bless them.

Steven would die, mercifully, after only a short stay in the hospital. His mother, his sister, and his best friend, Michael, all visited from Los Angeles, and Ron Parisi, a new friend of Steven's, was there. At the end, he saw the people who loved him. It's the way it should be.

I moved to a new apartment in the West Village only one week after Steven's death, and even though my work was the same, everything else was different. I still had my old friends Joe, Marvin, Hans, Ed, Andy, and Drey. But I started to create a new life. Ron Parisi was having a hard time, so I kept an eye on him. Ron was sweet and about to enter middle age. He managed to keep a positive slant on things, even though he seemed to be so alone in the world. His mind was eager to learn, and he shared anything he thought might interest me. We enjoyed being around each other. As a result, we had dinner at least twice a week for the next several years.

In 1994 Ron got a job working for Jay Garon, a literary agent for John Grisham. I knew Jay slightly from Fire Island. His lover, Gary, who claimed his life had been so affected by *Boys in the Sand*, wanted to meet me. So at Ron's request I was invited to dinner at Jay's. Jay was a heavyset, unattractive man with a sharp tongue, an unpleasant personality, and enough power to get away with it. I liked him. Gary was just the opposite: a hot Italian with a sweet personality who drank a little too much, and I liked him too. We had a pleasant meal, and as usual, I went through my repertoire of dinner-party stories.

"Wakefield, I think it's time you sat down and wrote your book!" Jay announced. "Have you ever thought about it?"

"I've thought about it a lot, but I've never found the time."

"Find the time. Just build it like you would a house. Make a plan. Do a couple of chapters and send them to me."

Jay sparked some old dream, and I began to think seriously about writing. It didn't take any money—that was good. But it would take a lot of time. Well, I had plenty of that. So I started. About six months later, when I had finished three chapters, I sent them to Jay. He got back to me in a few days, encouraging me to continue. I took his advice. Unfortunately, in less than a year Jay had a massive heart attack and died in his sleep. I continued to write because Jay made me believe that I could. I had a new dream. One I knew I could realize.

Now, when I walk on the streets of New York, I look for old faces, faces from the past, faces I used to see all the time. I even look for familiar faces I can't put names to. Faces I used to see at the baths and clubs. They're not there. It's as if a whole generation has been wiped from existence.

Shortly after Paul's death, when I first returned to the city, I ran into Alvin Beam on the street. Alvin was a gypsy dancer I'd known for years.

"My God, Wakefield Poole! I thought you were dead!" We hugged, and after a beat he asked in all seriousness, "Why aren't you?"

We laughed, talked briefly, and went our separate ways. I started to think about his question. Why am I still here? How am I HIV-negative? Maybe I'm still alive because I was a drug addict at the right time. I took so many drugs that I got to a point where I didn't think about sex. I didn't care about it anymore, and when I finally cleaned myself up, I was too fucking scared. As a result, I've been celibate since 1980. Funny, but there is life after sex, and hope is better than despair.

It feels good to attach something positive to a period that was, in all respects, the bottom of my existence. At these really low periods the Pollyanna aspect of my personality has prevailed, and I've always remembered the song "Look to the Rainbow" from my first show, *Finian's Rainbow*. In the song, one of the lyrics proclaims, "Follow the fellow who follows a dream."

I always have, and until I grow up, I always will!

Afterward: Seventy-Five

I'm now three-quarters of a century old. To be honest, considering the life I've led, I never thought I'd make sixty, but here I am getting ready to launch a new edition of my book. Knowing that I could make changes, I picked my copy from the shelf and began to read. It turned out to be an enlightening experience. Writing the book, I took memories and put them into words; on rereading, the process was reversed and the images flew by like a movie.

While writing the book, I strove to tell the truth as I remembered. The truth is still there but a few of my perspectives have changed. For example, as a child, I never felt sexually molested, yet re-reading this section I saw how some could draw other conclusions. I was usually the aggressive party and at no time felt threatened. I can only say, I have no unpleasant sexual memories of this early period of my life other than my mother catching me masturbating in the shower. Now that was traumatic! As challenging as some sections may be to the reader, other than changing a few misspelled names, I've decided to leave them as written, but I'm happy to have the chance to play a little catch up for you.

In April, 2003, I decided to retire. After fifteen years working for Calvin Klein Cosmetics Co., I was tired and it was time. I had a tough choice to make. I certainly couldn't afford to live in New York on Social Security. Royalties on my films had dwindled drastically, so once again, as I did in the 1970s, I'd have to give up New York and my longtime friends. Where would I go? It's said "You can't go home," but that's exactly what I decided to do—return home. I still had some family there, so Jacksonville it was to be.

The bank and I now own a very modest townhouse on the Arlington River. I live alone except for three cats—Floyd, Fred, and Mommy. Someone moved away from the complex and left Mommy. One stormy night I brought her in from the garden and she decided she'd stay. She's old, fat, and has no teeth but still loves to chase squirrels when I let her out in the garden. I feed a tribe of nine feral cats in the parking lot. I've had them all spayed and neutered so they're content to eat, stretch, and lie in the sun by the river. My life is pretty much the same. It's taken me several years to learn to relax, to get used to not having somewhere to go or something to do every morning.

I met a wonderful group of twenty or so gay men and women. We meet every Wednesday for dinner at different restaurants. Most of my family outings are food events as well so it's no wonder I've put on a few pounds. Southerners do a lot of eating. I've also started to play bridge again so life keeps getting better.

It hasn't been all roses! Controversy has always been my companion. So much so that sometimes I'm not even aware until I turn around and. like a shadow, there it is. I thought when I retired all that would disappear. With the release of my book, a collection of my films on DVD; appearances in the documentaries *Ballets Russes*, *When Ocean Meets Sky*, and *That Man: Peter Berlin*; combined with Jim Tushinski's commitment to make a documentary out of *Dirty Poole*, interest in my films began to rise.

In 2007, I received an invitation from Joe Yranski, the Senior Film Librarian of the New York Public Library to do a lecture in their "Meet the Maker" series at the Donnell Center. Porn at the New York Public Library! I couldn't believe they didn't make a mistake but was assured that they hadn't. Jim prepared a program using an interview format. It would include clips from my Broadway and television appearances as well as my films. We titled it "The Two Faces of Wakefield Poole." Everything was going along fine until we were advised that there could be no nudity in our program. We never considered including hardcore but to do a program of my films with no nudity would be impossible.

Joe Yranski was mortified that we were meeting resistance from his superiors. He had presented many offbeat programs (with nudity) at the Center with no repercussions, but they let Joe know, they were not happy about this program. Pornography is pornography! This was the beginning of an attempt to get me to walk out on the program. They couldn't cancel without repercussions but if I dropped out they could save face. We persevered but a few minutes before the event, they refused to allow a scene from *Bible* because you could see the cheek of Samson's butt through his mesh trunks. I was hurt, furious, and ready to walk out, but Jim convinced me that we should continue.

After my introduction, I told the audience about the censorship problems and announced that if anyone came to see skin, they might as well leave. It got a big laugh and we continued. For the entire program, sitting in the second row, pencil and paper in hand was one of the women of the board. I have no idea of her intentions or what she was writing but it was intimidating. Another conflict dealt with! I don't enjoy being a victim but these things keep happening. We repeated the program at the Miami Gay & Lesbian Film Festival and Long Island Gay & Lesbian Film Festival with no incident.

In 2010, the Fire Island International Film Festival declined to screen *Boys in the Sand* because it did not meet "community standards." Crayton Robey, the director of *When Ocean Meets Sky*, and Philip Monaghan, the owner of the house used in the third section of *Boys in the Sand*, were outraged. They decided to produce a charity event at Whyte Hall in the Fire Island Pines to show the film and raise money for the local health center. In spite of objections from several very vocal community members, Crayton, Philip, and other brave volunteers managed to pull off an incredible weekend. I arrived at the dock to find a huge banner advertising the event with a booth selling tickets and T-shirts. There were two screening and a cocktail party. Tickets were $50 and $75 and to my surprise, they both sold out. The cocktail party at the Frank Gehry House (used in the third section of the film) was also a knockout success. I will forever be grateful to Crayton and Philip for giving me a weekend I'll never forget. I felt as if I'd won the Academy Award.

Now, I'm just waiting for *Dirty Poole* to be finished and onto the big screen. Jim has re-mastered all my films and they look as good as or better than the originals. What a thrill it was to see them again and to see them looking so fresh.

We started filming interviews in New York, Los Angeles, and San Francisco. About half of the people we asked, mostly Broadway friends, either ignored the request or found some excuse not to participate. I wasn't surprised but was disappointed. Still, it was thrilling to see people I hadn't seen in years and the interviews we did get were exceptional.

In closing, I have one more story I'd like to tell. When *Dirty Poole* was first published, I sent copies to all my relatives. My Aunt Margaret and Uncle Vance, a Lutheran Minister, had two grown children, David and Rebecca. David had his mother's musical talent and had become the musical director /organist for the largest Catholic Church in Houston. In the late 1980's, he died from AIDS. It was a shock because he had not come out to them. They felt as though they didn't know their own son. For years, she had no answers to her many questions. That is, she said, until she read my book. Her note thanked me for being so open. She said she had learned so much that helped her understand David and the life he led. She blessed me and closed with the observation, "Gay life is so mysterious!" She was right. It is.

David Edward Byrd

The controversial poster for *Wakefield Poole Bible* (1973) by famed Broadway poster artis David Edward Byrd.

Paul Jasmin

Original poster for Bijou (1972)

Appendix

The Films of Wakefield Poole

Boys in the Sand (1971)
Bijou (1972)
Wakefield Poole's Bible (1973)
Moving (1974)
Take One (1977)
Hot Shots (1981)
The Hustlers (1984)
Split Image (1984)
Boys in the Sand II (1984)
One, Two, Three (1984)

Wakefield Poole's films are available from:

Gorilla Factory Productions
1-888-779-8817
www.gf-productions.com
sales@gf-productions.com

and

TLA Entertainment Group
1-888-TLA-DVDS
www.tlavideo.com

Printed in Australia
AUHW021250011221
356314AU00001B/13

9 781590 212295